Also by M. R. Montgomery

In Search of L. L. Bean
A Field Guide to Airplanes of North America
Saying Goodbye
The Way of the Trout

Many Rivers to Cross

Of Good

Running Water,

Native Trout,

and the

Remains of Wilderness

M. R. Montgomery

Simon & Schuster

New York London Toronto Sydney Tokyo Singapore

SIMON & SCHUSTER
Rockefeller Center
1230 Avenue of the Americas
New York, NY 10020

Designed by Paulette Orlando

Illustrations by Glenn Wolff

Manufactured in the United States of America

10   9   8   7   6   5   4   3   2   1

Library of Congress Cataloging-in-Publication Data
Montgomery, M. R.
   Many rivers to cross : of good running water, native trout, and the re-
mains of wilderness / M. R. Montgomery.
       p.   cm.
   1. Trout fishing—West (U.S.).   2. Natural history—West (U.S.).   3. West
(U.S.)—Description and travel.   I. Title.
SH688.U6M66   1995
799.1'755—dc20   94-40608
                                                                      CIP

ISBN: 0-671-79286-5

To my companions in the West—hosts, old friends, chance acquaintances. Their names are written in this book, a little farther down the trail.

All the rivers run into the sea; yet the sea is not full; unto the place from whence the rivers come, they return to flow again.

—Ecclesiastes 1:7

Contents

1.	Up in the Pines	13
2.	At Turtle Cave	30
3.	On the River with Crook	40
4.	Apache Country	55
5.	In the Sierra Bonita	77
6.	Over the Waterpocket Fold	95
7.	Cougar Country	108
8.	Saddlebag Trout	119
9.	Across the Great Divide	131
10.	Mud Volcanos	152
11.	Along the Snake	171
12.	San Juans, Sangre de Cristos	182
13.	Woodchuck Eaters	198
14.	Veltie's Camp	211
15.	Wild Horses	222
16.	Bullbats and Beer	233
17.	Sitting in Paradise	241
	L'Envoi	253

1

Up in the Pines

WHERE DOES THE WEST BEGIN? A HUNDRED DEGREES OF longitude on the sunset side of Greenwich, England, is the simple answer. West of that meridian, it gets drier, higher, colder. The soil thins; a short-grass prairie replaces the rich farmland of the Corn Belt. The West stops somewhere short of Los Angeles, by the way. The Pacific Slope was out West once, but no more. America is now truly bicoastal. If you tell someone in Los Angeles or Seattle that you live back East, they will say, "Boston?" or "New York?" If you tell a Westerner you're from Back East, he'll guess, "Chicago?" unless you're in northern Montana, where they tend to think, "Minneapolis?"

My own apprehension of the West is more vertical than horizontal. The best of the West begins at least a mile above sea level and gets better as you head up. Denver is a mile high, but still hot, dusty, and barren as Kansas. The same rule of thumb applies to Phoenix, Arizona, which is about as western in feeling, no matter how many saguaro cactuses they plant at the airport, as Dayton, Ohio. But get up in Arizona's mountains, around Prescott or Globe, and something changes in the light and the sky and the mood, and you're West again.

I was born a little short of a mile above sea level, over in the Big Dry of eastern Montana, just on the border between high plains and badlands. In Glasgow, Montana, everybody's idea of paradise was and still is to head a little farther west and a little bit higher, maybe just to the Bear Paw Mountains over by Chinook if you didn't have the time or the gas money to make it all the way to the Rockies. When you got up a thousand feet or so above the surrounding plains, you could find a pine tree and sit in the shade and listen to the water run in the creek. Some of us, when we get there, can't help going fishing, but the loveliness of running water appeals to everyone. I have never met a person who would turn down a picnic by the river.

The true West survives in and along its mountain streams. In my life I found and then lost two creeks that were little changed since the first Indian ponies grazed their meadows. It occurred to me, rather late in the day as with most sensible ideas, that if there had once been two—even if they are now ruined and I cannot take anyone there anymore—I could find new ones. Because two of the last, best pieces of Montana also just happened to have God's own trout in them, and because they were the finest examples of two very different landscapes I had ever seen or ever shown to anyone, there might be some principle at work here. Maybe it would turn out that any place where genuine, native, aboriginal trout still swam had kept its many charms, and not least the virtue of authenticity, of the preservation of wildness.

In my mind, a wild and wet and western place will not be defined by the absence of humanity; if you want that kind of wilderness you'll have to leave the earth. But wild water does not draw crowds. The dedicated and affluent fly fishers have captured the big rivers below the mountains. There they struggle against all imagined odds to convince a large fish to make a small mistake, and I leave them in possession of the field. If they think that is the West and they are winning it again, so be it. My serene place must have fish, the ones that belong there. But it will be marked by a notable absence of compulsive visitors with high, and often achieved, ambitions to wrestle trout.

We settled the West along running water, and when that land

was gone, a few dreamers invented a great foolishness called dry-land farming and drew the last few hundred thousand immigrants into the high plains around the turn of this century. Rain was supposed to follow the plow. That is how my parents and I ended up being born in the Big Dry. The rain followed the plow all right—over the mountains to the state of Washington—and never came back. We grew up with a great love for green grass and running water, having seen so little of it for so many years. This book is about places they did love and would have loved had they known them; all are in the West and all well over a mile high, up in the pines. In the dry country below the ranges, "creek" is a one-word sonnet and "pine tree" is an entire lyric.

Mountains make the West bearable. If they weren't there to catch the snow, the Great Plains would shade imperceptibly into the Great American Desert. Without them, there would be no Colorado River and no Columbia, no wide Missouri, no Rio Grande del Norte. The West would be as dry as lowland Israel, as desolate as the Sinai.

Desert folks, and that includes residents of the western high plains, understand that their very life depends on mountains. What did Isaiah threaten when he prophesied the Lord's mightiest curse? "I will make waste mountains and hills, and dry up all their herbs; and I will make the rivers islands, and I will dry up the pools." And what did Joel promise if the Lord's wrath were averted and He smiled upon Israel? "And it shall come to pass in that day, that the mountains shall drop down new wine, and the hills shall flow with milk, and all the rivers of Judah shall flow with waters."

Most of us depend on the plumber for our water now, and we have created our own savannas of front lawns and tree-lined streets. But Isaiah's threat should not be taken lightly in the cities of the plains. I have seen man make waste mountains and hills, and now I seek places that flow with waters as clear as new wine, as nourishing as milk.

ONE RIVER I WOULD HAVE TAKEN YOU TO SEE WAS A SMALL AND handsome stream in high ranch country. It cut through a level meadow dotted with haystacks and the beaver-slide stackers that made them. And then the cows ate it. Not directly, although cattle can do that, but miles of the river were killed with a bulldozer so that a few more bales of hay could be cut. I have told part of that story in another place. A few years ago, I looked again at the meadow around the East Fork of the Bitterroot River and saw something that had escaped my eye earlier, a fact of hydrology that I had just been shown in another high meadow hundreds of miles south of Montana in the White Mountains of Arizona.

Because the stream now ran in a deep machine-made cut, because the solids in the water were swept along directly through and out of the valley and there were no meanders or bars or willows to hold back the water and precipitate the burden of sand and silt, the stream ran at a lower elevation than it once did, and the water table in the high meadow had fallen down to the new level of the river's surface. They saved a few acres of pasture from erosion in flood time by digging down the riverbed, but now, for dozens of yards back from the bank and for miles on both sides of the river, it wasn't worth damn all for growing hay. The lushness of sedges and meadow grass was gone; their roots could not reach the water. Rich hay was replaced with droughty weeds. It wasn't even justifiable homicide to kill that stretch of water. No one comes to enjoy it anymore; I didn't see even a beer can on the shadeless bank.

A quarter of a mile from the gouged-out main channel, along one unaltered tributary called Cameron Creek, the streamside meadow looks just as well as ever. The hay in midsummer is tall and green and droops over the banks, and the tips of the blades drag on the water. The landscape has that peculiar charm of used but unabused nature. You could go there and admire it, but one hay field is a poor substitute for a whole valley, and I can hardly bear to look at it anymore. It is true that when first I saw it— Ross's Hole, also known as Sula Meadows—the land did not look the same as it did that September afternoon in 1805 when Lewis and Clark camped there and inquired of a large band of Salish Indians about how to get over the forbidding mountains that surround the meadows. But the little that's been left nearly natural does not look worse. Fences provide a geometric frame; hay mowers and grazing cattle stifle any woody invading plants; the steers are advertisements for organic beef on the hoof.

The tiny side stream still has trout, small ones, dwarfed as aquarium fish are stunted because there is not enough volume of water to make them robust. And uncles and grandfathers yet bring children and teach them how to fly cast on the little creek for lunch fish. They are supposed to put the native cutthroat trout back—things have gotten that bad on the East Fork—but often they don't. The fishing is of no consequence, and really, it never was. What mattered, what hurts to this day, is that it was a place where cattle and fences and haystacks and mint and trout and children and yellow-headed blackbirds and mayflies and frogs and a pair of dipper birds shared the water. Take out any one of them and it is diminished and less remarkable.

After this had happened, a friend showed me, among several wonders of his country, another brook. It was a long way from anywhere, in the middle of the Crow Indian Reservation, a fine and small stream of clear water with trout that lived under the banks and in the deep holes between the flinty ledges. I thought it was a new place to cherish, to think about in hard times, to return to, a place to go some June morning when the air was clear and you could see all the way to Wyoming. In 1988, under the haze of great wildfires burning in Yellowstone Park to the west, Joey Caton and I gathered by Hoodoo Creek, ate our lunches, and admired the trout. Well, the cows got that one a few years later.

The old cattle company that leased the reservation land west of the Bighorn River went belly-up, and a bunch of little outfits, some Indian, some not, got the lease and broke it up and ran in stock without much care for the rules and with no cowboys to herd the cattle from pasture to pasture. The cows ate the short grass off the sides of Hoodoo gulch, and they stood in the creek and ate the willows, and most of all they walked, cutting trails through the bunchgrass, crisscrossing the steep hillsides. Cows are lousy at climbing or descending a slope and they are creatures of habit everywhere, and so, to get from the benches down to the water, they hoofed in miles of cow-patted switchbacks to traverse a few hundred vertical feet.

The soil around Hoodoo Creek is a young thing, recently

eroded off the red rimrock sandstone, and it doesn't have much character or cohesion ("older than dirt" is a relative judgment). It makes dark gummy mud in the spring and soft red dust in the summer. In between those seasons, for a few days, the bitterroot, *Lewisia rediviva*, shows its multiple cerise flowers, naked against the just-greening prairie.

The last time I went into the Hoodoo, on a June day when the high benches were dotted with bitterroot and sego lily in flower, the creek bottom was covered with six inches and more of red silt blown in and washed down from the scarred hillsides. We looked for fish in vain up and down, from the springs where the creek began to the waterfall where it disappeared into a canyon unclimbable to man. A pair of mallard ducks landed in the stream and dabbled for a few minutes and then took off in quacked alarm when they realized someone was watching them. Just from being mucked about by ducks briefly, the water ran red for an hour. It still hadn't cleared when we left the creek and climbed back out of the gulch. Joey Caton, who had loved that canyon stream for thirty years and more, thought about it for half a day before saying anything. He had been composing an elegy right through lunch, and he was working on one that a visitor would appreciate—"What they did to Hoodoo," he offered, "it is like someone ripped a page out of the history book"—and that was all he would say about it.

Elegies for dead rivers should mention the settings. The East Fork ran below the towering Bitterroots that stood knife-edged against the western horizon. At Hoodoo you look west to the steep weathered limestone of the Pryors, or east to the great anticline that marks the beginning of the Bighorns. That is the eye's memory. In Ross's Hole, the aroma of mint crushed underfoot gave the nose a role in the enjoyment of the green grass in the high meadow. In the Hoodoo country, the warm scent of sagebrush complemented the dry heat of the prairie. In the Bitterroot valley, the water ran properly cool; in the Crow country, spring-fed Hoodoo felt shockingly cold.

What was most peculiar about these two places, much odder than their destruction, which has been a commonplace event on land public and private in the West, was their biological antiquity.

One was tamed and farmed; one was wilder, though ranched; but they were both unique, and their beauty was apprehended by people who wouldn't fish if you paid them to do it. Besides being handsome, those waters held, when things were good, the genuine native trout of their country.

What we are talking about here, and I am pleased to have gotten this far without using the word, is finding and losing and then searching again for an authentic western alpine ecosystem. It will have fish in it, but it has more. If I were a better botanist, I know exactly what I would do to find the original West—go looking for *Lewisia rediviva* and the fourteen other members of the genus. Flowers get you away from most dollar-bringing tourists, Boy Scouts, slick-rock mountain bikers, and Outward Bounders headed for some mental adventure at tree line.

More serious birders than I, the ones who never forget to pack their binoculars, could also find themselves in remarkable country. Just adding Williamson's sapsucker *(Sphyrapicus thyroideus)* and a dipper bird *(Cinclus mexicanus)* to their life list will take them to unusual and unabused places and leave a few hundred species for the next trip. But I know my weakness when it comes to finding the Golden West: there must be, in the words of that old drugstore-cowboy hymn, cool water, clear water, water. And if the water is all of those things, it will have trout in it. So we go where the fish are, but not to cast a fly more often than is necessary to be sure we have gotten to the right place.

IN 1890, THE NATIONAL CENSUS REVEALED THAT ALL ARABLE AND habitable land in the West had been settled, although, as I said, there were a few dreamers who weren't through sod-busting yet. Reflecting on the census, Frederick Jackson Turner addressed the American Historical Association's winter convention in 1893 with the news that the frontier had disappeared, the West was closed, the great escape valve of America had shut. He was ten years late with the news. You can tell when something's gone without waiting for bureaucrats to notice and historians to analyze. It's dead when you start holding memorial services.

Buffalo Bill Cody buried the dream when he organized his first Wild West Show in 1883. He knew it was history, so he recreated it and drug Annie Oakley and Sitting Bull and assorted geriatric mountain men and gunslingers and cowboys around the United States and Europe until they got sick and tired of signing autographs and went home and stayed there. Sitting Bull, who enjoyed touring immensely, was ordered home early and would later be murdered while "trying to escape." Cody carried on with replacements until old age and that new spectacle, the motion picture, caught up with him.

Well, sometimes a little western storytelling has its good points. A young Theodore Roosevelt, inspired by several of the oddest adventure novels ever written, went out to the Dakotas for his health, mental and physical, and became a mountain man, a gunslinger, and a cowboy. As a youth, Roosevelt was not allowed to read dime novels or attend Wild West Shows, but he was extremely fond of the work of Capt. Mayne Reid, an Irish immigrant who had gone west and then wrote about it in a series of juvenile tales. I want you to get just a flavor of Reid's style, and ask you to remember that his books were very good for Theodore Roosevelt and therefore, through the power of the presidency, very good for the conservation movement in America. Captain Reid believed in scientific nomenclature and attention to biological (the word "ecological" had not been invented) systems:

> About noon [and this is typical], as they were riding
> through a thicket of the wild sage *(Artemisia tridentata),*
> a brace of those singular birds, sage cocks or prairie
> grouse *(Tetrao urophasi),* the largest of all the grouse
> family, whirred up before the heads of their horses.

Now, here's the point: if Theodore Roosevelt, a great American, could put up with an occasional bit of binomial Linnean scientific nomenclature, so can we. It is good for us, not easy to chew but nutritious, something like buffalo *(Bison bison)* jerky. I will only do it once in a while, I promise, and almost always in the service of precision and clarity.

A few years after Roosevelt went out West and became robust, he made it to Cuba for the Spanish-American War, charged up San Juan Hill with, if slightly behind, a personally recruited brigade of like-minded amateur and professional Westerners, and that made him a war hero and a useful and successful candidate for vice president of the United States. It did not hurt his electoral chances that Buffalo Bill immediately added a pageant of Roosevelt's Rough Riders charging Spanish infantry to his original Wild West staple—Custer's Last Stand.

After an extremely disgruntled anarchist with a handgun assassinated Pres. William McKinley, we got our first dude-ranching commander in chief. As president, and not a moment too soon, Roosevelt began to save most of what's left of the West out there in the national forests and the national wildlife refuges and national parks and monuments and, heaven help us, in all those fragile arid spaces under the thumb of what has been the great oxymoron of this century, the Bureau of Land Management. Roosevelt's presidency was good for 40 million acres of national forest, five national parks, sixteen national monuments (the Grand Canyon, for one), four national game refuges, and fifty-one bird sanctuaries. Roosevelt had a particular interest in birds, although of a rather rough-and-ready sort. As a youth he shot and mounted his own specimens.

The very first wildlife refuge in the country, Wichita Mountain down in Oklahoma, was bought in 1901 and fenced and managed just to have a few buffalo (you remember the Latin, I'm sure) left in the country where the old Southern Herd had numbered in the tens of millions. Bill Cody approved of the idea, although he would have figured out a way to charge admission.

Critics of our federal land-management agencies have made a good living by pointing up the numerous failures, mistakes, misjudgments, and occasional fatuousness of the government, but Roosevelt pushed something that Americans have never stopped believing could be true. The West is still supposed to be like it was, to be preserved, and that is something we don't expect of any other quadrant of America.

It's gotten to the point where, back East, you can get a friendly

audience out to hear a proposal to turn a big chunk of the old Nebraska Territory—everything roughly from Lewistown, Montana,
to Belle Fourche, South Dakota, and north to the Canadian border, including Teddy Roosevelt's old ranch—back into the national bison range. The idea is to start buying every piece of
private property that comes on the market, put a fence around the
reserve, and give it back to the buffalo. My mother, who died a
few years ago, was raised square in the middle of the proposed national bison range, and let me tell you, if she had thought it would
work, she'd have left the promoters something in her will. But she
got out when the getting was good. The ones that stayed aren't
buying into the plan, and in spite of the good intentions of the
New York Times and National Public Radio, there'll be a national
bison range just as soon as they finish that ski lift in hell.

Most tourists don't need 20,000 square miles of free-ranging
buffalo. All some of us require is a buffalo snapshot; the rest of us
will settle for a buffalo burger.

But Americans want their West, and I'd like to show you some
of it. The good place is always within sight of running water. The
Old West isn't all locked up in a park or a federal forest or sitting
on top of some mountain where you have a view of the next
mountain. It's in the water. Even where it's dry now, in the badlands and canyons and kolobs and coulees and gulches and salt
flats, the scenery was shaped by water. The Native Americans had
that right: all creation starts with water. And the modern history of
the West begins on running water.

As best they could, and they were surprised how hard it
was, the Lewis and Clark party explored the new Louisiana Territory and the disputed Oregon country by river. The next Anglos
into the country had one thing on their mind and that was beaver
(Castor canadensis) pelts, and that meant following the Missouri to
all its headwaters and down the other side into the Columbia and
the Colorado and the Rio Grande until there weren't enough
beaver left in the West to eat a box of toothpicks.

It's a shame that Theodore Roosevelt was fonder of gunpowder than trout flies, because the one thing that got plain left out of the great conservation movement of the early 1900s was running water. Maybe it could never have been saved from all those dams and irrigation districts and hydroelectric generators and placer mines and a million rinky-dink little projects that mimicked the big ones on private and public land from Mexico to Canada. The trouble with western water is that it all belongs to someone; it is a commodity, an inheritance, a chattel.

It took the government about seventy years to get from the first national forests and national wildlife refuges to the first legally protected wild and scenic rivers. That's two long generations of abuse and neglect and exploitation that dwarfs what we did to solid land. In fact, if we wanted to pay the money, we could have a national bison range by the year 2000. We could restore vast seas of the old short-grass prairie and the tall-grass prairie and have grizzly bears and timber wolves from Montana to Arizona. All we'd have to do is relocate a few tens of thousands of people and a few million cow critters and woolies. But in truth, the Colorado River and the Columbia and the Missouri will be a series of stilling ponds from now until the next ice age.

But not every tributary, not every headwater, will ever be so violated again. We're back to our piece of inescapable jargon that sums it up, the unavoidable verbal pothole on the highway to happiness, "ecosystem." The federal government and some of the states have discovered that you can't just try to save endangered species; you have to save ecosystems. And up and down the water-catching western mountains, from the savannas of the Great Plains and across the true desert of the Great Basin and through the southern Sonoran Desert, the world, which is an old-fashioned way to say ecosystem, depends on running water.

Meriwether Lewis never came into the Crow country below Hoodoo Creek down along the Yellowstone. On the trip west the entire party went up the Missouri looking for the place where one tributary of the Mississippi would approach a tributary of the Columbia. On the party's return from Oregon, Clark came down the Yellowstone, passing the mouths of the Bighorn and Little Bighorn Rivers. Lewis split off and headed toward Canada to explore the Marias country north of the Missouri. On the way west they expected, as best we understand their sense of the continent, to find some low pass where a short portage would cross the Great Divide. They were hoping, if things really went well, for something like the Great Lakes (but without Niagara Falls) and water that ran both ways.

Thomas Jefferson, who sent them west, certainly had high hopes of finding such a place. The former ambassador to France was well acquainted with the great Canal du Midi, completed in 1681, an artificial waterway that allowed large vessels to pass from the Atlantic to the Mediterranean without the difficult and often dangerous passage across the Bay of Biscay and through the Straits of Gibraltar. And he knew that even the Alps were penetrable. Between the Rhine and the Danube, near Nuremberg, the divide was so nearly flat that it had attracted the attention of Charlemagne in the late eighth century, and work was actually begun, only to end with the arrival of the Dark Ages and the collapse of the Holy Roman Empire. Even as Jefferson planned to explore the West, money was being raised in Europe to build the Rhine-to-Danube, North Sea–to–Black Sea, canal. America, he believed, was in all respects superior to Europe and would reveal a way west.

There was only one angler on the expedition, Silas Goodrich, and he went along the Missouri with Lewis on the return trip. That may be why Clark, exploring the Yellowstone River, never noticed that it was chockablock full of trout. His eyes were drawn to the immense herds of elk and buffalo on the river's banks. If he noticed the bitterroot in bloom, and in an average year it would have been as he passed by, he never mentioned it. And he came upon the Yellowstone River far below the geysers and hot pots and boiling muds in what is now that national park. It was just as well. Yellowstone deserved to be publicized by a person with a sense of the dramatic, and there was one coming along in a few years, the irrepressible mountain man Jim Bridger. Neither Lewis nor Clark had any taste for the spectacular; their talent was perseverance.

Before the party split up temporarily on the return trip, and just south of Missoula, Montana, on the river named after the plant,

Meriwether Lewis dug a single specimen of bitterroot and packed it up to take home. That the bitterroot had beautiful bloom in season was irrelevant to the preservation and transport of the dried plant all the way from Montana to New Orleans and by ship to Philadelphia. He dug it because Indians had told him the tuber was edible. Lewis and Clark were interested in what we now call economic botany; that, and finding the easy way to the Pacific. The signs along the Lewis and Clark trail from South Dakota to Oregon show a stylized Sacajawea pointing west. It would be truer to life to show her leaning on her digging stick. In the hard country along the Missouri, there were days when she fed Lewis and Clark and the rest of the party with roots and bulbs and tubers.

Over in the East Fork of the Bitterroot and everywhere else in the drainage of the Clark Fork of the Columbia above the big falls near the Idaho border, in all those thousands of miles of river and stream, there was only one true trout, the Westslope cutthroat, *Oncorhynchus clarki lewisi*. It filled those waters, and in ancient times when glaciers backed up lakes along the Continental Divide and the water spilled in both directions, it had come east and occupied all the headwaters of the Missouri in the Rocky Mountains. (Lewis and Clark were somewhere around ten thousand years late to find their Great Lakes waterway from Missouri to Oregon. When the ice age ended, the lake that tipped both ways went out with the glaciers that had dammed it up.) Silas Goodrich was the first explorer to catch a Westslope cutthroat trout, and he did it east of the divide, by the Great Falls of the Missouri.

IN HOODOO CREEK, A TRIBUTARY OF THE BIGHORN RIVER, THE aboriginal trout was the Yellowstone cutthroat, *O. clarki bouvieri*, a brassy-colored, large-spotted cousin. Reservation waters usually didn't get stocked, and they never were planted so far off the tourist track. Hoodoo, tumbling down over a twenty-foot vertical fall, could not be invaded by modern migrating alien trout coming up from the Bighorn. Until they dammed the Bighorn back in the seventies, there were no trout in it; it was a warm prairie stream, meandering along 2000 feet below the Hoodoo. The native fish had climbed up into the country long before down-cutting Hoodoo Creek carved the barrier waterfall.

The Bighorn Mountains, although they lie in the rain shadow of the Rockies, catch enough precipitation to make up several rivers. The north-flowing ones are all tributaries of the Yellowstone and so of the Missouri. These waters made up the easternmost province of the inland empire of native western trout. Farther into the high plains, a hundred miles downstream and a few thousand feet lower than the snowcapped peaks, there were only warm-water prairie fish in the drainage: paddlefish, buffalo fish, catfish, sunfish. The province of western trout is tiny and always was. From eastern Montana to St. Louis, the Missouri always was the Big Muddy.

The disruption of the alpine native fishery started a century ago in the West, and Montana was as enthusiastic at meddling as any state. Norman Maclean, whose *A River Runs Through It* became the urtext for a generation of fly fishermen and other tourists, never catches a native trout in the entire novella. He and his father and brother Paul angled for introduced species, and that includes the large rainbow trout of the Big Blackfoot River. That they had not been there since the beginning of time was a fact of which Maclean seemed blissfully unaware.

Two of the introduced fish, the coastal rainbows of all hatcheries everywhere and the European brown trout, did more than outcompete the local fish; there would be consequences for the scenic landscape that no one imagined. They grew large, sometimes larger than the native fish they were displacing, and they attracted anglers from across America and from foreign countries. If you want to see a swarm of men and a few women in rubber overalls, all you need to do is head for one of the West's "blue ribbon" trout rivers.

Anglers are a fairly morose group of tourists, extremely focused on proving that they are smarter than fish. The benefit to the local economy is obvious. While residents do fish, reasonably scientific surveys indicate that most of them fish with worms (and even dig their own), and somewhere between 80 and 90 percent of them say they go fishing just to get out of the house. It is the tourist anglers and those quasi tourists—people who move to Idaho or Wyoming or Colorado or Montana because the fishing is good—who spend serious money on western trout.

A few anglers on a stream are a visual pleasure, bucolic characters in a rural landscape. A river like the Bighorn awash with drift boats ferrying fly fishers, a river like the upper Madison lined for miles with one wading angler after another, is an urban scene with a borrowed view of mountains. Well, those anglers are happy although they do not know—and if they know they do not care—that the fish they harass are not authentic. The out-of-place rainbows and brook trout and brown trout are modern improvements in the land above the plains, on a par with ski lifts, interstate highway truck stops, restaurants with wine lists, and motels with cable television.

THE ABORIGINAL FISH ARE NOT NECESSARILY ISOLATED OR ALWAYS distant from the nearest gas station. They hide out in small refugia, in little corners. They are the fishy equivalent of the old Hole-in-the-Wall Gang: they don't know their time is up; they won't admit the West is tamed. I have given up talking about them to anglers who own more than one fly rod or who have luggage manufactured expressly to carry fishing tackle. "Oh," they say, "you like those little cutthroats," and then there is a pause and the first driplet of condescension: "Easy to catch, aren't they?"

That is true. If you want to, they are easy to kill, and so were the buffalo and the passenger pigeons, and as far as we know, so were the woolly mammoths. Our American elephant may have been exterminated by the first humans to reach the Great Plains. That was another disappointment for Thomas Jefferson, along with the broken dream of a waterway west. Lewis and Clark had orders to keep a sharp eye out for lurking mastodons and mammoths. Fishing, like most exploitation of wildlife, only got hard after there were too many of us and too few of them and we started to make a game out of it.

Depending on how fine a line you draw, whether you are, as biologists say, a lumper or a splitter, anywhere from five to twenty-five species and subspecies of western trout survive. It had been my experience that all places where I encountered them were good country, finer places than the valleys already overrun with anglers carrying enough equipment in their pockets to outfit a small tackle store. If that happened by chance, perhaps it could be planned. Looking for the species and subspecies might bring everything that goes with them, wildflowers and bear tracks and the smell of mint underfoot and, if one were lucky, arrowheads.

Finding out where the wild things are is particularly easy when they are fish, and not just because they are confined to a very small fraction of the earth's running water. About a dozen of the aboriginal trout—I am "splitting" now—are officially threatened and, in one case, endangered species under federal law. The few that are not officially listed are still of special concern to state agencies, who have at long last realized that native fish are particularly adapted to local waters, to extremes of turbulence and turbidity and wide variations in temperature from season to season and from dawn to dark. But that is only part of the reason for government concern. Over and over again I have heard biologists explain what they are doing—their tedious efforts at preserving and restoring these fish—with the simple factual statement: "They belong there." And when you find your rare and wild fish, you will be as close to the Old West as ever you can be, and if you want, you can even touch one. This is not advisable with buffalo and impossible with most wildlife.

The few streams and lakes that hold native fish are well inventoried. The listed species have state and federal officials assigned to their preservation. The only problem in finding specific destinations was convincing these wardens of the gene pool of one thing: I didn't care how big the fish were as long as they were in running water in handsome country worth visiting for its own sake. Apparently, few people make a phone call to locate average-size fish, and no one ever asks a fisheries biologist what the landscape looks like. That is odd, because field biologists are great admirers of the natural world. And they spend so many hours doing paperwork that they love to be outdoors. Even the ones who have handled too many trout to give a damn about angling like watching the light change on the hills and listening to the water.

One by one, they gave me the names of many rivers to cross. And different as they were, each one turned out to be in exactly the right place.

2

At Turtle Cave

AFTER CLIMBING SLOWLY OUT OF THE HOODOO GULCH FOR THE last time—traversing the long way across the steep slope and then switching back just like a cow would—I took off my fishing vest and tossed it in the bed of Joey Caton's pickup truck. I had packed in, among other things, two empty 500-milliliter plastic bottles and a 100-milliliter bottle of pure formaldehyde. My plan had been, when we found the virginal Yellowstone cutthroat trout of Hoodoo Creek, to put a few into a nine-to-one dilute solution of scientific pickle juice so that a friend in the icthyology business could confirm their aboriginal authenticity. Now the hollow thump of the bottles on the metal bed mocked me.

I will confess to having hoped the trout might even be a new sub-subspecies. *Oncorhynchus clarki montgomeri* had a nice sound to it, if my friend was in the mood to name it after me. In a generous moment—while reflecting on all of this in my room at the Lariat Motel in Hardin, the night before I planned to meet Joey up in St. Xavier and head for the back country—I had also thought that *O. c. catoni* would be a gentlemanly gesture.

But this was a depressing beginning for an odyssey. I had come to the one last place in the world that I knew for sure was still pure and wild, and it had slipped away while my back was turned. If I had brought along a companion who detested (or barely tolerated) fishing, that person would at least have wanted to touch Hoodoo Creek as we knew it when it was good. You can drag someone almost anywhere, even over twenty miles of rutted track, if you promise them clear water, clean water, at the end. And even if you had to tell someone to be careful about the rattlesnakes (Joey managed to meet one while looking for trout in a side-spring trickle), that person would still admire the water, cautiously. But now there was no joy in being beside it, running cloudy and rusty brown, and the rattlesnake, well—it had captured the ground around the clear-flowing spring.

Given that Joey and I were twenty miles off the pavement and every last trout in Hoodoo Creek was long gone, we moved on to the backup plan. This scheme had been on our minds every time we went into the high country west of the Bighorn River canyon. It all had to do with Joey's turtle cave. Years ago, out hunting deer with Martin He Does It, the tribal game warden (and medicine man), Joey had gotten caught in a summer thunderstorm (there are no effective hunting seasons on the Crow Reservation, and not many deer anymore) and took shelter in a cave. It had a big turtle carved on the wall, he would say, holding his arms out to the side, bent at the elbows, his wrists back toward his head to show a turtle the size of a washtub. Every time we were in the back country we would go looking for the turtle. In three trips we never got close. Oh, we checked out plenty of caves, but Joey never thought they looked right. He would know it when he saw it, he said. Twenty years is a long time to remember what a cave looks like, but he was always right when he said, "Something's wrong with this one," before we walked up to it. There are caves all over back there. Everyplace the limestone crops out, running water has dissolved out hollows and deeper caves. We looked in dozens and didn't find as much as a beer can, which was surprising; you'd have thought we weren't even in Montana.

Part of the problem was we kept stopping here and there to look for arrowheads, or we'd take a run down the power-line right-of-way to look at the tepee rings, or we'd cut across the Pryor road to some exposed Cretaceous bedding and go poking around for dinosaur teeth. This time, I was so depressed by the massacre of the Hoodoo trout that I began to care more about the turtle than usual. There ought to be something good left around here besides dinosaur bones I thought, and we'd better find it.

The Crow Indians came late into the country. They got here just a few decades before Lewis and Clark showed up, and they spent very little time in the high country west of the Bighorn River. They lived down in the valleys, where the good and fattening grass grew; they called the Little Bighorn River the Greasy Grass, because that valley had the richest grazing. The tepee rings between the Bighorn and Pryor Mountains on a bench above Grapevine Creek are surely not Crow, for they are surrounded by worked flint. By the time the Crows came to Montana they were well supplied with trade goods: pots and pans, metal arrow points, and not a few muzzle-loading rifles. The Crow high ground was and is east of the river at the very beginning of the Bighorn Mountains that run from there to Sheridan, Wyoming.

One of the reasons the Crows tended to stay out of the Hoodoo, Martin He Does It had told Joey Caton, was the rock carvings—the petroglyphs—on the canyon walls and inside the caves. The Crows figured whoever made those spooky pictures was probably still hanging around. The Crows absolutely never went up on the Pryor Mountains, the range between the Absarokas to the west and the Bighorns. Pryor Mountain was already occupied by Little People, He Does It had explained. When Joey told him he had found a cave with a drawing in it, Martin wasn't interested in taking a look.

A lot of western tribes were afraid of the Little People. The description, from places as far apart as the Crow country and the Flathead territory west of the Continental Divide, was quite consistent. Little People were almost perfectly round; they were nearly all belly. Sometimes they were more oval, but always barrel shaped, with short arms and legs that stuck out of their bodies. Some of them didn't even have necks, and all you could see, besides their squat bodies, was hands and feet and the feathers in their hair. Like most malevolent dwarfs anywhere in the world,

Little People stole babies and food and medicine, especially to-bacco, and were incredibly strong for their size. Joey believes in Little People, and he's not alone. Every time someone digs up an infant human skeleton in Montana or Wyoming, the newspapers report that it could be, at last, proof of the Little People's exis-tence.

In between trips to Montana, I had been reading what I could find on petroglyphs in the area and never found a description of a turtle image in any of the books or journal articles. As a matter of fact, there aren't many regular turtles in eastern Montana. Along the Bighorn River you'll see more fossil turtles (or the casts of turtlelike Cretaceous critters) sticking out of the old marine shale than you will real turtles sunning on a rock. But there were pecked-out petroglyphs of Little People in many of the books and journals, although the authors never called them that. The Native Americans who did the rock carvings were long gone before the Plains tribes moved in or before the Salish and Nez Perce bands came up the Columbia to Montana. The later cultures made paintings on rocks rather than carvings, paintings with horses in them usually. That gives them a date sometime after the first Spanish mustangs made it up to Montana.

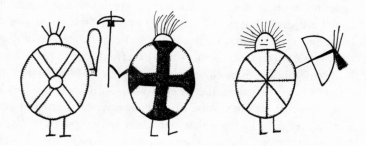

The petroglyphs that perfectly match the oral tradition of Little People are actually stylized pictures of warriors from the days be-fore horses. They are foot soldiers, and they are carrying shields in front of them, shields big enough to cover the whole trunk and the legs down to the knees. Skinny shins and feet and forearms stick out from behind the shields, one hand usually grasping a lance, less often a bow. Sometimes a head (though seldom a neck) shows; more often just a few feathers protrude from behind the top of the shield. They are excellent cartoons of the oral-tradition Little People. The Crows had shields, too, but on horseback one carries a much smaller shield, just enough to protect the vital organs of the upper body.

There are well-known Little People/warrior petroglyphs up in the Pryors. I was hoping for one, along with the enormous turtle, somewhere on the eroded saddle between the Pryors and the Bighorns. We motored slowly along the benches between the gulches looking for the turtle cave, and it never looked right, not all morning and not after lunch. The most curious thing we saw out on the sagebrush high ground was a large porcupine headed north toward the Pryor road. We both thought it was a badger for a moment; the undulating, low-slung gait confused the eye. By our best reckoning, that porky was already two miles from the closest tree and, the way it was headed, twenty miles from the next tree. We decided it was lost, not a good omen for us.

"I remember," Joey said, "that I was trying to get up-canyon from Martin, because he had moved some elk, and I was hurrying to get up where the canyon runs out and they would have to come up into the open, and I remember the sagebrush was higher than anywhere else. I was driving our old Jeep station wagon and bouncing through this high sagebrush before the rain hit." And then it started to look like this was exactly the right place and he had remembered it accurately. The sagebrush was higher than usual; it came up above the wheel wells. Ordinary Crow Reservation sagebrush doesn't come up to your knees. I must tell you— and this is why I chose that particular quotation from Captain Mayne Reid—as our pickup bounced through this veritable thicket of wild sage, a pair of those singular birds the sage grouse, the largest of all the grouse family (now classified as *Centrocercus urophasianus* and pronounced *kentrokerkus* if you want to impress an ornithologist), whirred up before our horsepower.

* * *

IF THERE IS A GENERAL RULE FOR ONCE-OCCUPIED CAVES IN COLD climates, Joey's turtle cave fit the bill. The now dry creek bed had cut a coulee down through a limestone outcrop in ages past, and the turtle cave was on the north side of the creek. Morning to afternoon it would gather in the low light of winter. The opening of the turtle cave was just as Joey remembered it. You had to stoop a little to get in. The only problem was the turtle. "It looks just like it, but it's too small," Joey said. And it wasn't exactly a turtle; that is, it was a magical turtle. On examination, it had distinct arms and legs with three-clawed hands and feet, a short tail, and no neck. It was carved just through the oxidized exterior of the limestone, which has a warm brown color, and so the turtle/whatever was startlingly white. If I had to make the call, I'd say it was more like a muskrat than a turtle.

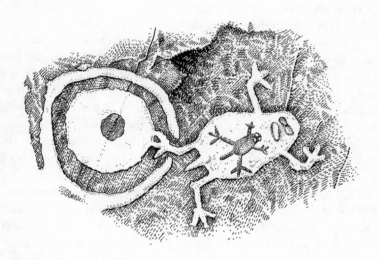

It had a humanlike face, a bifocal face; two eyes looked back at us from above a downturned mouth. On its belly or inside its belly was an exact miniature duplicate of the large carving. The artist had created it all by carefully leaving the oxidized brown surface intact for the miniature, making a brown bas-relief baby turtle. The drawing, as best people know who make a study of these things, is unique. It's the only one there is; it is something private between the artist and his god, not something public like a drawing of warriors that narrates a battle. "But too small," Joey repeated. The creature is coming out of a carefully cut round ring, one foot still inside the circle. That is a very common petroglyph motif—a circled bull's-eye—and you can make of it what you will, Freudian, Jungian, or idiosyncratic.

We were not the only people to ever see it. Well up in the rear of the cave there was a neat inscription carefully and legibly scratched through the brown surface:

Dennis Rule
Dec 10 1882

That's six years and six months after Custer's Last Stand, fifty miles away to the east-northeast over on the Greasy Grass.

Across the cave on its western wall there is a less elaborate version of the same turtle, also with the smaller one inside it, but there it is rendered sideways; you cannot see the face. The short tail is clearly oar shaped in side view, like a muskrat's, but it is carefully crosshatched to show its scaliness, like a turtle's. Still, this figure is no more than a sketch compared to the finished ventral view that Joey had noticed years ago. And outside the cave on the overleaning limestone by the entrance are several remains of more bull's-eye circles, most of them partially rubbed off either by buffalo a long time ago or, more likely, by cattle of the last century.

One of the problems with the high plains is that there is a real shortage of things for bovines to scratch on. The first telegraph companies had trouble maintaining the poles; they were like magnets to the itching buffalo. The polish on the rock that had erased most of the drawings looked too fresh, too shiny, to be as old as buffalo doing. It looked a little close to the ground, too. Range cattle aren't short, but they're no buffalo. You may have noticed, if you hang around cows much, that they almost always come over to look at you. I can never figure out whether they are trying to decide if you're good to eat or whether they just think you might be stiff enough to make a good rubbing post.

After I sketched the turtle and copied down Rule's name and date, I bent my head to go out the entrance and noticed a piece of flint lying on the floor. It was a large and perfect scraper, a big flake of flint with a resharpened and serrated edge. It was just lying on the surface, as if someone had left it there recently. Caves are a bit like garages with the doors left open; everything blows into them, and they fill up with dust and sand. That scraper should have been buried. I suspect someone else looking for arrowheads and petroglyphs had dropped it, perhaps while taking their own photograph of the turtle or after copying down their note about Dennis Rule. It was too nice a stone tool to throw away.

We got out of there directly because it looked like a thunderstorm was coming. If it rains enough while you're on the dirt track, you may get to stay all night and all day until it dries out. Four-wheeling in Montana gumbo is just a way to make big slippery useless mud balls out of rubber tires.

Back at Caton's Store in St. Xavier, Joey was getting our stuff out of the pickup when he said it again: "The turtle's too small." I asked him if his father had ever seen it, and he said yes, and I said, "OK, but let me do the talking when we go inside."

"Mr. Caton," I asked, "you remember the turtle drawing in the cave over there past Grapevine Creek [which of course you pronounce "crick" so that people will understand you], the one Joey found?"

"Sure."

"How big was it?"

"Little thing," he said, "about so." He made a circle with both hands, touching his thumbs and forefingers.

If you took the average of what they had remembered, you'd

have reality. The whole turtle drawing is about eighteen inches across, including the bull's-eye. That is a pretty good rule about most stories people tell you out West: take the average.

We leaned on the counters in Mr. Caton's store, which is well stocked with inexpensive Swiss Army surplus uniforms because that is the cheapest warm clothing he can find and it gets cold on the Crow Reservation and unemployment runs between 60 and 80 percent, depending on how you count it, and we talked about the back country, which we agreed was getting long on cattle and short on game animals and seemed to be getting very short on fish. Mr. Caton remarked that some of the tribal members were asking about trading in their .308 and .306 deer rifles on account of the shortage of game. They were looking to swap for something in the assault-weapon category. He was not sure he wanted to broker those deals.

Whether there were fish or not was of no interest to the Crow Indians. Historically, they wouldn't touch fish if they were starving. Plenty Coups, one of the major chiefs when the reservation was laid out in the 1880s, had a mentally challenged brother. The brother's name was Eats Fish.

"Makes you wonder who would draw a turtle," Mr. Caton said. "Wasn't any Crow did that." Well, we talked about that too—or, I'll admit, I gave a lecture and then tried to ease it up with a story at the end. The monologue went something like this:

Although the turtle drawing seems to be one of a kind, that doesn't mean turtles weren't an important part of the mythology of the western Indians. In several cultures, it's Turtle that makes life on earth possible. Turtle (usually after some prodding by Muskrat or Loon) brings the dry ground up out of the primordial ocean. He or she (it varies) carries the world up on his or her back so that human beings have a place to live. Sometimes it is Muskrat who talks Turtle into it; sometimes it is Loon.

When the Flatheads, one of the people that believed in Turtle, got religion, they got it by choice. Two of them walked from the Bitterroot River valley in Montana to St. Louis, Missouri, because they had heard from their Canadian cousins that the Black Robes had the answers about life after death, and the closest place to find a priest was St. Louis. Among other things, they had to walk over the Continental Divide and then through Blackfoot country and then Crow country and then Cheyenne country and Sioux country; all of those people were enemies. They got their Catholicism, but they had trouble giving up Turtle. One old woman got in a serious argument with Father Ravalli, a Jesuit priest from St. Louis who had been talked into coming west. She could swallow it all except the part about God making the world in six days. It was Turtle, she said; he holds up the world; we live on his back.

"And who holds up Turtle?" asked Father Ravalli, so the story goes. He was a man who preferred to work as a good Jesuit should, by logical argument and gentle persuasion.

"Another turtle," she said.

"And that one, who holds up that turtle, if not God?"

"It is no use, Father," she said; "it's all turtles. It's turtles all the way down."

I'll admit, when you write it out, that seems like a long story for a hot humid afternoon. But some Montana people will go on about things. I believe what you get out West is a sort of polarized conversational output. Some people won't say boo and some of us will bend your ear. The total amount of talk, like the two estimates of the turtle drawing, averages out to about what you'd expect.

And then we got to talking about Custer, which you usually do on the Bighorn, and there was more talk than normal that year because a television company was in town filming an *American Experience* program on the battle. And that got us going on the subject of battlefields, and I asked Joey Caton if he'd ever been to the new state park at the site of the battle of the Rosebud, which happened just a few days before Custer's mistake, and he said no, and I said we'd go tomorrow, which we did.

And after looking at the Rosebud, we were going down to Sheridan, Wyoming, which is approximately on the way back around from Rosebud Creek to St. Xavier if you're not in a hurry. I cannot get away from running water anyhow, and I particularly wanted to see Sheridan, because that's where Big Goose Creek comes into the Tongue River. Those waters, in the last two weeks of June 1876, were the site of the greatest trout massacre in the history of the United States Cavalry.

3

On the River
with Crook

ROSEBUD CREEK, LIKE THE LITTLE BIGHORN, IS A PIECE OF WATER
with more history than it needs. It comes out of the Rosebud
Mountains (hills, really, compared to the Bighorns right behind
them) on the eastern edge of the Crow Reservation, runs north
and east through the Northern Cheyenne Reservation by Busby
and Lame Deer, and finally drops into the Yellowstone at the town
of Rosebud, between Miles City and Forsythe.

If you take out a map of Montana and look at the Yellowstone
valley, you'll get a quick lesson in the politics of war and peace.
There are two Indian reservations side by side, the Crow and the
Northern Cheyenne. The Crow Reservation runs to some 3500
square miles (and used to be almost twice as large, almost 6000
square miles, or 38 million acres). The Cheyenne got about a
tenth as much, around 400 square miles. The Northern Cheyenne
were among the victors at the battle of the Little Bighorn (and the
battle of the Rosebud), but the Crows were on Custer's side—or,
more exactly, Custer had a handful of Crow scouts, all of whom

had the good sense to quit and go home a day early. The Crows also had the luck not to be in anybody's way and to be natural enemies of every Plains tribe that was in the way of wagon tracks, railroads, telegraph lines, and settlers. My enemy's enemy is my friend, as they still say in parts of the world.

The battle of the Rosebud was one of those unplanned events that war is too willing to provide. It happened just nine days before Custer's last fight on the Little Bighorn. There were three army groups operating in Montana that summer. General Terry's command, with Custer on the point, was heading west from North Dakota; General Crook was moving north from central Wyoming; and General Gibbon was wandering around somewhere between Bozeman and Billings, north of the Yellowstone. What they were after was the various Indians who were off the reservation. Grateful as the citizens were for the eventual success of the three United States Army forces, one is not surprised to learn that only Custer, Terry, and Gibbon got towns or counties or rivers in Montana named after them. That is because Custer died gloriously, Terry and Gibbon saved the separated survivors at the Little Bighorn, and Crook quit while he was ahead.

General Crook, already a noted Indian fighter from the Apache campaigns down in the Arizona Territory, had a perfectly straightforward military policy: you found villages (*rancherias* as they were called in Arizona and New Mexico), shot anyone who stood up, and burned the food and dry goods and hauled off anything that would be useful. In the euphemistic jargon of the bitter end of the twentieth century, his policy was ethnic cleansing and the process was destruction of the infrastructure.

In Arizona he had been a lightning raider, making his men carry their own rations and ammunition whenever possible; he eschewed the baggage trains and wagons of other commanders and built a mobile strike force. Indeed, he had relied on Native Americans for most of his fighting men. Some change occurred when Crook came to the plains: perhaps it was the vastness of the territory, the lack of obvious places to find and destroy an enemy, the sheer sense of endlessness. Moreover, his past success in Arizona and his later triumph in 1883, when he would pursue Geronimo

deep into Mexico and force the surrender of the Chiricahua
Apaches, had always depended on pitting Indian against Indian.
When he trailed Geronimo into the Sierra Madre, he had 193 Indian fighting men, carried on the payroll as scouts, and only 42
army troopers, all of whom lagged at least a day's march behind
the scouts.

But he who had led small forces swiftly now commanded a pon-
derous army, freighted down with its own baggage, supported by
teamsters, mule skinners, and packers. A few Crow scouts were
his only hired Indian allies. He remained a methodical man, given
to riding a durable mule (named Apache) rather than a showy
horse, and almost obsessive about preparations—logistics, rations,
and camp sanitation. He had always believed in overwhelming
force, and he avoided skirmishes.

There was no rendezvous point for the three forces, and each
one had moved away from the telegraph wires that had provided
some indirect connection before the summer campaign began.
Crook, whose enormous force outnumbered Custer's, stolidly
marched north from Fort Fetterman (near modern Casper,
Wyoming) with his thousand troopers and civilian packers and
teamsters and Indian scouts. He made a semifortified forward
camp where Sheridan, Wyoming, sits today.

Sheridan is one of those western towns with no intrinsic charm
but a terrific scenic backdrop. Except for the orderly and civic-
minded Mormons of Utah, Westerners regard land-use zoning as a
form of socialism if not communism, and one man's estate is another man's trailer house on the lot next door. The Bighorn Mountains rise directly west of Sheridan without foothills to obscure the
view, although with considerable clutter along Big Goose Creek in
the immediate foreground. Western towns just sprawl until it gets
too far from downtown to build.

The reason for setting up camp on the Tongue River was simple: at the confluence of Big and Little Goose Creeks and the
Tongue, Crook had a perfect water supply for his sprawling collection of men and beasts. The trapezoid of land bounded by the
creeks, the river, and the steep Bighorn Mountains was more easily defended than a camp on the open prairie.

From Sheridan-to-be he headed north for the plains and detached a few hundred men to go downstream along the Rosebud to find a rumored Cheyenne village and clean it out. By splitting his forces, he came very close to being the hero of Crook's Last Stand.

While nearly half his fighting force descended on the village, he would wait for their return to the upper Rosebud, and then the entire command would move northwest to the buffalo range along the Yellowstone. It was assumed that when the army found the Northern Herd they would find the Sioux and the Cheyenne. Crook was right about the buffalo. A substantial band of Cheyenne, Ogala, Sans Arcs, Miniconjoux, and Unkpapas were following a herd on the rolling plains west of the Rosebud and also spoiling for a fight. They made contact with Crook's force on the upper Rosebud, the battle started, and then the Indians fell back, and back, and back until they had drawn his army out and fragmented it into manageable bites. He barely got his men together before they would have been overwhelmed piece by piece. Crook retreated after burying his dead and headed back to the base camp on Big Goose Creek. His troopers, half of whom were recently converted infantrymen mounted on rank mules, were no match for the horse-adept Indians on a movable battlefield.

Meanwhile the Indians went on back to their big camp, the one on the Little Bighorn, with the interesting news that the army was in the area and the even more unusual news that the United States Army didn't seem to have much stomach for a fight. It is impossible to tell what emotion Custer felt when, nine days later and for the first time in his career, the Indians were not frightened by some bugle blowing and a volley of carbine fire. History is speculative without survivors, but I suspect Custer was astonished even before he was afraid.

THE BATTLEFIELD AT THE ROSEBUD IS JUST AT THE MARGIN BETWEEN foothills and high plains. Near the entrance and outside the boundary of the state park is a steep rocky scarp that was used as a buffalo jump, a killing ground, for thousands of years. If you duck through the three-wire fence and climb the cliff (there weren't any No Trespassing signs), you look northwest toward the plains down an expanding triangle of nearly flat ground, a perfect place to get a small herd of buffalo started and one that inevitably pinches them in between two coulees until there's nowhere to go except over the precipice. Certain death traps, Civil War battlefields for example, have the capacity to make the mind's ear imagine the rattle of musket fire. When I am at a buffalo jump, I hear the faint rumble of hooves. It is worth the climb: it helps to understand what went wrong. The plains stretching out to the northern horizon were exactly the wrong terrain for Crook to pursue Indians. There was no wall to put them up against.

Recognizing that he was outnumbered, outflanked, and outhorsed, Crook called it a day and headed back for his base camp in Wyoming, not to stir for two weeks, when he was reinforced and persuaded to head east into Sioux country. Indeed, having been routed by the large party of hostile Indians, having suffered considerable unavenged losses, and having knowledge that Terry's command—Lieutenant Colonel Custer, Major Reno, Captain Benteen—was headed directly for the aforementioned aroused aborigines, Crook's men, with his blessing, simply retired from the Indian campaign of 1876 for a few weeks, went back to Big Goose Creek, and started fishing.

While it had begun as innocent recreation and a change in the camp diet, angling became an obsession overnight when the army returned to Sheridan. At Big Goose, just two days after the Little Bighorn fight, Crook's aide-de-camp, Capt. John Gregory Bourke, was summoned from his tent by a Capt. Anson Mills, Company M, Third Cavalry, to verify that Mills (with the unspecified assistance of two enlisted men) had caught 146 trout, beating Mills's own camp record of "over 100"—a record set on the very day of the battle of the Little Bighorn. The first fishing contest in the history of the West was under way.

These were, of course, cutthroat trout, a fish very likely absent from Rosebud Creek, although Crook and his men did not have the leisure to angle while they were there. This Rosebud water, like that of the nearby and well-named Powder River, is of poor quality, sedimented, not of high-mountain origin, and subject to a lethal combination of high temperatures and low flows in the summer. Bourke, by the way, could not have used the name "cutthroat." That perfectly descriptive word was invented in the summer of 1883, when Charles Hallock, a distinguished author and editor of piscatorial matters, caught dozens of them on a trip to Montana Territory. Hallock was fishing, by one of those accidents of redundant proper nouns, on Montana's other Rosebud Creek, a hundred miles to the west of the battlefield Rosebud, over in the Beartooth Mountains: "we caught fish there which I have never seen on the same meridian or anywhere else.... Its distinctive feature ... was a slash of intense carmine across each gill cover, as large as my little finger. It was most striking. For lack of a better description we called them 'Cut-throat' trout. Have any of your correspondents," he enquired of *The American Angler,* "taken any like them anywhere along the range?"

Like many good ideas, Hallock's "Cut-throat" title was scorned at first by the academics and angling writers who had not really noticed the fish's most obvious feature. David Starr Jordan, America's premier icthyologist (and later president of Stanford University) was shocked at such a coarse and crude appellation for the fish he preferred above all other American trout for its beauty and vigor. One correspondent to *The American Angler* suggested that while "cutthroat" was accurate it was "a terribly repulsive name. Let me suggest that he [Hallock] change it to Sioux. That expresses his idea [of war paint] and gives a pretty sounding title." But Hallock won; by the time Jordan published his magisterial *American Game and Food Fishes* in 1902, it would be "cutthroat" trout all the way down.

The western Rosebud, where the name was born in Hallock's keen observation and clear style, still has trout in it, but thanks to the usual genetic pollution of the West, it's clean out of cutthroats. Brown trout swim where it nears the Yellowstone, rainbows in the middle, and brook trout in the headwaters. It also has seventy or eighty cabins around the shore of Rosebud Lake, the largest of several ponds formed by glacial moraines along the stream. There Hallock found "an unvisited lake, and there was no boat." Still, the borrowed vista of the Beartooths is as striking as ever. Those same mountains drove Hallock, rarely at a loss for words, to admit: "I have never attempted to write up that trip because my pen could not do justice either to the sport or the marvelous scenery which we found there in the heart of the Rockies."

By and large, none of the early visitors to the Bighorns were capable of describing the country; instead, they concentrated on the facts. "My notebooks," Bourke wrote of the days just after the battle of the (eastern) Rosebud, "about this time seem to be almost the chronicle of a sporting club, so filled are they with the numbers of trout brought by different fishermen into camp; all fishers did not stop at my tent, and I do not pretend to have preserved accurate figures, much being left unrecorded."

The mood of this defeated army was elevated by trout fishing far beyond the wildest claims of any promoter of Walton's gentle sport or by any Saturday morning cable television fishing show. The defeat at the Rosebud, the mass grave of comrades, the anxious retreat—all were forgotten; repressed, one supposes, in what can honestly be called an orgy of angling.

The whole camp's sudden fascination with fishing amused a band of a hundred Shoshone warriors who had come over from the Wind River country in western Wyoming to tag along with Crook and count coup on their enemies, the Cheyenne and Sioux. The Shoshone, who traded with Columbia basin tribes, ate trout and salmon with gusto. After watching the soldiers fish for a few days, the Shoshone volunteered to show them how warriors fished. Like anything worth doing, it could be done on horseback.

They piled brush across Big Goose Creek, making a sort of water-permeable weir; and leaving a few men at the temporary dam, a half dozen Shoshone retreated downstream and then came charging up the creek bed all abreast, lashing at the water with coup sticks and lances. Hordes of trout fled upstream and pressed against the brush dam and were promptly plucked out of the water and tossed on the bank. That, a Shoshone told Bourke with pointed emphasis, was the way *men* caught fish.

General Crook was one of the few officers in camp who had no fascination with trout. His taste ran to gunpowder, and he daily provided the mess cooks with elk or bear or buffalo. He was not immune, however, to the social pressure to try his hand at the sport. The fishing had improved immensely after the Little Bighorn; the same hot weather that bloated the mutilated naked bodies on the hills up there had brought on a hatch of grasshoppers in Wyoming. And the Indians, decamping and heading back toward the Black Hills, had set fire to the summer-dry prairie. The smoke was visible on the horizon to the north, and the prairie fire apparently got the swarming grasshoppers on the move. This sudden increase in their numbers along the Tongue perked up the trout and provided the anglers with unlimited quantities of live bait. Armed with artificial flies, "General Crook started out to catch a mess," Bourke wrote, "but met with poor luck. He saw bear tracks and followed them, bringing a good-sized 'cinnamon,' so it was agreed not to refer to his small number of trout."

They had all been fishing with artificial flies, not an article of equipment that you would imagine a fighting force would carry, but summer campaigns in the old Nebraska Territory had always included recreation and scientific observation. George Bird Grinnell, then employed by the Peabody Museum of Harvard University, had accompanied Custer into the Black Hills in 1874, one of several naturalists and journalists on the expedition that had put the Sioux on the warpath to begin with. Grinnell would have been at the Little Bighorn in '76 had he not been overworked and recovering from a bout of influenza. He regretfully resigned his place on the guest list.

Fly-fishing had been a mildly successful tactic until the spate of grasshoppers attracted the all too focused attention of the trout, and the fish started to refuse inappropriate artificial lures. This phenomenon is well known to fly fishermen of the scientific bent who call it selective feeding. The fires also aroused Crook's interest in the country to the north, but not too much. Rather than looking for Custer's command with a reconnaissance-in-force, Crook, with a small party, decided to climb the Bighorns behind his camp and scout the plains from a safe distance using a spy glass. They went as high as the permanent snowfields of summer and peered off to the north. Unsurprisingly, they saw nothing.

The rolling land toward the Little Bighorn was lifeless, empty, and burnt.

I am not shocked at Crook's sudden loss of enthusiasm. Many good generals have avoided battles they could not win. What seems more phenomenal than the urge to fish rather than fight was the almost unreal abundance of trout in Big Goose Creek and the Tongue River below it. Bourke, whose job included keeping a daily history of Crook's command, reviewed his diary years later:

> I find the statement in my note-books that there must have been at least fifteen thousand trout captured in the streams upon which we had been encamped during the period of three weeks, and I am convinced that my figures are far below the truth; the whole command was living on trout or as much as it wanted; when it is remembered that we had hundreds of white and red soldiers, teamsters, and packers, and that when Crook finally left this region the camp was full of trout, salt or dried in the sun or smoked, and that every man had all he could possibly eat for days and days, the enormous quantity taken must be apparent.

Streams are variably productive, depending largely on the constancy of their flow and on the nutritional quality of the water. Rivers coming out of the Bighorns are highly productive of microorganisms. The mountains are a mix of limestone strata and leach out the phosphorous and potash that support bacteria and algae, the first links in the food chain. The Bighorn River itself is so rich in these chemicals (they are the same as the last two numbers on fertilizer bags in the familiar three-number code) that it would be unsuitable for industrial processes, should Hardin, Montana, ever get a business more complicated than an alfalfa-seed mill. It is technically polluted by nature herself, clean but much too rich. Big Goose, pouring down off the eastern end of the Bighorn Mountains, also has ideal water quality for nourishing the invertebrate prey of its trout.

When I telephoned one of the local fisheries biologists, he was a little unsure of what I would find in Big Goose Creek. Where it runs through the outskirts of Sheridan it is heavily fished, he cautioned, and above town it is surrounded by private property, and the Fish and Game Department didn't know, or need to know, much about those upper reaches. Well, it never hurts to ask, I remarked, and he gave me the name and telephone number of the landowner whose property guards the creek where it comes out of the mountains.

The telephone, or, to be more accurate, the telephone company, is not always a precise instrument. The landowner, a Mr. Lambert Neidringhaus, had two telephone numbers. One listing was correctly spelled "Neidringhaus," and the second was under "Niedringhaus." The fisheries biologist gave me the one spelled "Nie . . . ," the wrong spelling. I have since learned that Mr. Neidringhaus, whom I did not have the pleasure of meeting, would not answer the mislisted telephone, although it was his. I like a person who is punctilious about spelling, but that does seem a little fussy. Unable to call ahead and ask, all we could do was drive up Big Goose Road until we got to the dead end, and that would be *chez* Neidringhaus.

I WAS NOT WORRIED. WEST OF THE MISSISSIPPI I HAVE RARELY BEEN refused permission to trespass in order to fish. And I had Joey Caton with me, and he is the very model of low-key, dirt-kicking, ah-shucks diplomacy. On the other hand, there are some ranch gates I don't bother to go through to ask. It's hard to explain exactly how to tell which ones are a waste of time, but generally any gate that's obviously carved by a professional sign maker, that has a name like Circle R Ranch with all the letters done the right size and a coat of varnish, is a loser. There is a tendency among new arrivals in the West to shut the door after themselves and bolt it. Any gate that looks like it's been painted lately is chancy. There are some things that new money can't buy, and a gate that's been through a blizzard cycle is one of them.

The Neidringhaus spread turned out not to have any gate. Big Goose Road just ran out in a circle driveway. (Not circular. Circle, like the one in that great Western song: "I wish I had a circle drive-way, I'd just keep on goin' round, wouldn't stop to get my clothes, just keep headin' back to town.")

We also turned up Miss Marion Neidringhaus, who was sitting on the grass with her back up against a big ponderosa pine tree reading a book. The odds on finding someone reading a novel out on the lawn in Wyoming on a weekday are long.

"You are lost," she asserted, and introduced herself.

I gave her my name and answered, "I am not lost. I am looking for General Crook's fishing grounds."

"Well, you're not lost," she agreed.

"Could I go up and fish?"

"Why not?"

"I haven't got a Wyoming license."

"No problem. I had a date last night with the game warden. No, just kidding. But you won't see one. Just watch out for rat-tlesnakes."

I said something like, June was too early to worry about rat-tlesnakes.

"It's never too early to worry about rattlesnakes," she said.

It might not have been too soon to look for snakes, but it really was too early to expect much in the way of fishing. Big Goose Creek was still bitter cold; we had seen snow up on the Bighorns as we drove toward Sheridan. All I wanted to do was see what we could find for trout. I just wanted to know if the creek was still all right.

Captain Bourke had been up Big Goose Creek several times and was struck by its abrupt change to a plunge-and-pool stream, quite unlike the placid waters where it ran through Crook's camp near the Tongue River: "The dark-green water in front rushed swiftly and almost noiselessly by, but not more than five or six yards below our position several sharp-toothed fragments of gran-ite barred the progress of the current, which grew white with rage as it hissed and roared on its downward course." It still does, al-though today anyone foolish enough to commit the old pathetic fallacy and ascribe human emotion to running water would be beaten about the head and shoulders with a copy of Wordsworth's complete poems. It grew white with turbulence certainly, both above and just below the small dam where the town of Sheridan extracts its drinking water, water so innocent and clean that the testing company once suspected the town had sent bottled mineral water, not the real thing. Usually you can't get within a mile of a domestic water-supply intake, but Big Goose Creek, protected by the Private Property signs all along the road and innumerable rattlesnakes, is one exception.

There were no Yellowstone cutthroat trout in the creek; that was one thing the Fish and Game Department knew for sure. What was there, I found out by fishing with an underwater fly, were unusually large fish for a small high-gradient river. Fish don't all look alike, even of the same species. We caught a couple of feral rainbows and one brook trout, and they were all chunky, healthy, bulky fish. The brook trout was an admirable specimen, worthy of being painted as a model of the species. Winslow Homer would not be able to distinguish it from his beloved Adirondack natives. Most brook trout planted in Rocky Mountain streams are a pathetic shadow of their eastern selves. They tend to overpopulate and thus stunt themselves, and they are also often inexplicably pale. It is hard to explain, but they can have the same appearance as a human being who's having a bad day; they look *drained*. The worst example I have seen are the brook trout in the upper Big Hole River by the Big Hole National Battlefield. They look more like sardines than trout. You have to turn them in the light to see the remnants of their characteristic pink spots.

Miss Marion's brook trout (which I was only borrowing to take a picture of) was, on the other hand, in fabulous physical condition—deep bodied, colorful, and stupid. It would have made a perfect model for a Winslow Homer watercolor, and yet I could not admire it. Handsome it was, and yet wrong it was, lost it was, alien, anomalous, anachronistic it was. The effect was something like seeing a wristwatch on an extra in a western movie. A hundred generations in Big Goose Creek and the brook trout will still look like it was recently arrived from Maine. It will never be part of the western wilderness; it will always be an artifact of modern human ingenuity, a creature of improvements in transportation, as out of place on the plains as an Airstream trailer or you or me. We can see ourselves without going west.

It would have been wonderful to find, before the stocking ruined it, what Big Goose Creek would do for a Yellowstone cutthroat. At least we have Captain Bourke's record, and I find it altogether believable.

On the outing where he found the water white with rage, at the first steep section of Big Goose Creek, which would put him at the Neidringhaus estate and right in the area of the Sheridan water-supply dam where Joey and I were fishing, he tried unsuccessfully to fool the cutthroats "with all sorts of imported and manufactured flies of gaudy tints or sombre hues—it made no difference. After suspiciously nosing them they would flap their tails . . . and then, having gained a distance of ten feet, would provocatively stay there and watch us from under the shelter of slippery rocks." Lacking the modern nymph imitations that are the elite angler's equivalent of worms, or any gaudy fly remotely shaped like a grasshopper, they settled for catching live grasshoppers and dangling those in the water. "The change was wonderful: in less than a second, trout darted out from all sorts of unexpected places—from the edge of the rapids below us, from under gloomy blocks of granite, from amid the gnarly roots of almost amphibious trees."

A mule skinner by the name of O'Shaugnessy who had been brought up in the salmon districts of Ireland was the self-appointed guide on this trip, and he baited up a willow branch and string-fishing-line outfit with grasshoppers for Captain Bourke, who wrote that O'Shaugnessy told him he would find

a fine big fish, "a regular buster, in the hole beyant." O'Shaugnessy had been unable to coax him out from his retreat, but thought that, if anything could tempt him, my bait would.

I cautiously let down the line, taking care to keep in the deepest shadow. I did not remain long in suspense; in an instant the big fellow came at full speed from his hiding-place, running for the bait. He was noble,

heavy, and gorgeous in his dress of silver and gold and
black and red. . . . He was pretty to look upon, weighed
three pounds, and was the largest specimen reaching
camp that week.

Bourke got the colors right. Yellowstone cutthroats are at once
all four tints, silvery and brassy and black-spotted and showing an
almost fluorescent red at the gill covers. A big male during spawning season and for a few weeks afterward may have a rosy belly.
Three pounds is exceptional for a stream-run fish, but if a displaced Eastern brook trout could grow to more than a pound in
Big Goose Creek, I find Bourke's three-pound native cutthroat
quite believable. Although he does not say so, I suspect the
poundage was checked on the quartermaster's scales. It was, after
all, a mock-serious fishing tournament.

Abruptly, and for no obvious reason, Crook concluded that he
should communicate with Fort Fetterman, get his telegrams, and
decide what to do next. The appeal of fishing and bear hunting
had run its course; it was time to get back in touch with headquarters. "Up to the end of June, no news of any kind, from any source
excepting Crow Indians, had been received of General Terry and
his command," Bourke noted, "and much comment, not unmixed
with uneasiness, was occasioned thereby." It should be said, as
Bourke did not, that the Crow Indians had provided the unbe-
lieved news that Custer's command had been massacred.

The appeal of fishing having also palled on us, Joey Caton and I
went up-country too, forty-two miles north on the interstate from
Sheridan to Crow Agency, where we had met that morning. Crow
Agency is just up the highway from Garryowen, a village named
after the marching song of the Seventh Cavalry. From Crow
Agency, if you look due north, up on the first bench you will see
the small buildings at the Little Bighorn Battlefield National
Monument and the tourist stores near it. After meeting in the
morning, we had left Joey's truck by the Indian curios store across
from the entrance to the battlefield. The entrance and the store
are both on the Lame Deer highway, the road we had taken in the
morning, making a pretty drive to Busby and then south to the

Rosebud battlefield. If you walk behind the store, as we did that afternoon, you get an unobstructed view of the river valley, a better one, in fact, than from the battlefield and cemetery. Where you see the alfalfa fields now, that was the Greasy Grass. If Custer had gotten as far as the Indian curios store, he could have seen the whole array of tepees scattered along the Little Bighorn. It might have changed his mind about the wisdom of a frontal assault, but I doubt it.

I noticed Joey was looking southwest toward the Bighorn River canyon and the high country south of it. Another evening thundershower was darkening the hills between us and Hoodoo Creek. I said something like it was good fishing down in Sheridan and wouldn't it have been good if Big Goose still had cutthroats in it. I thought because he was staring moodily in that direction that he was thinking about the missing fish in Hoodoo.

"I guess we found that turtle," he said, changing what I had imagined was the subject. "But it's still too small."

4

Apache Country

IF HOODOO WAS GONE AND THE DARNED TURTLE WAS TOO SMALL, I was ready to write off Montana for a while. I wanted to start all over again the following spring and look for new high country that someone was keeping a better eye on. The sensible thing to do in North America is head south early and follow the summer north, and I had a hint of where to begin. The Big Goose trout derby is not the only mention of cold water in John Gregory Bourke's *On the Border with Crook*. Captain Bourke kept a poet's eye on running water while he was on that Mexican border in the Apache campaigns, and he kept an angler's eye on what was in it. Almost casually, writing of Fort Apache, Arizona, he remarked that the river by the fort was well supplied with trout. He gave no other physical description of the country, but I could see it in my mind's eye. There would be pine trees, and I was betting on apple trees. So I would begin there, high above the Sonoran Desert, on the river with Bourke.

Albuquerque seemed close enough to the Arizona mountains; and I had been to Phoenix once in my life, and that was enough. Albuquerque sees the occasional fly-rod-toting tourist; it is the closest large-plane airport to the lower San Juan River near Farmington, New Mexico, a destination blue-ribbon river. The headwaters of the San Juan and a few more high-country streams in the San Juan Mountains of Colorado still hold wild and native fish of two rare and threatened species, but few bother with them; too small and too innocent are the aboriginal trout of North America for too serious anglers.

The San Juans are the Continental Divide in this country, separating the Rio Grande (which flows to the Gulf of Mexico) from the Colorado River drainage (which is headed for the Gulf of California). When it was good—and that was a long time ago, before sheep, cattle, lumbering, and extensive row-crop agriculture—the main San Juan was home to Colorado River cutthroat trout *(Oncorhynchus clarki pleuriticus)*, an always beautifully colored fish with the potential, in large waters, of reaching handsome sizes—fish as long as your leg, as they boast in Colorado. They were replaced almost everywhere by stocked rainbow trout, which bred with them and won the battle of the genes, and elsewhere lost habitat to more prolific brook trout and more aggressive brown trout. They are as rare in New Mexico as restaurants that don't offer a choice of green or red chili on everything you order. East across the divide, but still in the San Juans, the Rio Grande cutthroat trout *(O. c. virginalis)* survives in small headwaters near the divide and also in the Sangre de Cristos on the east side of the Rio Grande valley. That is a fish worth knowing in unabused country, and we will find it before we are done.

The trouble with the lower San Juan, the cold tailwater river below the Navaho Dam, is that the fishing is too good to be true and all the trout are as long as your arm and the banks are lined with fly fishermen who conflate size with importance. Controlled water and stocked fish have nothing uniquely western about them. Things out of place are curious but not satisfying. In the same way, it makes no sense to me to visit Lake Havasu, Arizona, to admire the authentic London Bridge so carefully transported to that recreational mecca: there are no tides, for starters, and no fog, for another.

A few hours drive southwest of Albuquerque, across the border into Arizona, one of the rarest trout in the world swims in the headwaters of the Salt River above Fort Apache, a fish so obscure that it was not even identified as unique and given its proper name until 1972. This is the Apache trout, *Oncorhynchus gilae apache*, one of a pair of fairly primitive and intensely isolated trout that survive in the middle of the great desert that surrounds them. It is found in the midst of the White Mountain Apache reservation and streams in the abutting Apache Sitgreaves National Forest. The other in the duo is the Gila Trout *(O. g. gilae)*, a very few of which still swim in the old Mescalero Apache stronghold of the Gila Mountains in southwestern New Mexico. The Gila trout is on the endangered species list, and visitors are not allowed to touch one. There is very little to report on an impalpable trout. You do not have to eat a trout to know it well, but you do need to catch one, hold it for a moment, and release it. Just looking at a trout in the water is bit like going to a museum and looking at the art through a bottle; the view is distorted and the visitor disengaged.

Even the best of museums, those do-not-touch places, have begun to provide artifacts that the visitor can handle or wear. This is the curatorial version of catch-and-release fishing. These objects are usually imitations and re-creations, but they satisfy the urge. A few miles north of Albuquerque, for example, at the state park in Bernalillo, you can climb down into a restored kiva. Inside the museum you may grind corn with a metate at one exhibit and then, a few feet down the aisle, don the improbable iron headgear of a Spanish conquistador and examine your image in a mirror. These moments of make-believe would not be half so satisfying in Boston or New York. Just outside the museum runs the Rio Grande; behind the building, surrounding the restored kiva, lie the crumbling adobe walls of an authentic pueblo. It is the same with fish and other wild things: there are places where some belong and others do not, and we should travel toward them, not expect them to come to us.

Both of these desert-bound trout-water alpine environs are remote from all other similar landscapes. One crosses, however easily by automobile, vast reaches of inhospitable and beautiful desert to find them. Besides trout, which are merely my symbol of surviving wilderness, these old Apache and Gila refuges have their mountain lions in abundance and very nearly still have that ultimate indicator of western wilderness, the grizzly bear. That animal is extinct south of Yellowstone Park, but it held out as long as it could against the armaments of trappers and ranchers, surviving in the same country as the desert trout.

If you went to Cliff, New Mexico, on the Gila River and looked northeast toward the Mogollon Mountains and the Gila Wilderness, you would see the last stand of the grizzly in New Mexico, an animal killed in 1931 on the old LC ranch. It was the last of the breed that once swatted Gila trout out of the mountain meadow streams. The last Arizona grizzly went down in 1935, just on the eastern edge of the White Mountains between Clifton and Blue, Arizona, not far from where Apache trout survived high in the White Mountain Apache Reservation.

You have to admire the grizzly. It may be extinct in the Southwest, but it took fifty years of intense government trapping to finish it off. It lasted longer than Coues's elk, the original great deer of the country, an elk with palmated antlers—with broad flat areas between the tines making it something of a cross between moose antlers and the deerlike tines of Rocky Mountain elk. But great predators cannot survive without abundant prey (think of the educational television movies that do show an accurate ratio of dinners to diners: wildebeest by the hundreds of thousands, lions by the score), and after the turn of this century, most of the prey animals in New Mexico and Arizona were cattle and sheep. Predation became thievery, either from the herds or from the hunter's game pole. Wolves too went down in the dirty thirties.

Aldo Leopold, the great ecologist of our century, killed some of the very last wolves on the Mogollon Rim between Fort Apache and Gila. The idea was to increase the number of deer by reducing the number of four-legged predators. Trapping reformed him from a being reflexive government employee into a reflective independent thinker; the insight came as he watched the light go out in his last wolf's eyes.

Neither bears nor trout nor wolves seem possible on the road out of Albuquerque toward the Fort Apache country. The traveler's back is resolutely turned to the mountains; the windshield reveals a vast arid plain interrupted only by mesas. The last hint of high country is in the rearview mirror, to the north and east. Ahead and to the left, west and south, where the trout are said to live, the terrain promises only monotony.

The interstate highway from Albuquerque to Gallup and on to Winslow, Arizona, replaces old Route 66, bits of which survive. Old 66 bisects downtown Gallup—endless storefronts offer Indian jewelry on (perpetually) Half Price Sale. Over in Holbrook, Arizona, stands one of the great artifacts of the early age of automobile travel, the Tepee Motel. This cluster of white stucco tepees is scattered across a half a city block, right on Route 66. They have been recently (late eighties) refurbished and glow white in the street lights. "Everyone stops and takes their picture," the night clerk remarked to me one evening, "but most people don't get a room."

IT IS NOT NECESSARY TO TRAVEL AS FAR WEST AS HOLBROOK BEFORE turning south toward the White Mountains. I did it only to see the Tepee Motel. The hurrying traveler will leave Interstate 40 at Sanders, just across the border (and the Continental Divide) into Arizona, and start down Route 666 to St. Johns and then make a choice of ascending the mountains either through the old Mormon settlement of Springerville on the east or through the old mining and cattle town of Show Low to the west. Springerville, totally unprepossessing, sits on the earliest transcontinental highway, U.S. 60, which runs from Newport News, Virginia, to Santa Monica, California, but has none of the fame, probably because it has none of the rhythm, of Route 66. Still, when you are in Springerville, understand that you are standing where the first automobile, a Pathfinder driven by A. L. Westgard, passed through Arizona on the first transcontinental auto trip in the history of the United States.

The original and eponymous Mr. Springer was a man who opened a general store and made the mistake of extending credit to the numerous cattle rustlers, stage robbers, and assorted ne'erdo-wells who had congregated in the valley. This put him out of business in less than a year, and when a U.S. post office was established in 1876, the residents put in for the same "Springerville" as a joke, not realizing or caring that it would hang around the town's neck forever.

Show Low, the next town west on 60, got its name from the card game that was played in the Old West much more than poker ever was, no matter what you see in the movies. That's the British game of Seven Up, the source of that now meaningless litany "high, low, jack, and the game!"

Two partners had opened a stagecoach stop where Show Low is now. It was remarkable, in 1876, for its cleanliness. Popular as it was, there wasn't enough business to support the two of them, and the partners agreed to a winner-take-all game of Seven Up. The two men, Corydon E. Cooley (a former scout with our old acquaintance Gen. George Crook) and Marion Clark, were tied at six, within one point of the seven required to win the game. Cooley had already shown a high trump and the jack of trumps to pull even, and Clark realized that his hand did not hold a solitary low trump to show. He told Cooley, "If you can show low, you win." Show low it was, and one supposes Cooley summed up his winning hand by intoning "high, low, jack, and the game." Show Low it is, a small mercantile center at the foot of the Mogollon, a staging area for visitors to the Apache reservation and the White Mountains.

Alternatively, you can reach either Springerville or Show Low by heading a few miles farther west than Sanders and head south through the Petrified Forest National Park. Whichever way you travel, the first hint of anything in the trout way of business is a faint blue shadow on the southern horizon that ever so slowly deepens and solidifies into a mountain range. The White Mountains begin to be visible to the southbound motorist around the town of Snowflake, which might give the traveler the wrong idea of the local weather, however accurate an idea of the weather before him in the mountains. It was founded by two Mormons, a Mr. Flake and Mr. Snow, and has nothing to with trout country. Like so many ranges, the White Mountains will disappear again south of Snowflake, blocked out by the foothills as you approach.

Water, as you travel the high ground of the Colorado Plateau toward the mountains, is scarce to nonexistent. Occasional dry washes cross the highway, and, lacking culverts, the road just dips down to wash level and then bounces back up again. It was a rainy May when I visited, and there were temporary signs along Route 666, the southbound highway, warning that the road was closed ahead. It was not; they were just late in picking up the folding signs. Sand and gravel still lay on the blacktop at several washes, and the damp high-water mark on the sides of the washes was visible and plenty high to stop a vehicle. I have endless enthusiasm for Indian artifacts, and thinking that the previous day's thunderstorms might have sluiced out something in the relic line, I stopped at the second wash and spent half an hour walking up the edges of the gully, poking at interesting objects with a fishing staff. There were a few pottery shards in the debris, and I took them home with me.

Running water in the washes was evidently a rare event. There was no low-growing greenery, nor any cottonwoods. This was very intermittent water, not to be relied upon in any season. Driving across and walking on the high desert is a useful enterprise for people trying to understand the West. Except for mining towns, there are no old settlements, not even single ranches, very far from reliable running or standing water. Windmills and steel water tanks extended the reach of habitation and accounted for the final settlement that closed the frontier in the 1890 census.

The importance of springs, creeks, and "tanks" (which is southwest talk for natural waterholes) made water part of the naming of the landscape. In Arizona, where "coyote" is a common attribute in place names, there are thirteen different Coyote Springs, three Coyote Tanks, two Coyote Waters, and five Coyote Wells. However, in this land of such scarce running water, there is only one single solitary Coyote Creek.

Moving water, so precious and so rare, became part of the dreamworld of western life, the very definition of peace and tranquility. Lieutenant Bourke, our biographer of Gen. George Crook, was from well-watered Pennsylvania, but he developed an ear for

the mythical power of western water (and a keen eye for the presence or absence of trout). His description of the peaceful death of
one of Bourke's Indian fighters captures the sensibility perfectly.
Old Jack Long, he wrote

> was in camp with one of the commands on the San
> Carlos, and broke down entirely; in his delirium he saw
> the beautiful green pastures of the Other Side, shaded
> by branching oaks; he heard the rippling of pellucid
> waters. "Fellers," he said, "it is beautiful over thar; the
> grass is so green, and the water so cool; I am tired of
> marchin', 'n I reckon I'll cross over 'n go in camp"—so
> poor old Jack crossed over to come back no more.

It was likely that malaria did in Jack Long. Wherever water from
the mountains reached down to the tropical heat of the desert,
there was malaria in Arizona Territory.

The road out of Show Low up to Pinetop, the last town before
you enter the Apache reservation, has considerable promise if you
have trout on your mind. In June local landowners, mostly retirees
escaping the heat of Tucson and Phoenix, set out roadside tables
with fresh stone fruit for sale, peaches and nectarines and apricots.
Twenty miles ago it was high desert sagebrush and prickly pear
cactus; suddenly it is cold-climate fruit for sale. Pinetop started
out as an off-reservation saloon for soldiers from Fort Apache and
didn't progress much further until the automobile put it within
reach of the desert towns to the west.

Its social history is pretty plain to an observer. There's an abandoned fish hatchery, relic of the age of introducing exotic trout.
Several small trailer parks are mostly occupied by mobile homes
that appear not to have moved since they arrived, including a
number of vintage Airstream "bullets." Mountain resorts had, out
in the western deserts, a period of boom right after World War II
when reliable automobiles were available but air-conditioning had
yet to reach the consumer market. When home air refrigeration
become common in the sixties, most of the small resorts stopped
growing. This accounts for the evident venerable age of the permanently parked trailers.

Second homes for the masses were many years down the road. Condominiums arrived in the brief savings-and-loan bubble of the eighties. The developers left their mark; for miles the road to Pinetop is new and four lanes wide, with the faltering beginnings of a continuous strip of businesses from Show Low to Pinetop. Off in the woods, condominium second-home developments cut into the pine forest. It is not quite working. On any given night, Pinetop in the nineties seems to have more empty beds than occupants.

WHAT BROUGHT ME TO PINETOP WAS THAT GREAT MOTIVATOR, UTTER ignorance. I didn't know what an Apache trout looked like, didn't know where to find one, and even if someone drew an X on a map, it would be on some Forest Service back road or tribal logging track, and they get surly at rent-a-car companies when you take their shiny vehicles into the boondocks. In Pinetop, at the Arizona Game and Fish office, a fellow named Jim Novy knew where the fish were in the national forest and had offered to show me. The Apache trout is a "fish of special concern," as they say, not on the endangered species list but the object of considerable management efforts, all attempts to repair the damage done in the past by stocking and in the present by continued degradation of the habitat (which means three things out West: mines, cattle, and chain saws). After a day with Novy I would get a look at tribal waters where environmental problems were limited to chain saws. The Apaches don't raise cattle for profit; they raise Rocky Mountain elk and sell hunting privileges for considerably more money than you can get for beef critters.

Jim Novy turned out to have one of the less common personality traits in America, although we find it a little more often in the West than back East. It is hard to describe; it is not the romantic man (or woman) in nature; the West is too much tamed for that. Westerners who commune with nature full-time usually turn out on close inspection to be immigrants, dropouts, druggies, or survivalists. People usually talk about Westerners being easygoing, but that has intimations of indolence or laid-backness, which are not appropriate. For some reason, the word I think of is "amicable," maybe just because it sounds a little more old-fashioned than "friendly," a word much cheapened by the tendency of people who think it is friendly to say "Have a nice day" too often. At a large supermarket near my home, the store once offered a full refund of the price of your groceries if the checkout clerk forgot to say, "Have a nice day."

The amicable Westerner, and everybody whose name appears in this book is one, is pleased to have guests and takes great pleasure in showing people his or her world and is confident that you will like it and is personally complimented when you say you do. It is the obverse of tourism marketing or regional chauvinism; it is more a way of indicating, without saying it in so many words, that I choose to live here because it is good country, and now I will share it with you. I will give you an example that has nothing to do with wildlife or trout or running water, an example that steps outside of Anglo westernism but is entirely of the amicable persuasion.

Before leaving New Mexico for the White Mountains, I traveled north of Santa Fe to look up an old high school friend who writes books because he cares about the language and who raises garlic for a living. On the way I came to Zia Pueblo, one of the smallest of all New Mexican pueblos both in area and population. I dislike the idea of driving into Indian reservations or pueblos just to look around. Even when it has been organized into a revenue-producing event, as at Acoma Pueblo or Taos, it seems like voyeurism. But if you have a purpose, that is different. It seemed like a good idea to buy a piece of pottery, and while pueblo pottery is widely available in shops throughout New Mexico, it is also possible to buy it directly from artists who have not signed exclusive contracts with galleries, or so I had been told.

Zia is just an unpaved main road, a large Catholic church, and a few dozen adobe houses. On one there was a small and faded sign saying "Pottery" and some newer, mysterious decorations, including red-white-and-blue crepe paper bunting over the front porch. I knocked on the door and was swept into what turned out to be a high school graduation party for the potter's granddaughter. Nothing would do but that the visitor, besides looking at some fine pottery, eat a full meal, drink lots of Kool Aid, and have a piece of the graduation cake. I was introduced to the entire family and the guests who arrived as if I were planning to move in next door. Pueblo houses, by the way, are indistinguishable from regular housing forms on the inside: Sheetrock-and-plaster walls, electric baseboard heat, and wall-to-wall carpeting. There were two framed pictures in the living room: the Sacred Heart of Jesus and John F. Kennedy.

I found something I could afford and bought it from Mrs. Chije (although some men now make pottery, it is traditionally and properly a women's art) and headed off. Her husband walked me to the car and thanked me for coming to the graduation party and then said: "You must come back for the Corn Dance; that is the best thing at Zia Pueblo. We have dancing in the parking lot behind the church and all different kinds of food for everyone, and you will like it very much."

"When is it?" I asked him.

"August fifteenth."

I apologized. I couldn't come that year, but if ever I was in New Mexico in August, I would come to the Corn Dance and look for him and his wife and say hello. And then it occurred to me that the date of August 15 was familiar to me from years spent working in the largely Roman Catholic city of Boston.

"Isn't that the feast of the Assumption?"

"Oh, yes," he said, "that too."

That is what I mean by "amicable." It is a way of being friendly and at peace with the world. We will have our Corn Dance and you really should come. And the Virgin? She can come too.

Jim Novy's Apache trout are, for the most part, clear across the White Mountains from Pinetop on the east side of the reservation, closer to the towns of Alpine and Springerville. Over there, the fish are in small tributaries of the Salt River, or, to break it down further, headwaters of the Black and White Rivers that make up into the Salt. The Mogollon Rim, pronounced *Muggy-yawn* in Arizona, makes up a divide between the Salt River drainage, all headed off through the desert for Phoenix and the lettuce ranches that surround it, and the Little Colorado, which flows north across the tilted Colorado Plateau to the big Colorado, where it hits the river fifty miles north of Flagstaff. The divide is almost imperceptible. Little Colorado waters and Salt River tributaries both arise on the top of the Mogollon east of the Apache reservation, but the Salt's cut down through the rim and escape to the south, while the Little Colorado's found their way out to the north and west. Historically, both river systems held Apache trout, due to interbasin transfers as lakes formed and then disappeared high on the rim. But as Jim Novy put it, "We lost them in the Little C." That may be partly because the Little Colorado was easier to stock with aliens, but it has more to do with the natural terrain.

Both the Salt and the Little Colorado were regularly stocked with all the typical imported trout (brown, brook, and rainbow), but the headwaters of the Salt—the forks of the White and Black that dropped down through the Mogollon Rim—made up into cascades and waterfalls, natural barriers to upstream migration from the roadsides where fish were always stocked. The Little Colorado's tributaries, making a gentler descent across the north-sloping top of the Colorado Plateau from the Mogollon Rim, lacked those natural barriers and were perfused with exogenous genes. The difference in the topography of the two river basins is obvious to someone who arrives at Pinetop from the two basic directions. The Mogollon Rim is invisible coming down south and uphill from Holbrook along the Little Colorado; only the high White Mountains show against the skyline, and the road is gently graded and the ascent almost imperceptible, except for the last few miles to Pinetop. If you come from Phoenix or Tucson headed north through the Salt River basin, the Mogollon looms like a continental landfall in the ocean of desert, and the road itself, where it has to cross the downcutting Salt River, is steep and windy and canyonesque to the point of vertigo. For myself, having been both ways and hoping to return someday, coming up through the Salt River Canyon will remain a unique, one-time experience.

The closest national forest Apache trout to Pinetop and to visitors are just outside the eastern boundary of the reservation at the base of Mount Baldy, the highest peak in the White Mountains. It is the local sacred mountain, although if it has an Apache name, no one will admit it. I think it does not; it is just plain Mount Baldy. In the national forest, its slopes are part of a designated wilderness area; on the reservation slopes it is a ski area, run for profit by the White Mountain tribal government. One can exaggerate the Native American respect for the land.

These particular Apache trout, on the national forest side of Mount Baldy, are one part of Jim Novy's career-long restoration projects. A small creek coming down the northeast slope of the mountain had been dammed for livestock purposes back in the 1930s. This is Lee Valley Reservoir, and like all the Little Colorado drainage, it was devoid of Apache trout. The reservoir still holds aliens, plus a few restocked Apaches, but the feeder creek has been renovated, as they say in fisheries-speak—that is, poisoned out and restocked. In addition, like most Little Colorado streams, Lee Valley Creek lacked the dramatic pitch that makes for barriers to upstream migration, and a complicated concrete-and-steel waterfall barrier had to be constructed just upstream of the reservoir. We walked around the lake to look at it, and it was an admirable and effective piece of small-scale civil engineering. At this point I realized we were standing in a wilderness area, and that meant tons of concrete and structural steel had to be rowed across the lake and carried the last hundred yards by hand. Not even the preservation and re-creation of wilderness allows for the use of machinery and motorized vehicles in a designed wilderness area. Upstream of the barrier, Lee Valley Creek meandered through a healthy *ciénaga*, a sedgy marsh ungrazed by cattle. The running water is off-limits to fishing until it's certain that the Apache trout are reproducing, but it should open before the end of the nineties.

"That," Novy said, pointing at the creek, "is what a trout stream is supposed to look like. It's the last one you'll see today that looks right." The basic problem, he explained as we drove south along the eastern edge of the reservation-forest boundary, was plain old cattle. "They truck them up, drop them off, and leave them for the summer. The cow, now that is an animal that won't move ten feet until it's starving to death, and they spend most of the time standing in the creek." As if on schedule, although he was surprised himself to see them up in the national forest so early, we encountered the first cattle of the year standing in Burro Creek chewing on the vegetation.

"It gets to the point," he said, "where we have an endangered plant up here, the Arizona willow. They used to line the creeks, and now I don't see two of them in a day's work."

We stopped at Stinky Creek, which didn't seem to deserve the name, and looked at some new fencing that paralleled the banks. "Those are live stock exclosures," he explained, "and it's not easy to get permission to build one. We have to jump through a lot of hoops. You go to a public hearing and say the cattle are ruining the streams, and they'll tell you it's the elk; we got too many elk, and that's the problem."

Several dusty miles later, we got to Centerfire Creek, where the long process of proving that elk and cattle do different things to running water was under way. About two miles of the creek is fenced in with standard three-strand barbed-wire cattle fence. Sections of the top wire at each end of the valley were covered with plastic tubing so that elk and deer jumping the fence wouldn't accidentally cut themselves on the wire. This, then, is the experimental situation: a meadow with no cattle, but elk access. Then, to settle the issue of how much grass elk eat, rectangular patches the size of a one-car garage were further fenced, elk-high, to compare elk-grazed meadow with completely protected turf.

The grass, you could see without getting out a ruler, was a little higher inside the elk exclosure than outside. But the difference between the meadow inside and outside the cattle exclosure was dramatic and visible. Up to the fence, where cattle could graze, the grass was golf-course-fairway short and sprinkled with dandelions just coming into bloom. Inside, the new grass was higher than the worst kind of rough (to stay with golf comparisons), and dandelions had been choked out by the hay. There was one difference that I did not see until Novy pointed it out: in the elk-only meadow there were old seed heads, dried and brown, left from the previous fall. Outside, in cow country, they'd been eaten long before they could mature.

I said that the seedheads were pretty obvious once somebody pointed them out, and was a little chagrined that I hadn't noticed.

"We all learn something every day," Novy said. "I thought I knew a lot about stream habitat, but there were some obvious things I never saw until we got some hydrologists in here to look at the problem. The Forest Service has a thing called 'Jaws,' and a couple of those people came in here and surveyed." ("Jaws," it turns out, is a deliberately mispronounced acronym, GAWS, for general aquatic wildlife system.)

"There were two things I missed right here in Centerfire. Anybody could see that the stream was getting wider from the damage, cows trampling the banks, chewing up the willows and the bankside sedge. What I didn't see was just as important, down-cutting and embeddedness."

Down-cutting is one of those counterintuitive quirks of natural meadows, or, more precisely, unnatural meadows. The reason you get meadows in the first place is the natural tendency of running water to flatten things out and run as slowly as possible. A stream will carry silt in from the surrounding high ground and drop it along the bed. Little obstructions or vegetation will change the stream course, and over centuries it will meander back and forth across the meadow several times, always leaving more silt and sand and gravel behind until it reaches something approaching equilibrium. Water may seem to enjoy running, but it desires entropy. When cows start chewing on its edges, a creek picks up speed and starts to carry more sediment out of the meadow. It both gets wider and cuts down into the land. The water doesn't get any deeper; it's the whole stream from surface to bottom that gets lower. And that does real harm, not just to trout but to elk forage and cattle pasturage, as the water table in the meadow drops down to the new surface level of the creek. Sedges, the preferred forage of both elk and cattle, start to die as the water table drops below their root systems, and you end up with shallow-rooted but drought-resistant grasses and, of course, our old lawn pest the dandelion.

Embeddedness, a word you can hardly say twice in a row without stumbling and cannot find in a dictionary of ordinary civilian English, is just a problem for the trout. In natural streams, gravel and sand is sorted out by moving water and deposited in beds of like-sized particles. The bottom will have areas clean of silt where trout can dig spawning nests. With severe bank erosion and down-cutting, the silt filters into the gravel and fills the interstices, and the bottom begins to look like eroded concrete—a smooth surface with the gravel just peeking through. That is embeddedness, and it kills fish by attrition as each year fewer and fewer can spawn successfully.

As far as the banks of Centerfire Creek went, beyond the lowering water table and the destroyed spawning beds, it was a horror show. I have a photograph of Centerfire pinned on the wall to remind me of what happens when cattle are given unrestricted access to trout water: a bank higher than a man's head is cut back on a scarred slope. Bare soil is exposed to at least five yards from the edge of the stream, and there isn't a blade of grass showing for fifty yards up and down the brook. "They claim the elk did that," Novy said with a wry laugh. "You take a look when you're on the reservation, where they've got as many elk as any place in the West, and tell me if you see something like that."

We drove on south, passing small creeks and open meadows. A pattern began to become obvious even to a tourist. The national forest lands are divided into individual contract grazing areas, and these are fenced. When you get a good grazing meadow with water in it, you see that the fences, the boundaries, are set so that the abutting grazing areas have a share of the water. The fences cut across the creeks and meadows; they are never parallel to or protective of the streams.

Not typical, but illustrative by example, was a place called the Hay Ground, a broad and somewhat rocky meadow south of Centerfire where three different boundary fences met at a common place square in the middle of the creek itself. I wondered out loud if it wouldn't make sense to take water out of the creek, pipe it down to a watering tank, and give the cows a drink without letting them trample on the trout. "We're working on it," Novy said. "But the problem is we don't own the water. It all belongs to the Salt River Irrigation District, and they're awful protective of their rights. We have hearings, and anytime we talk about doing something like this, they worry about their water and the cattlemen worry about their grazing rights, and it goes slow." It seems odd, at least to an Easterner, to think of a national forest that doesn't own its own running water, but that's the reality in the West. "I think we'll get our stock tank," Novy said. "Some year."

Below the three-fence intersection, Hay Ground Creek ran a few hundred yards through an increasingly rocky meadow and then disappeared into a steep canyon headed for the Black River far below, south of the Mogollon Rim. We stopped on a logging road above the stream, parked, and walked down through a grove of ponderosa pines, slipping through the last barbed-wire fence that separated one of the grazing leases from the small amount of unpastured meadow. You could see instinctively why the lower end was not leased for pasture. There was some grass, but it was on the edge of a steep thickly wooded hillside that plunged off to the southwest—a good place to lose a cow, permanently.

It was an admirable small stream, clean bottomed with slightly undercut banks on the outside edge of the meanders and interrupted here and there by boulders. "You could fish from here up to the fences," Novy suggested. "You won't find much above them," he added, gesturing toward the intersection of the grazing-right barbed-wire boundaries.

He didn't want to fish. Most fisheries managers end up over-dosed on fish and pick another hobby. Novy still likes to fly-fish for trout, but when he does he leaves Arizona and heads for Montana, where, as he puts it, they have "real fish," by which anglers mean *big* fish. We found places to sit, soft grass in between the shattered basalt rocks that poked up through the meadow. The morning's low clouds had burned off, and the grass was dry and sun warmed. While we ate lunch, fish started rising in the creek here and there, all close to the bank, except one that rose steadily at the head of a small pool where the water slipped between two angular boulders. I was in no hurry to fish—all I wanted to do was get a close look at a trout or two—and with the weather turning so fair after a rainy night and a cloudy morning, there didn't seem to be any hurry at all.

We ended up chatting about deer hunting, with which I have minimal experience and for which I have only mild enthusiasm. Jim, it turned out, had a passion for very large mule deer with big antlers and really wouldn't mind getting his name in the Boone and Crockett record book. Along the Mogollon and over on the Kaibab country in northern Arizona, they have very big deer and a lot of them with curious multitined and irregular antlers, what trophy hunters call nontypical antlers. That was his heart's desire, a big nontypical mule deer. I admitted to being, on those rare occasions when I had gone deer hunting (a sport with little charm in the overpopulated East), just after one to eat. "Well," he said, "then you want elk."

After lunch, Jim said he would take a short hike down into the canyon to see how many of his Apache trout had migrated downstream into the plunge pools below the Hay Ground. "Impossible to fly-fish," he added, gesturing toward the thick brush that rimmed the lip of the meadow where the creek disappeared over the edge. I was happy he had something to do. Even when the results are unpredictable, watching someone fish is soporific, and he knew exactly what was going to happen. After all, he was intimately acquainted with every fish in the brook.

THE AFTERNOON WAS INCREASINGLY CLEAR AND WARM, WITH JUST AN occasional puffy fair-weather cloud. Trout were rising steadily; all was right with the world. There was no reason to expect a sizable fish. Not only was the stream small, but Apache trout were never notable for their size. A twelve-inch stream-borne Apache is a monster in its own small environment. There are now annual world records for Apache trout, all caught out of a single lake in the White Mountain reservation, and most of the trout have reached their considerable size, up to five pounds or so, by two years of heavy feeding in the fish hatchery before they are transferred to Christmas Tree Lake.

In half an hour, most of it spent on my knees (fishing little brooks while standing up is counterproductive, as any fish you can see will certainly see your standing figure), I caught twelve fish up to ten inches and missed six. They were all rising fish, cast to deliberately, and even in their alpine innocence not as easily caught as some of their cousins. While they didn't much care what the fly looked like, they were extremely sensitive to what anglers call drag, that is, what happens when the fly is not drifting downstream at exactly the same speed as the surface of the creek. When the fly goes too fast, too slow, or crosswise, it drags a wake and simply looks wrong.

If you are not in the mood for a gaudy fish, something in the line of a Colorado River cutthroat—a fish pretty enough to be a hobbyist's pet if it were not so difficult to rear salmonids in home aquariums—I think you will agree with me that the Apache trout is the most beautiful of all delicately colored trout. The textbook definition says that they are golden yellow or olive yellow (they vary from stream to stream) with pronounced black spots scattered evenly over the body. The first thought I had upon landing one was that it had exactly the same basic coloration (if you erased the spots) as a palomino. The ground color of the body was a rich deep golden tan. Its fins, excepting the tail fin, were tipped with a bright blond yellow, exactly like the mane and tail color of a show palomino. No trout photographs well, but the Apache is particularly difficult; the palomino blondness melts into a bland iridescent silveriness whether you photograph the fish in sun or shade.

The true diagnostic mark so far as I have been able to discover, is one that they share with no other fish of any species. The black pupil of their eye appears to extend in a black bar, slightly narrower than the diameter of the pupil, toward their nose and tail, just so:

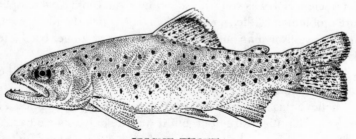

APACHE TROUT
Oncorhynchus apache

They are masked, mysterious fish. Several species of fish have vertical eye bars, including some of the aquarist's cichlids, but the horizontal bar is unique.

Apache trout, even if small, are hefty fish. They are deeper for their length than other trout, and the long dorsal (back) fin runs well to the rear on their body, almost as far back as the ventral fins behind the cloacal vent. This gives them a front-heavy look, not distorted but muscular. There is a Mexican idiom for a strong fish, a big saltwater fish like a yellowtail or a yellowfin tuna: "*tiene espaldas*"—the fish "has shoulders." Indeed, the strongest of saltwater fish have a muscular development concentrated forward of their dorsal fin: all the tunas, the dolphin (mahimahi), and the various jacks, including the Pacific yellowtail. Pound for pound, as they say in prize fighting and fishing, such fish are stronger than the more symmetrical ones. A ten-pound jack could tow a twenty-pound cigarette-shaped barracuda backward without much effort. Well, for all that it is a small trout, the Apache has shoulders.

We spent a few more good hours traveling Forest Service roads, stopping at streams and a few mountain reservoirs that Novy managed. At the end of the day we parked at one small pond, Acker Lake, named, Jim explained, for an old Arizona Superior Court judge. Jim stocks Montana grayling (*Thymallus* spp.) in ponds where inlet or outlet streams are Apache trout habitat; the grayling don't compete too much for food and don't interbreed at all. Their purpose is just to keep the anglers happy while the Apache trout recover to their maximum potential. Jim had stocked Acker Lake the week before and wanted to see if things had gone right. "It's not a science. Try as you will, sometimes you can have a temperature problem or acidity, and they'll go belly-up or they'll all escape over the spillway on you," he said. "I always try to get back a few days later and just look.

"If you wouldn't mind, you might try to catch one. They'll eat any small nymph."

I believe this is the only time a fisheries biologist regarded a fly rod as a scientific instrument, but it was the only tool we had. We walked the shore of the lake looking for dead fish and did find one grayling that had bellied up on the surface and been blown into the shoreline grass, but that, Novy said, was to be expected. While he went below the dam, looking for escapees, I stood on the wide berm of the earth-filled dam and cast to the circles made by rising fish, expanding circles made visible by the low glint of a cloud-filtered sunset. The fish were well out from shore, but reachable from where I was standing on the dam. The worst drooping back cast found nothing but air as it looped out over the low ground below the dam. Small grayling, nine and ten inches long, came to the sinking fly and almost hooked themselves as they took the fly and turned. Grayling are beautiful little fish with a large dorsal fin twice the size, proportionally, as a trout's, and the fin carries iridescent violet spots against a blue-gray ground color.

I got a little too intent on the fishing; the long May twilight made no strong announcement that evening had arrived. I was embarrassed when I looked up and saw Jim sitting quietly on a rock, apparently waiting for me to quit. I thought, and I told him, that I didn't mean to keep him out so late.

"If I wanted to leave, we would have," he said. "I don't get that many chances just to sit and look at the country."

"Lots of grayling," I told him, and added that they seemed fine and had good appetites, seemed to be in no shock from the stocking.

We walked back to his truck, and as we had each been doing all day, we both stooped over to pick up the occasional small piece of trash along the way. The forest was almost litter free, but we had managed to find a few beer and soda cans, some plastic cutlery and paper plates, an empty cigarette pack, and the inevitable piece of litter in fishing country, one of the half-pint foam cartons that angleworms are sold in. I was smoking filtered cigarettes that summer and had been field-stripping the front end (sprinkling out the tobacco and shredding and wadding the paper into tiny round bits) and then putting the filters in my shirt pocket. We put all the trash (and I emptied my pocket) into a genuine government-issue green-and-yellow Forest Service litter bag.

On the way back to Pinetop we chatted amicably about stocking policies of the past. "Man," he said, meaning humankind in general—he does not use slang, so it was not a form of address—"you know, we just like to tamper with things." We talked about the problems of genuine multiple use of the forests, which in the past has meant multiple users but not any coordinated program. "If we could just convince them that they'd have better grazing if they'd let us fence their cows out of the creeks," he argued, "well, that would be a start, seeing those meadows come back to the way they should look."

There was money for it, he added, $10 million in the Arizona Heritage Fund that could pay for cow bubblers and fences and replanting of streamside vegetation. The other problem was anglers themselves. He didn't know what the figures were for the national forest, but on the White Mountain reservation, less than 2 percent of the anglers were stream fishermen. "And they have trouble catching Apache trout in the lakes," he added. "The darn things won't eat salmon eggs and marshmallow baits."

Back at the Game and Fish office, we said our goodbyes.

"You ever want to come elk hunting," he said, "you tell me, I'll guide."

I haven't yet, probably won't, and to this day don't know why he offered, and I don't want to ask. If you made me guess, I'd say it was because I pick up trash, which is not the worst habit to get into. Either that or he invited me because I liked his little beautiful fish. Sounds funny, but I'd bet it was the trash.

5

In the Sierra Bonita

The first sign that you've entered the White Mountain Apache Indian reservation, coming northeast just a mile out of Pinetop, Arizona, is the tax-free cigarette store. (And if you are using a road map, you will think you have entered the Fort Apache Indian Reservation, but the tribe says it's White Mountain, and so it will be.) The reassertion of aboriginal independence makes for commercial opportunities. Some of the things that seem to have been included in the package of "so long as the waters run and the grass grows" are high-stakes bingo and low-tax butts. White Mountain, however, is not a treaty reservation, and that has had a major influence on its history and, in particular, on the management of wildlife in the mountains. If you are used to treaty reservations—lands where the Indians have retained traditional hunting and fishing rights, places where game is taken year-round without limit—the White Mountain country will seem very odd indeed. They have game animals; the land holds elk and deer in abundance.

The treaty reservation I am most familiar with, the huge Crow Reservation in Montana, has been hunted to the point of scarcity because there are essentially no rules. It still has good fishing in the main Bighorn River; the Crows don't fish. As you go along Interstate 90 approaching the Crow country from east or west, the highway is repeatedly posted with Deer Crossing signs, and in spring and early summer, the carcasses of road-killed deer on the shoulders are even more numerous than the warnings. But once you hit the reservation there is no need for deer-crossing markers, so scarce are the animals. In many trips along that road, I only once saw a deer on tribal land. It was in the wide median strip of the highway between Billings and Hardin, and it was being chased across the interstate by a Crow with a telescope-sighted rifle.

Because the White Mountain (then Fort Apache) and San Carlos Reservations were created by executive order of the president (in 1871 and 1872, respectively), the federal government retained control of all aspects of law and order. Early in this century, when the concept of wildlife management caught on, the Arizona Game and Fish Department and the United States Bureau of Indian Affairs imposed seasons, bag limits, and rules of fair chase on the executive-order reservations. Much as this may have irked the Apache—who regained, by lawsuit, control of their wildlife in the 1960s—they did get generations of practice at obeying laws intended to maintain and increase the population of game fish and animals. Since taking over management, the Apache have been more protective, less egalitarian, than Arizona's lawmakers. The first Apache program that varied from state practice was the end of the era of stocking alien trout and the beginning of the restoration of the native Apache trout. In game management they turned their herd of Rocky Mountain elk into a major moneymaker for the tribe.

Outside the White Mountain Apache Reservation, Arizona's elk are managed on a maximum-sustainable-yield basis so that hunters with various permits may take elk of both sexes and all ages. This insures that as many license holders as possible get something for the freezer. On Apache land, the tribe manages elk on a maximum-income basis. Every fall a select group of several dozen reasonably wealthy outsiders are allowed to shoot one trophy elk, defined as an animal with at least six antler points on each side of its considerable rack, and to pay, at last count, $15,000 for the privilege. It brings the tribe nearly $1 million annually. No other elk may be hunted, except for a limited draw for trophy elk open to tribal members. The result is elk everywhere, in numbers matching what you otherwise find only in national parks. The policy is unusual, but so are the elk. Except for the always rare and now extinct Coues's elk, the Apache had no tradition of unrestricted hunting of elk in the White Mountains. The animals were introduced after the reservation was established.

As to the fish, the Apache people historically had no stomach at all for angling but have developed a taste for catering to fee-paying anglers. They may have had, although no one remembers, a religious aversion to eating fish. They also eschewed pork, particularly that staple of late-nineteenth-century army fare, Underwood's deviled ham. The red demon on the label apparently evoked a superstitious fear. It is this aversion to pork, by the way, that encouraged some authors in the nineteenth century to conclude that various western Indians were actually the Lost Tribes of Israel. That doesn't explain the problem with fish. Trout, having scales, are perfectly kosher as they come from the brook. Our friend from pages past, Capt. John Bourke, remarked that in his more than twenty years of acquaintance with the Apache nations, some of these dietary prohibitions were overcome by necessity and familiarity:

> Pork and fish were objects of the deepest repugnance to both men and women; within the past twenty years—since the Apaches have been enrolled as scouts and police at the agencies—this aversion to bacon at least [although not to deviled ham!] has been to a great extent overcome; but no Apache would touch fish until Geronimo and the men with him were incarcerated at Fort Pickens, Florida, when they were persuaded to eat the pompano and other delicious fishes to be found in Pensacola Bay.

That may be true, but soldiers at Fort Pickens and Fort Marion, Florida, also recounted that the Indian's preferred quarry in salt water was the manatee, a mammal that produced red meat. The casual mention of scouts by Bourke should be fleshed out for readers unfamiliar with Gen. George Crook's many and successful campaigns against various bands of Apaches, including Geronimo. The several Apache clans or extended families had no particular loyalty to other Apaches, and in fact, Crook argued against putting these unaligned disparate Apache tribal units together in a single reservation. What Bourke calls scouts were, in Arizona, actually mercenary soldiers, not just the one or two wise trackers of Hollywood movies. In the long campaign across the border into Mexico that resulted in the surrender of Geronimo, Crook's fighting force consisted of more than 250 armed Apache scouts and fewer than 40 U.S. Cavalry officers and men. At times in that campaign, the scouts moving on foot were days in advance of the cavalry, whose chief role in forcing the surrender was psychological rather than combative. Geronimo could understand being pursued by other Apaches, but the sight of blue uniforms a hundred miles south of the border apparently convinced him he could not escape punishment.

A very few tribal members fish for fun on the reservation, children mostly. However, many are employed as wardens or as fisheries assistants or in one of the two federal hatcheries on the White Mountain reservation. Those facilities provide trout for several western reservations, and one is now devoted, for better or for worse, exclusively to rearing the trademark Apache trout. When I mentioned fishing on the reservation to Jim Novy, he assumed I was going to Christmas Tree Lake, because that's where the big fish are. I said I didn't think so. I wanted my fish in running water; it is an old preference. "Well," he said, "if you do go to Christmas Tree, look at their eyes."

THE ROAD TO WHITE RIVER, THE CENTER OF ALL TRIBAL GOVERNMENT on the White Mountain reservation, drops down from Hondah, a tribal tourist store and casino, winding through the Mogollon to the still-forested lower ground along the East Fork of the White River itself. The original government center, Fort Apache, is a few miles downstream where the East and North Forks meet. There is very little historical material left at the old fort; it was picked over when it was abandoned. The mess hall's wood stove, for example, is in the hands of the Game and Fish folks, and they use it to heat their big platform-tent elk-hunting camp.

I was supposed to meet the senior fisheries biologist at White River—an appointment made by telephone and confirmed by both mail and telephone—but when I got to the tribal Fish and Game offices, he was, as they say, in the field. There does not seem to be a special vocabulary for fisheries managers. Even if they are scuba diving or rowing a boat, they're in the field. It was a difficult morning as the staff tried to get in touch with him by radio and as they smiled nervously at their patiently waiting visitor. The assistant fisheries biologist was in the building but unfortunately tied up in an educational meeting, which, it turned out, he would have loved to skip for a chance to get up in the hills with anyone, even a tourist.

Several garbled radio-telephone messages later, it appeared that the only possibility was to find one of the tribal game wardens and have him lead the tour. This person turned out to be David Kitcheyan, an imposing figure of a man originally from the neighboring San Carlos Reservation. Considering that I didn't know where I was going and he wasn't sure where to take me, we had a successful, amiable day.

Kitcheyan, before switching to game law enforcement, had been a tribal policeman for a dozen years. He has massive shoulders and that rolling trooper's gait which comes from too many hours sitting in a cruiser and from carrying too many heavy objects—radios, night sticks, and revolvers—on his belt. We headed off for Deep Creek, a tributary of the White River, and the very stream that was the type location for the official nomination of the Apache trout. This required some map study, because Kitcheyan's worldview, much like a traditional Apache's, did not include trout. He knew the country like the back of his hand, but the only things written on it were logging roads, game trails, and elk herds. We (I did help with the map a little) found Deep Creek without any trouble, except for a problem with the creek itself. It had

been an unusually rainy May after a good snowpack winter, and
Deep Creek was running at full tilt, pounding down the south
slope of the Mogollon. At places, while still sitting in the truck
with the engine running, we could hear the streambed rocks rat-
tling against one another. From a distance the creek looked like a
set of stairs; there were no plunges and pool, only vertical and horizontal rapids.

The only place even remotely fishable was the least scenic,
where the creek pooled up against a logging-road culvert and was
temporarily slowed to a roiled but slower-moving deep hole. For
all the tumult, the water was clear and unclouded by silt; erosion
was well under control upstream. We could see fish holding near
the bottom, and after a while I managed to get one to come up and
look at a fly, only to refuse it. The drag on the fly was almost impossible to solve because the pool above the culvert had two back-
eddies, one on each side of the pipe, swirling against the concrete
abutments and the left and right banks, one turning clockwise, the
other counterclockwise. A third strong current ran directly through
the pool and into the culvert opening. It was like fishing in an ani-
mated, moving, Möbius figure eight—line, leader, and fly all
tracking off in different directions. Finally one of the smaller and
dumber (less robust and less educated?) trout swam up and ate the
fly and came to hand and got its photograph taken. It had, like the
fish over in the national forest, the same wonderful masked eye.

We tried to find a better place. I am not sure I was able to explain exactly what the problem was with trying to fish in Deep
Creek, but Kitcheyan was perfectly willing to set off for higher
ground. What I wanted, and what he and I tried to find on the
topographical map, was a high meadow where Deep Creek or a
tributary would meander and run slow and be fishable. We never
found one—but, good heavens, did we find elk as we went just a
few hundred feet higher on the mountain. It was calving season,
and cow elk heavy with unborn young would slip away from the
road as we rounded one tight turn after another. Cows with calves
next to them eyed us suspiciously from the open ground under
the tall pines. Best of all, we came upon a cow trailed by a calf
crossing the dirt track in front of us. The cow moved a dozen yards
downhill from the road and stopped, waiting for the calf.

The little one, mostly legs like all young of the deer tribe, bobbled its way across the road and decided to hide from us, perhaps on some signal from the cow, perhaps on a whim, if elk have whims. It stopped on the shoulder of the logging road, lay down in the short grass, pulled its feet and head in toward its chest and, once in the fetal position, it quite slowly and deliberately closed its long-lashed eyes. It wasn't Bambi but it was cute.

While we were watching the calf (Kitcheyan was at least as charmed as I was and wanted to see if the calf would open an eye and check on us—it did), a small black-and-white bird flitted across the road and perched vertically on the branchless corrugated bole of a mature ponderosa pine. It was clearly of the woodpecker persuasion, but I had never seen one like it, although I had been looking at western woodpeckers on and off for forty years, field guide in hand. This trip, for once and rarely, I didn't have a bird book in my jacket pocket, and so I just jotted down some notes of the obvious field marks: nearly solid black except for white wing bars and white head stripes, and lacking the usual ladder-back bars of most small woodpeckers. On later research, it turned out to be the relatively scarce, even rare, Williamson's sapsucker *(Sphyrapicus thyroideus),* in this case a male. It is restricted to high mountain country in the deserts of northern Mexico and the southwestern United States—in short, to the kinds of places where you might find isolated populations of elk or rare fish. As I have said, it doesn't matter whether you go looking for rare birds or odd trout or mountain lions. Choose your own grail and head uphill. You will have a satisfying quest.

A YEAR LATER TO THE DAY, WITH EVEN MORE CONFIRMATIONS AND phone calls, I returned to White River and met Kelly Meyer, a young man from Wyoming who is the hands-on assistant fisheries biologist of the White Mountain Apache Fish and Game Department and excellent company. It was he who was stuck in a meeting the previous year, he who would have loved an excuse to get outdoors. He took me back to Deep Creek, which flowed gently that summer. We ascended it to (by the map) an elevation of 8000 feet and spent a few hours examining a large number of extremely wild Apache trout. None were big, but they filled every niche in that tumbling mountain stream and would take a fly if you could float it naturally over their alert black-banded eyes. Nothing had trampled the bank except elk; there was no hint of angling pressure, no brookside trails, no bits of trash or pieces of nylon leader material tangled in the low-hanging bushes that sheltered the water from the sun.

Kelly, when I was unhooking the first fish, asked if I had noticed the eye. "They don't all have the bar," he said. When I said I thought all Apache trout did, he replied, "They used to."

I did not recall that conversation until the following winter, when I was reading up on the Apache trout in the bible of such things, Behnke's *Native Trout of Western North America.* Behnke notes that the Apache trout, of which there are several types from different remnant populations, is extremely difficult to raise in hatcheries. They are wary and excitable and have to be fed by unobtrusive means, as they would flee from any looming human form, refuse food, thrash against the sides of the imprisoning tank. The hatchery program, a cooperative effort of the tribe and the U.S. Fish and Wildlife Service, has the stated goal of raising nearly half a million Apache trout annually, equally divided between fingerlings and catchables—the last being trout over eight inches long. Catchables (a neologism, but a useful one) would include the annual infusion of a few world's-record bruisers at Christmas Tree Lake. This drive for productivity worries Bob Behnke:

> To reach this goal will require a large hatchery brood stock. Along with the unavoidable selection for certain hatchery-favored characteristics (disease resistance, artificial diet assimilation, tolerance of high-density rearing, etc.), program managers have decided to select for males that sexually mature at a younger age (age 2 versus age 3). Ironically, to accomplish its grand goal of restoring Apache trout and delisting the species under the Endangered Species Act, this large-scale propagation program will sacrifice the trout's natural genetic diversity.

It very well may. That is what Jim Novy was hinting at when he said that if I went to Christmas Tree Lake, I should look the fish in the eye. I have seen photographs of those lunkers in popular journals of sport. Some of the hatchery production has already evolved in the unnatural world of human-engineered production. The bar across the eye is faint, partial, or missing altogether. Part of the problem has been that the original successful brood stock— the fish that could survive hatchery confinement—all came from the upper East Fork of the White River, and those fish, even in their native stream, occasionally have absent or partial eye masks. The frequency of this aberration has only increased in the factory confinement of the hatchery.

They do have a program for improving the brood stock. Each spring, male wild trout (there are eight distinct races of Apache trout in separate small creeks) are taken from two of the wild stocks, stripped of their sperm, and the wild genes are bunged back into the hatchery brood stock. This is called preserving het-erozygosity, but it is actually the creation of a new, ninth, polymor-phic race of Apache trout unlike any in the natural world.

The law of supply and demand is a difficult one with which to argue. Only some 2 percent of all anglers who visit the White Mountains are stream fishermen; the others want lakes and large fish, and exotics do outgrow Apaches in the mountain lakes. Still, the tribe wants its own historical fish everywhere. It may be im-possible to suit the anglers and the tribe without changing the fish; that is the usual result when we try to improve things in na-ture. One hopes at least the eye bar will flourish. After all, the Lone Ranger without his mask is just another retired law enforce-ment officer with expensive tastes in ammunition. An Apache trout without its mask is what? *Oncorhynchus apache hatcheryi?*

On and off the reservation, the better solution may be simply to find streams free of trout or to poison out the introduced species (this is called restoration in fisheries-speak) and transfer Apache trout directly from native streams to new waters without passing them through a genetic and behavioral factory. The only problem is that it takes several years for natural reproduction to succeed, and the streams must be closed to angling. Still, if conditions are right, transplanted fish will fill every niche available in a new home, and if they evolve, they mutate toward greater rather than lesser wildness and appropriateness.

THERE ARE HALF A DOZEN PLACES OUTSIDE THE WHITE MOUNTAINS where Apache trout now live, and one of them, if you're not in a hurry, is on the roundabout way back from Pinetop to Tucson and Phoenix and the airplane home. These are fish that were live-trapped and transferred; they include one stock that has gone extinct in the White Mountains. The exiles include fish from Ord Creek, a tributary of the North Fork of the White River on Fort Apache Reservation. Ord Creek trout were regarded by those who knew them as the most colorful of all Apache trout. Efforts to reclaim and restore Ord Creek, where the Apaches were barely surviving amid a swarm of introduced eastern brook trout, resulted in the extermination of the resident Apaches by overenthusiastic poisoning, but fortunately, transplanted Ord Creek fish swim in the southern Pinaleno Mountains south of Globe, Arizona, and in other refugia.

To find them, you just make a big swing to the southeast from Pinetop to Globe to Safford, Arizona, down in the cotton-growing country along the Gila River, passing through the town of Pima, home of the cotton of the same name touted in advertisements for men's shirts. The mountains will disappear behind you, and you will have considerable difficulty believing that there are trout in your future as you drive farther and farther south into the land of cactus, roadrunners, and Gila monsters.

As you approach Safford, a substantial ridgeline appears to the west, and difficult it is, in the flat desert light, to estimate its distance or height. The road map informs you that it is Mount Graham and that it rises to a height of 10,717 feet, which seems highly improbable until a quick measurement of the mileage (a thumb's width on the road map, calibrated on the map's mileage scale) reveals that it is more than twenty miles south and west from Safford to the peak. In the clear air, it looks like a mere mile or two from downtown to the foothills.

I suppose Safford has its charms if you are in the cotton business. When I was checking out of the motel early the next morning, the pleasant woman at the desk congratulated me on my prompt departure. "They're gonna be spraying the fields," she explained. "It was on the radio weather this morning, and we're all gonna be sneezing and coughing for a week." Cotton, for all its cachet as a natural fiber, requires more insecticide per acre than any other agricultural enterprise, possibly excepting a golf course. "We used to all work in the fields," she said, "and we never got sick when we was kids. But now I don't know what they are spraying; all I know is I'm gonna be miserable by noon." As I headed south on Route 666 toward Mount Graham, the first crop dusters, sturdy biplanes, were taking off from the airport east of the city center.

I stopped at the turnoff to Mount Graham to buy a fishing license at a small store that looked like someone's retirement investment. Parked outside was a huge high-technology fire-fighting van, and inside were a dozen Apaches, all members of some elite federal group of smoke stompers. One of them said they weren't going to a fire; they were just headed for a position, from whence they expected to be deployed. Arizona gets more lightning strikes per acre than any other state in the union—this caused by the combination of desert heat welling up into a persistent wet air mass that swings in on the jet stream from the Mexican Pacific Ocean. They call it a monsoon, and it is, although a rather dry one.

The firefighters were stocking up on junk food and soda pop and looking at the pictures in copies of *Hustler* and *Playboy*. They made what sounded like jokes, but in Apache—a soft and musical tongue all out of keeping with the implied ferocity of being the language of Cochise and Geronimo. The woman behind the counter assumed I was headed for the reservoir down the road; that, she said, was where everyone fished. I told her I had heard that there were trout up on the mountain.

"Did you?"

I said I had.

"Well, I never," she said. "I guess there could be," she added in a tone of voice that amounted to saying, under her breath, "but I doubt the hell out of it."

Mount Graham is the home of several University of Arizona op-
tical telescopes, and they are building another one, much to the
annoyance of the professional environmentalists. The high country is home to an endangered species, the Mount Graham red
squirrel, and the argument is that more construction (and more
traffic) will threaten the animal, which looks exactly like any other
red squirrel to the untrained eye. Otherwise the forested slopes of
Mount Graham are just about as pristine as you will find in any national forest. For one thing, there is no logging except for the occasional citizen salvaging dead trees for firewood. This is not
because the Forest Service wouldn't like to log the country but
because it's too far to the nearest sawmill and the haulage kills the
profit. This may be the only forest in North America where economic considerations have produced conservation.

The road up Mount Graham, a paved recreational highway
called the Swift Trail, dates back to the days of the Great Depression and the old Civilian Conservation Corps. It has some finely
built stonemasonry retaining walls on the mountain side of the
road, although, as I recall, not a single modern guardrail anywhere.
It winds up to the ridgeline in a series of switchbacks, starting
down in the sagebrush and juniper and rising through a deciduous
oak forest to, at some 7000 feet above sea level, a mixed conifer
forest of pine and spruce. The occasional Mount Graham red
squirrel flirted with individual extinction by deciding to cross the
Swift Trail, but for twelve windy miles I did not see any roadkill at
all.

I was headed for Grant Creek, which took its name from one of
the early army posts in the Apache wars, Camp (later Fort)
Grant—after the general and president—situated on the western
side of Mount Graham where the mountain stream came down to
the high plain. The attraction of the mountain was obvious to the
cavalry; it produced that rare Arizona ecology: cold running water
and green grass. John Bourke and George Crook were there when
Camp Grant was established, and Bourke noted that the site "offered many inducements which could not well be disregarded in
that arid section; the Graham Mountain, or Sierra Bonita as known
to the Mexicans, is well timbered with pine and cedar; has an

abundance of pure and cold water, and succulent pasturage. . . . " The one thing it did not have, Bourke noted, was trout. For trout in Arizona you had to go up to the White Mountains. There Camp (later Fort) Apache was built where "two branches of the Sierra Blanca River unite," rivers "stocked fairly well with trout, a fish which is rare in other sections of the Territory."

Fort Grant was also, although they did not realize it, well stocked with mosquitos and malaria parasites; and it was eventually abandoned for that reason among others. The old fort is now a major federal penitentiary, and the Spanish name of Sierra Bonita survives as well. Just a mile from the prison sits the town of Bonita, which consists entirely of a barroom with two outhouses.

Rising up the mountain and winding around it to the headwaters of Grant Creek, you come first to Hospital Flat, a small campground with a tiny stream running down the middle of the meadow. There is a beautifully scrubbed Forest Service comfort station with his and hers chemical toilets, a gravity-fed drinking-water supply, and a memorial monument to the Eighth Cavalry, who established there, so the plaque says, a hospital for soldiers taken ill down in the swampy country around Camp Grant. Actually there is no record of any use of the Hospital Flat for straightforward medical purposes. It was, however, a popular spot for soldiers to go on leave, bringing their women with them. It would be called these days, to be polite about it, Rest and Recreation Flat.

The small brook in the middle of Hospital Flat has some Apache trout in it. They are, as Bourke noted, not native to Mount Graham (although they may have been, in some prehistoric past) but stocked fish, transferred there from the White Mountains back in the early 1980s. I suppose I could have fished in Hospital Flat, but it would feel kind of funny if anyone stopped and watched. Some creeks are small enough you can jump across them; this one was so small a cricket could hop it.

Grant Creek, just a few miles up the road, was much more promising. There was space for two cars to pull off the road, and the flow of water was audible even before I turned off the ignition. The creek tumbled down, crossed under the road through a culvert without pause, and disappeared downhill through a bouldery-bottomed stand of mature ponderosa pines. Near the stream above the road there were two informal stone fire rings and no signs prohibiting their use. A hint of a foot trail led downstream, but it petered out fifty yards downhill from the road, and the banks of the creek had no tracks except the paw prints of a skunk. Mount Graham red squirrels, oblivious of their predicted imminent demise, chattered like red squirrels do everywhere, a clattering note that always reminds me of a model airplane's glow-plug engine starting up.

The brook was all plunge and pool, some natural, some man-made. You could see where fisheries people had tried to increase the proportion of pool to riffle by digging logs in crossways to the stream bed. Most of them were washed out, angling into the stream instead of barricading it. The sound of falling water masked any traffic noise from the road, which had been busy all morning, mostly with Forest Service and university vehicles, plus a few recreational visitors. The mountain gets a lot of day use, 180,000 visitor days a year as the Forest Service calculates such things. The popularity is understandable; a half hour's drive up the hill is the same, so far as changing climate and botany, as driving from Tucson to Montana.

I liked Grant Creek enormously. There was mint growing in a few places, considerable western skunk cabbage, and fiddlehead ferns just unrolling. I think if it had not been for the fire rings and the fiddleheads, I would have been content to catch a few trout, put them back, and head for Tucson. And then there was also the noticeable abundance of trout. I walked along the stream and could see, as soon as I topped out over a pool, trout fleeing for the shadowed banks, scurrying down under shelving rocks, dashing up under the foam of small waterfalls. I also had a salt and a pepper shaker in my fishing vest. I like tomato-and-bread sandwiches when I'm traveling; they make a break in the constant cholesterol of western cuisine. And I had some aluminum foil. The breakfast sausage patty in Safford had been the size of a salad plate, and I had asked the young lady in the cafe to wrap it up. I told her I'd have it for lunch. Saving food—I guess that comes with remembering World War II and ration stamps and having parents who survived the Depression.

This was all quite accidental, one of those serendipitous convergences: trout, fiddleheads, salt, pepper, aluminum foil, and a fire ring. I was about to eat an officially listed "threatened" species, and I was thankful for the narrow window of legality. If these had been "endangered," I would have had to stick with tomato sandwiches.

After walking no more than a quarter of a mile down from the road, I came to a fall where Grant Creek dropped over a substantial cliff and I was looking down at the tops of mature pine trees. There was no point in going any farther; I had already walked by a hundred trout, and all I needed was one for lunch. Halfway back up to the road I had noticed a particularly deep pool, one about the size of an old-fashioned claw-foot bathtub. It had a small waterfall at the head and a deep undercut bank on the left side as you looked downstream where the water pushed back under a fallen log. If there was a fish big enough to cook, that was the likely place. The sun had gained and was almost overhead, shining down through the wide-spaced ponderosa pines, hitting the surface of the water and penetrating down to the gravel and sand in the pools. As will happen when first light directly hits the bottom and warms the water, a scattering of small aquatic insects started to hatch. One was a tiny bluish mayfly, and I saw some housefly-sized dark brown caddis flies. (I mean the small houseflies, the ones that are hard to swat, not the big bumbly ones.) I let this activity all happen for ten minutes by the watch and started back upstream, fishing as I went.

Apache trout are a little bit easier to catch than wild brown trout; that's a scientific fact. In White Mountain streams where they mingle—the lower forks of the White River, for example—Apaches make up less than 15 percent of the total trout population but are caught in larger numbers than the more numerous brown trout. That statement should be amended with a caution that most of the Apache trout in the lower river are stocked fish, not wild.

The ones in Grant Creek were not free for the taking, however. While they didn't seem to be too particular about what kind of fly

I used (mountain trout seldom are), they were exquisitely sensitive to unnatural drag on the fly. If it floated naturally, they ate. If it tugged just a little bit at the surface tension, they would watch it and let it be. If it dragged noticeably, it frightened them and they fled.

Up at the bathtub pool, three different fish were rising, one at the tail, one at the head just below the waterfall, and a third beside the log that lay in the water on the far bank. I decided to eat the one by the log.

It took fifteen minutes to catch him. Twice the fly's dragging wake spooked the fish, and I had to roll back on my haunches and squat quietly (I was fishing from a kneeling position) and wait for the trout to come back out into the feeding lane, just at the visible edge where the fast water in the pool slipped by the slower current next to the log. I changed flies twice, more for something to do to pass the time than to deceive the fish. He (as he turned out to be on inspection of the appropriate internal structures) took the fly quietly, jumped twice, ran back under the log once, and then came to hand easily and died quickly.

I enjoy cleaning fish, but then, I was the child in the family who enjoyed scooping out the pumpkin insides at Halloween. Trout insides have a perfectly clean if distinct smell. Even the stomach (and one must look inside the stomach) with its acidic gastric odor is not unpleasant at all. The contents of the gut were predictable: a single black elytra (the opaque wing cover) suggested a previous snack of beetle; two small black ants had made a fatal slip somewhere upstream; a single mosquito larva was still wriggling; and there were a pair of identifiable mayfly larva and two battered caddis flies. The rest, absent a microscope to look at surviving hard body parts, was just a smush of insectness. The main thing was that the stomach was fairly well packed. For a clear and not very productive-looking freestone brook, Grant Creek appeared to be nutritious. (Over in the White Mountains, near Springerville, there is a Rio Nutrioso. I bet it had trout in it two hundred years ago.)

I made a small fire with the butt ends of some deadwood, pushing the branches together as they burned until I had a bed of coals as big as a building brick. I put the sausage out on a rock by the stream, expecting that magpies and Steller's jays would clean up after I left. There was just enough grease on the inside of the tin-foil package for a temporary nonstick coating. I sprinkled the fish with salt and pepper, put six tightly rolled fiddleheads, cleaned of their brown fuzz, on top of the trout, and made a neat drugstore wrap longways and then rolled the ends of the foil up tightly and put the package, fiddlehead-side-down, right on the coals.

It is easy to tell when tinfoil trout are done. If the fire is not too hot, the coals will burn through the aluminum foil in just a few places, and the escaping steam, once the trout gets up to near the internal boiling point, will tell your nose it is time for lunch. I guess it took about fifteen minutes, but time is nothing when you are lying back on your elbows drinking a reasonably cold beer (I meant to put the can in the stream, but forgot) and smelling wood smoke. Threatened species, I should tell you, are something like stolen fruit, delicious but with a slight aftertaste in the conscience.

After drowning the fire and policing the area, I came off the mountain shortly after noon and headed for Tucson. The map showed a road dead-ending at old Fort Grant at the base of Mount Graham, and there was time, so I took it. The Arizona desert is a popular place to build prisons. You go by one between Globe and Safford; there's another one on the Swift Trail at the base of Mount Graham; and Fort Grant turned out to be a third. Grant Creek was invisible, either drawn off for irrigation or just perco-lated down out of sight into the high desert.

I went into the saloon in Bonita and had a truly cold beer. The highway map showed a gravel road heading west out of Bonita to-ward Willcox, a town along the interstate and on a direct line to-ward Tucson. The bartender said it was a fine road and mostly paved and would save an hour's drive if I was headed west.

I'm glad I took it; I found something I was looking for. The one thing that had seemed lacking on the road up to Hospital Flat and Grant Creek was an apple tree. I had never been within a few miles of trout without passing an orchard or an old gnarled apple tree in someone's backyard. All I had seen of any note on the way into Mount Graham was an enormous Gila monster crossing the

road just uphill from the state prison. But if you run the road between Fort Grant and Willcox, you will understand the inevitabil-
ity of the intersection of apples and trout streams. Mile after mile
of orchards line the road, some older abandoned ones but mostly
new ones planted hedgerow style with dwarf trees (the apples are
normal; it's just the tree itself that is diminished). The state agriculture station in Willcox was obliging with information. They figure about 5000 acres of apples in the valley and an annual
production of 200 million pounds of apples, right smack in the
middle of Arizona. The water comes from wells; the surrounding
Pinaleno and Galiuro Mountains capture the water and ship it
down where it has been percolating into the Willcox basin for a
few million years. They grow a high-sugar Granny Smith and ship
it to Washington State as an additive in apple juice canneries. The
good money, and they're hoping for more, comes from shipping
table fruit to Taiwan and Hong Kong. If Japan ever opens up for
agricultural imports, they're ready in Willcox—the major table
fruit is the Fuji apple, developed in Japan.

Tucson. Well, it was there at the end of the day. I don't think I
have ever seen a town as large with as little soul or center to it. In
1993, when I was there, it was still obviously recovering from the
savings-and-loan boom of the 1980s. Cutting around town, headed
for Phoenix the next morning, I drove by miles and miles of partly
occupied condominiums. Someone was watering and mowing the
grass, but the yards were empty and there were no shades or cur-
tains on window after window for mile after mile. There were no
For Sale signs. The neighborhood was an advertisement on its own
hook. I'm sure it will recover. After all, it has maximum sunshine,
reasonable temperatures, terrific lightning shows in the surrounding hills, and it's only a few hours drive to tall pines and short
trout. I like Arizona, but I think I will always return to the state's
mountains through Albuquerque and drive through the hard country across the Colorado Plateau and down to the Mogollon. That
way you see only Gallup, a small western town with few dreams
and absolutely no illusions.

6

Over the
Waterpocket Fold

THE ARIZONA EXPERIENCE OF FINDING TROUT SURROUNDED BY saguaro cactus and trackless desert inspired me to think about Utah, the only state in the union with a fish named after it in Latin, *O. clarki utah*. The official English name is Bonneville cutthroat trout, from ancient Lake Bonneville, a vast inland freshwater sea until it dried up into the Bonneville salt flats and the highly saturated Great Salt Lake. In a few cold streams on the edges of the ancient lake bed there still are trout.

The Salt Lake City airport is a popular landing field for fly fishermen. There are no trout in the Great Salt Lake, just as there are no waters in Casablanca, but these anglers are not so misinformed as Rick Blaine pretended to be. Idaho and Wyoming are just a hundred miles away to the north and northeast.

Two hundred miles due east, Utah's own Green River below Flaming Gorge Dam is a mecca for people interested in very large trout—alien rainbows and a curious fish with no scientific name, the Snake River finespotted cutthroat, which lives in the cold tail-water and submits to being caught over and over again. From Memorial Day to Labor Day, every plane disembarking passengers emits several anglers, easily identified by the rod cases they carry.

I was headed in the reverse and perverse direction, southeast toward Las Vegas, Nevada, away from all waters where important fish swam. It was wrongheaded travel by choice, chasing off after Bonneville cutthroats. The more time I have spent on famous rivers, the less I have enjoyed the angling. The trouble with big fish is that they attract people who are interested in bragging. If you combine that human trait with a second one, the urge to bet on a sure thing, you will understand why blue-ribbon trout streams do not attract a random sample of either humanity in general or anglers in particular.

The rivers most likely to cater to fishermen in search of heroic fish are easy to identify. All you need is a copy of the state's special regulations. Any river with what is called a slot limit is a candidate for the list. These are streams where anglers are allowed a few fish, usually two, under a certain length, usually twelve inches. These are "lunch fish." The law will also allow one large fish over twenty (or more) inches in length. This is the trophy fish. Trophy fish are frozen, sent to a taxidermist, cast in a mold, and recreated in plastic and painted to look more or less like the original fish. Most guides try to discourage the practice, as a large fish that lives in the pool below the big rock (or any other identifiable lair) can be caught over and over again. This is good for their business. The basis for modern catch-and-release fisheries management is elegant science, but the political energy that makes it work comes from market forces at the point of sale, and the guide is on the river and the taxidermist is not.

While waiting in the rent-a-car line, I struck up a conversation with a person who was toting a pair of fly rods in their distinctive aluminum tubes. He was headed for the Snake River country with five compatriots, all set on catching monstrous brown and rainbow trout. When I said I was headed south, looking for native cutthroats, it was he who, as I have mentioned before, responded with a peculiarly eastern facial expression, the affable sneer, and said, "Easy to catch, aren't they?"

The Hertz rental line was interminable, due entirely to a minimal staff and this party of six big-fish anglers bound for Wyoming. They had two problems that were occupying the time of the only available clerk. They all wanted to sign on the rental agreement as authorized drivers, and five of them were tipsy, which is what happens when you start in on it before lunch at 35,000 feet. They planned on rotating the job of designated driver for the duration of the vacation. They were having a roaring good time in a six-way conversation about food and drink and trout, and having trouble finding their driver's licenses and paying attention to the clerk's instructions about where to sign and initial all six copies of the rental contract.

While I was being served, they tore off, not without grabbing one of my two bags and throwing it in their rental van and hauling it up to Jackson Hole. It was returned to me three days later in New Harmony, Utah, after several telephone calls from various isolated pay phones to Delta Airline's capable and concerned lost-baggage department. As a general rule, if you have to have a problem while traveling, try to have it in Utah, where politeness and the work ethic are encouraged by the Mormon culture. Fortunately, the bag they left was the one with the short fly rod and fishing vest in it. (It was not a short fly rod for short fish; it was a four-section pack model that fit nicely on the diagonal of a suitcase.) Unfortunately, the bag they absconded with held the hiking boots and hip waders and rough clothes. I was headed to Boulder Mountain doomed to fish in street shoes and city pants. But Boulder Creek on Boulder Mountain was really a side trip, and if the bag hadn't shown up by the time I got down to Cedar City for the big expedition, well, I'd just have gone to the Zion Cooperative Mercantile Inc. and got outfitted.

The interstate south from Salt Lake City tucks between the Wasatch Range and the desert, rising steadily as it pulls away from the Great Salt Lake. It heads up into the foothills as if engineered to escape the heat. South of Provo it climbs faster, and you begin to have faith in the prospect of trout. The one indispensable indication of the possibility of trout anywhere in the lower forty-eight states is cold-winter vegetation—an apple orchard or a lilac bush is the most obvious domestic plant material, just as aspen trees are indicator species in the uncultivated landscape of the West. Thanks to reservoirs and their cold tailwaters, there are trout in the deserts as well, but natural trout streams are never far from aspen, pine, or fir trees.

As the highway approached Nephi and the turnoff to Boulder Mountain, cherry and apple orchards appeared. In mid-June the cherries were bright red on the small trees, mile after mile. I stopped in Nephi looking for something cold to drink and saw a small boy standing by the side of the frontage road waving a homemade sign promising cherries in exchange for cash. There were three boys in this retail agricultural business, it turned out, and they had commandeered the abandoned tourism information center in the front of a shopping mall parking lot. It was an open-sided structure with empty racks that had once held brochures touting the various attractions of Juab County. The boys were taking turns waving the sign, selling the cherries (75 cents a quart), and spending the proceeds at the Burger King across the street. I got the distinct impression that the cherries had been pilfered. This was not a brilliant Holmesian deduction. I asked them where they got the cherries, and two of them pointed at each other and said, "His place," and the third one laughed at the explanation.

The route to Boulder Mountain, some 200 miles southeast of Salt Lake City, is for most of the way a road to Lake Powell, the reservoir on the Colorado River behind Glen Canyon Dam. That accounted for the only slow traffic—people trailing huge power-boats through a countryside as dry as the inside of a self-cleaning oven. The road follows the Sevier River valley before ascending a tributary canyon to the top of the Aquarius Plateau. The Sevier drains the Great Basin slopes of the Wasatch and Aquarius Plateaus and also part of the Pine Mountains in southern Utah, carrying the water out into the flat plain of the old Bonneville Lake bottom near the towns of Deseret, Hinckley, and Delta. There the flow disperses into irrigated fields and disappears. The sparse headwaters of the Sevier rise in the windblown and water-cut landscape that means Utah to tourists—Zion, Bryce, and Canyonlands National Parks are all in the north-south range that makes up the water boundary between the Great Basin and the Colorado.

Somewhere back in the last ice age, when glacial dams backed up temporary lakes and waters spilled across ancient divides, cutthroat trout native to the Pacific Ocean watershed—almost certainly from the Snake River drainage—spilled over into the headwaters of the Colorado, most likely into the Green River east of the Wasatch and Uinta Ranges, and from there they moved down into the main Colorado and ascended its accessible cold-water tributaries. Downstream and west along the Snake into what is now Idaho, another shift in the ice made a path for these same Snake River trout into the Malad and Bear River headwaters, and from there down into the Bonneville/Salt Lake basin. The subsequent postglacial isolation resulted in two subspecies of trout, one on each side of the divide between the Colorado and ancient Lake Bonneville. *Oncorhynchus clarki utah* would colonize streams flowing into the Bonneville basin, dispersing all around the Pleistocene lake from the Wasatch and Aquarius Plateaus on the east to mountain streams in Nevada on the west. On the south edge of the Bonneville basin, the Pine Mountains between Cedar City and St. George rose high enough to generate, and maintain to this day, trout-water streams. The boundaries of Utah are utilitarian and modern: straight lines running ordinally to the compass points. The frontiers of Utah trout are irregular and subtle.

Over east in the Colorado drainage, the same Snake River stock evolved into another variant, *Oncorhynchus clarki pleuriticus*, the Colorado cutthroat trout. These also migrated across what would be the mapmakers' modern lines and survive today in Wyoming, Colorado, and Utah.

BOULDER MOUNTAIN IS THE HIGHEST POINT OF THE AQUARIUS Plateau, and Boulder Creek flows off its east slope into the Colorado via the Escalante River. Utah is short on Spanish names; although it was once a province of Mexico, Spanish settlement never reached it. It was 1776 before anyone from the old settlements in New Mexico ventured as far northwest as present-day Utah. Two Franciscans, Fathers Dominguez and Velez de Escalante, led an expedition to find a trail that would link Santa Fe with the missions then being founded in upper California. They gave up after fording the Colorado and setting eyes on the Great Basin. It would be sixty years before other Europeans entered the country, and they would be looking for beaver. Dominguez was the leader of the expedition but got nothing named after him. In a sense, neither did Velez de Escalante: the real family name was Velez; Escalante was just the family's hometown in Spain.

The Escalante drainage, Utah fisheries managers thought, should not have any Colorado cutthroat trout in it, not because it is in Utah but because it is so far south along the big river that cold-water-loving trout would have trouble making it that distance down a waterway named for the burden of red silt it carried. The southernmost known Colorado trout in Utah had been found in the upper Fremont River (named after the explorer), which is more rightly called, using its other official name, the Dirty Devil River. The Fremont/Dirty Devil enters Lake Powell just uplake of Bullfrog basin. The headwaters of the Fremont also rise on Boulder Mountain twenty miles, as the crow does it, north of Boulder Creek. But by the time the two drainages reach the Colorado, more than a hundred miles of river separates the mouths of the Fremont and the Escalante, which flow, respectively, north and south of the Waterpocket Fold, a vast bulge of Triassic sandstone that separates the two rivers. Just downstream from the mouth of the Escalante, on the east bank of the Colorado, the San Juan River enters the main stream, flowing east to west out of New Mexico and Arizona. The San Juan was once home to Colorado River cutthroats, so, clearly, at some time in history they had gotten as far south as the Escalante.

Boulder Mountain streams that run west into the Sevier would have held *O. c. utah* historically, but as in most of the West, the native fish had been supplanted by eastern brook trout and European brown trout, or else they had lost their genetic uniqueness to conquering hatchery-stock rainbows or Yellowstone cutthroats. The Escalante/Colorado River drainage waters in the Boulders were also, as far as anyone knew, all stocked with aliens. In 1982, while conducting routine samples of fish populations, the Utah Department of Wildlife Resources sampled the East Fork of Boulder Creek, a small stream that feeds into a man-made reservoir. They caught the usual suspects—mostly brook trout, some rainbows, and a few unidentified cutthroats that were remarkable for their bright coloration. Yellowstone cutthroats, of which literally billions have been propagated all over the western United States, are a fairly dull silvery fish with brassy notes and lots of black spots. These East Fork fish were bright red even on their bellies, and their spots somewhat fewer in number and larger than the prolific black dots on a typical Yellowstone fish.

My directions to this odd and isolated population of red-bellied fish were simple enough. One drove to Torrey, Utah, where the road forked, and instead of heading for Canyonlands National Park and Lake Powell with everyone else, one turned south toward Teasdale and Grover (not major metropolises) and kept a sharp eye out for a sign saying Garkane Power. The East Fork of Boulder Creek, back in the Eisenhower administration when such things were allowed without regard to niceties, had been tapped for hydropower. There would be a small reservoir high on the East Fork, and the red-bellied, possibly Colorado, cutthroat trout swam somewhere upstream from the reservoir. According to the mimeographed fisheries report where I first read about these fish, the East Fork "has been substantially impacted by hydropower development. Currently, only about 3.0 miles of the East Fork upstream from the King's Pasture reservoir has not had flows reduced."

There is an aptitude for euphemism in bureaucrats' prose; they must have a stylebook that provides soothing synonyms for ordinary English. I knew this, but I was still surprised when I got there.

The road up to the reservoir, the Dixie National Forest ranger had remarked, was "certainly not meant for ordinary cars." A pickup could make it, he explained, unless it rained. If it rained, I would need four-wheel drive. If it rained hard, I shouldn't go at all. "The last half mile's the worst," he added. "If you get as far as a place where you can't drive any farther, you're close."

As it turned out, the road angles in at the creek, leaving the pavement a mile away from where the East Fork meets the highway. What you eventually come upon, taking the dirt road toward the upper reservoir, is a dry creek bed. Off in the distance through the aspen trees, a three-foot-diameter concrete pipe is visible, snaking down the fall line of the valley. Inside the pipe is the entire flow of the East Fork of Boulder Creek. As the son of a civil engineer, I had to admit it was a nice piece of construction. On the other hand, as a writer, I thought that putting a creek inside a pipe was more drastic than the phrase "substantially impacted" hinted at. One gets used, out West, to water being drawn off trout streams for irrigation or temporarily dammed for hydro, but to say that the only part of the stream where "flows had not been reduced" was upstream of the pipeline was masterful understatement. I am still learning how to decode government cant, but I believe that a federal "substantial" is synonymous with "total," just as habitat "degradation" is what most people would call "destruction."

On the other hand, it may be a faint shudder of revulsion that propels the bureaucrat toward euphemisms. Father Velez de Escalante's diary of his search for a way from the Rio Grande valley over the Continental Divide and across the Colorado River gives an example of that motive. Just as they crossed the modern Colorado-Utah border at a point due east of Boulder Mountain, they came across two Indian women. They "were so poorly dressed," Velez de Escalante wrote, "that they wore only some pieces of deerskin hanging from the waist, barely covering what one cannot gaze upon without peril." I am reminded of a federal forester with a great affection for the land who could barely stand to look at what his agency had done to a small stream. He named that previously undefined creek in the middle of a horrible clear-cut Oh My God Creek.

The road, if you crossed the washouts very slowly, was satisfactory all the way to the fence around the power company's reservoir. Inside the fence were about fifty amicable beef cattle, all steers and heifers, no cows with calves and no bull to keep an eye on. By and large, range cattle are harmless, but the less testosterone or maternal instinct, the better. The same is true for bears and buffalo. The fence had a built-in opening for pedestrians, an angled passage too narrow and too short in a straight line for even a calf to get through. Absent No Trespassing signs, I trespassed.

The shoreline around the reservoir was free of human footprints—remarkable in the modern West at a place you can reach by high-clearance automobile. But there are two Garkane Power reservoirs, one down by the road where the water comes out of the power plant and this one feeding the pipeline penstock. The lower one is right by the highway, gets more stocked fish and thus more attention. In addition, there are four natural lakes within three miles of the lower reservoir, all accessible by ordinary cars or easy walks. King's Pasture Reservoir was clearly on the bottom of the food chain of Utah anglers.

The East Fork of Boulder Creek turned out to be a fine trout stream and a perfect example of what good intentions have done to western waters. I picked my way through the cowpats to the lower end of the stream, which was conveniently cow chewed. There were a few clumps of willows for shade and cover, but most of the bank just above the reservoir had been browsed to the ground, so that fishing, even in street shoes, was easy. In small streams, getting too close to the water is a mistake in any case. Near the lake, the creek held brook trout up to ten inches, as eager as they were numerous.

I walked upstream a few hundred yards and climbed over a drift fence that marked a boundary between the private property around the reservoir and the Dixie National Forest land that surrounded it. There were still a few cow pies by the creek, but old ones, leftovers from the previous summer's grazers. At the fence, the proportion of open stream bank to willow-covered bank changed dramatically, virtually reversed itself. What had been an open stream with occasional willows in the private inholding changed to a shaded stream with infrequent access through occasional browsed openings. The streamside grass was taller, and there was less of that most obvious of all indications of overgrazing, the dandelion. If you want trout out West, or just a campsite without cow flop, the farther you get from dandelions the better you will do.

The trout—or the ones I could catch; I am well aware of the uselessness of a fly rod as a census-taking device—changed immediately above the fence line. It is not very often that you get such a clear and simultaneous transition of fauna and habitat. They were small rainbow trout, relics—like the brook trout downstream—of some stocking program years ago. They did not look at all like modern hatchery rainbow stock.

I should make a distinction here between wild stream-bred trout descended from hatchery-born fish and recently planted pan-sized hatchery production. You can always spot the latter. All hatcheries for the past forty years or so have been working with the same basic genetic form of the rainbow trout. They are pale, wan creatures with rounded tailfins (from crowded swimming in a concrete raceway), and they usually show some sign of sunburn on their dorsal surfaces. Their adipose fin, the soft floppy fin between the back fin and the tailfin (dorsal and caudal fins in fish-speak), is usually shrunken and deformed by ultraviolet radiation. These wild—feral, to be precise—rainbows were descendants of an earlier generation of stocking programs.

From the beginning of stocking in the 1890s until the years shortly after World War II, the majority of hatchery fish were put in rivers as fingerlings. After the original introductions had caught hold, local hatcheries would strip eggs from wild fish in nearby waters and rear them to fingerling size and return the baby fish to the home rivers in hopes of augmenting natural reproduction. Excess hatchery fish would be used to expand the range by stocking fingerlings in new waters. In those early years, when hatcheries were working with essentially wild fish, the reason for stocking them at such a small size was simple economics. In nature, rainbows spawn in the spring. By the time summer comes, the fish, no matter how well you propagate them in the hatchery, are just a few inches long. The only way to get them up to catchable size was to hold them over for more than a year and plant them back fourteen to eighteen months after they hatched, and the cost of that kind of rearing program couldn't be justified.

What the country needed, fisheries managers decided, was a trout that could be raised to catchable—meaning eatable—size in six months. This was possible with modern technology—with sci-entifically formulated fish chow, antibiotics to reduce the diseases of overcrowding, and temperature-controlled water to keep the fish eating at maximum metabolic efficiency. If it sounds like trout are raised like broiler chickens, that is because it is true. The problem when eggs from wild trout were used was that the end of the six months came in the fall, at the close of the fishing season. What was needed was a manufactured trout that could be deliv-ered to the stream just in springtime to be caught by anglers, bopped on the head, and taken home for dinner.

The solution was an elegant piece of biological engineering. Managers started selecting hatchery brood stock for a single char-acteristic: delayed spawning. Generation after generation they took the fish that came latest into breeding season and crossed them. They moved the spawning dates from early spring to late spring, then summer, then early fall. Finally, managers created a race of rainbows with delayed puberty and a discombobulated bio-logical clock. By the 1940s, several hatcheries had independently achieved the same goal, a rainbow trout that spawned six months late—in September instead of March. By force-feeding and ma-nipulating the water temperature for maximum growth during the winter, hatcheries could take eggs in the fall from these off-sched-ule fish and present an ardent public with something big enough to fry in April.

What they had also created was a fish incapable of thriving or breeding in the wild. It was as though they had made the fish equivalent of a tomato plant that would only sprout in October. That might be fine for a greenhouse, but you would not expect much of a crop in the open field. And as tomatoes have, when bred for a single purpose, lost much of their savor, so the new trout had lost most if not all of their capacity for survival. Fall-spawned, spring-planted, catchable-size rainbows lose weight slowly all summer, and very few, if any, survive the winter.

By deduction, one would have to conclude that these thriving East Fork rainbows were relics from a much older introductory stocking of capable fish. There was also a morphological clue. One of the variations in rainbow trout is that some subspecies tend to retain what are called parr marks into adulthood. "Parr" is the word for small trout (and small salmon), and all of them carry splotchy dark vertical bars along their sides, apparently for camouflage, in the first months of life. Baby fish spend their first summer at the fringes of streams and within patches of submerged vegetation—the vertical parr marks help break up the body outline and make them less obvious to predatory adult fish. These chunky little East Fork trout, certainly adults, still bore distinct parr marks. The various races of six-month-wonder hatchery rainbows, on the contrary, lose their parr markings by the time they are stocked, as do all coastal rainbows *(Oncorhynchus mykiss irideus)*. Several races of interior rainbows (*O. m. gairdneri* for the most part) keep their parr bars for life and resemble these East Fork fish. The other possibility was that these rainbows had crossed, as happens easily, with the aboriginal Colorado cutthroat trout, a fish that also keeps parr marks into adulthood.

As I worked upstream, the valley narrowed and steepened and the creek started to gain pitch, tumbling over itself in low half waterfalls. As the character of the flow changed, so did the trout. I have a few barely adequate photographs of trout taken near the fence and then successively higher upstream. (A good color photograph of a trout is a scarce item in the amateur scrapbook. Much of their coloring is iridescence, not pigment, and good rainbow fish photographs are as rare as good rainbow weather photographs). But to the eye, with every hundred yards of upstream progress, the trout metamorphosed gradually from rainbows to cutthroats. The round black spots grew larger and less frequent, as though the melanin had migrated into clumps. First a faint red cutthroat mark at the gill opening appeared, and then, a few yards uphill and a few fish later, it became a crimson slash. A wash of faded rose on the belly turned brighter and redder with every upstream move. The rainbow along the side of the fish faded to nothing, as if transformed into the increasing general coloration.

I turned after releasing the last fish and looked down toward the King's Pasture Reservoir. I hadn't gained more than 200 or 300 feet of elevation and half a mile of creek run, but I had managed to climb, in low-cut shoes, up out of alien modern trout country into the aboriginal home of Colorado River cutthroat trout. It is not everywhere that you can stroll through a hundred years of history and an eon of evolution in a few hours.

It was a short distance, but it gave the sensation of walking backward along one of those time lines that schoolchildren make and post above the blackboard when they are studying history. At one end, just downhill from King's Pasture, sat a 1993 Ford Explorer with automatic transmission, air-conditioning, and shift-on-the-fly four-wheel drive. I could imagine the fish in the creek downstream being hauled in generations ago, before the power project was built, as fingerlings, probably in milk cans on a buckboard. And every step up the river from the drift fence was a journey back toward Eden's grace. I had angled farther and farther into the past, moving back down the chain of being, watching the genetic code (or the outward expression of it) revert with time and distance. The double helix unwound and recombined and was made original flesh. Rainbow-trout genes were kicked off like dirty boots until at last the small trout in the headwaters were native and fine.

A hundred miles away in any direction, other tourists were seeking their West. They were drawn to the huge water- and wind-cut sandstone spires, sheer cliffs, and deep box canyons, all first shaped when this desert was green and riverine. We were all looking for the same thing, the Old West. Their goal was sculpted rocks of magnitude, free of city grime and graffiti, all glowing against the sky. And I had desired with all my heart these aboriginal fish burning bright in the noonday sun.

Yes, such trout are easily caught. But who, when remembering America's Zion, ever wept for it, that it was easy to see?

7

Cougar Country

I HAD PLANNED TO DRIVE THROUGH BOTH BRYCE AND ZION National Parks on the way from Boulder Creek to New Harmony, Utah, a small town midway between Cedar City and St. George. An afternoon doubleheader of scenery was irresistible. Besides looking at certified spectacular rocks along the route, there are very few reasons for a tourist to go to New Harmony (population ca. 600). It is well off the interstate and has no services. It is called New Harmony because it replaces plain old Harmony, built down on the floodplain of Kanarra Creek (which becomes Ash Creek a little downstream of New Harmony). The original town was flooded out repeatedly around the turn of this century.

A few visitors come to buy apples; the town is a local center for commercial orchards. Quite a few pass through on their way to go deer hunting in the adjacent Dixie National Forest. The least likely reason anyone would show up would be to go trout fishing. Angling was so unusual that one of the two outfitters in the town turned down my business. In twenty years, no one had ever asked him for a trout-fishing trip, and he passed me along to another outfitter who, as he put it, "did odd things like that."

The sixty miles of highway from Boulder Creek to Bryce

Canyon follow the ridgelines, only occasionally dipping downhill to negotiate a way around some intractable geology before returning to the high road. The highway runs along the literal watershed, the dividing line between the Colorado and the Sevier Rivers. In a way, they are both dead-end rivers. Precipitation on the Colorado River slope is headed for the Gulf of California but will never get there, having been entirely withdrawn for municipal and agricultural purposes before it gets to Baja California. Sevier River water runs toward the Escalante desert, the southern edge of ancient and arid Lake Bonneville, and ends up in agricultural fields.

The divide is stunning slickrock country, and probably should be in a national park of its own except for the way the highway was engineered. The two-lane paved road is on the skyline, and western scenic roads tend to be down in the valley so that visitors can lift up their eyes unto the hills. All the way to Bryce I was peeping over the edge and down into the canyons, which is, literally, not uplifting.

I got to Bryce and changed my travel plans. It had nothing to with the scenery; it had everything to do with the scenery. Utah 12 cuts across the north end of Bryce Canyon National Park, and the first federal curve I drove around revealed a crenelated cathedral of Navajo sandstone in the distance and an automobile in the foreground stopped in its tracks in the middle of the road to allow its occupants a leisurely view of the wonders of geology. On average, during this off-season weekday, every half mile there was a pleasure vehicle as dead as roadkill in the travel lane or moving so slowly as to be effectively inert. The same thing happens in Yellowstone, where a handy moose or a grizzly bear sets off an instant traffic jam. But because the rocks weren't going anywhere, I couldn't understand the need to stop before you got to one of the numerous scenic-view pullouts. I gave up on going through Zion as well. It was a long enough drive, and I wanted a route where everyone maintained course and speed, and so I lit out for the interstate.

The reason I needed an outfitter in the Pine Mountains was a mixture of common sense and federal law. The only three streams in the area with Bonneville cutthroat trout in them were up above

9000 feet, more than a mile higher than the surrounding desert. Two of them were in a motor-free wilderness area, and the third was accessible only by a trail restricted to all-terrain vehicles. The common-sense part was not trying to walk in on a short holiday. I was after trout, not blisters.

The outfitter who "did odd things" was Ms. Karen C. LeCount, and on the telephone she seemed pleased to add a fishing expedition to her repertoire. After we made a date, she took the trouble to drive over to Cedar City and talk to the Dixie National Forest trout biologist to make sure she was taking me to the right places. What she knew about already, her basic business, was cougars. Karen is a graduate in wildlife biology with a specialty in carnivores and a successful guide for mountain-lion hunters. When it isn't cats (and one is allowed to hunt lions year-round in alternate sections of southern Utah), it's deer hunters; and when it isn't hunters, it's recreational horseback camping trips, including an annual one for women only. The demand for trout tripping had been and perhaps will be nonexistent.

Besides cougars and deer, the other available big game animal at New Harmony is the Rocky Mountain elk. Unfortunately, from the outfitter's point of view, the elk are right in New Harmony, which makes hunting them very difficult, what with backyards and swimming pools and apple orchards and people looking over your shoulder all the time. Elk hunters will do almost anything to get a nice head of a taxidermized *Cervus canadensis* up on the wall, but they would rather not be watched by housewives and small children while acquiring the animal.

The Pine Mountains west of town are potentially excellent elk habitat, and that inspired the Department of Fish and Wildlife to swap some Utah bighorn sheep for some Wyoming elk and transplant them to the western region of the Dixie National Forest. They turned the elk loose right behind New Harmony at the base of the mountains, expecting them to move on up into the forests and glades and add a new animal to the local alpine landscape. Apparently they got some smart elk who took one look at the alfalfa fields and apple orchards of New Harmony and settled in to stay. The orchards now have twelve-foot-high fences around them to exclude the elk, who still haven't shown any gumption for moving onward and upward. New Harmony is neat and orderly, like all Mormon towns, except for one result of the local elk herd. The orchardists have taken to tying flimsy plastic bags to their fences to spook the elk, and the result is a lot of tattered ZCMI and Wal-Mart bags fluttering in the wind and eventually tearing away and scattering through town.

I understood before arriving that Karen LeCount owned mules and hunted lions, but I had no real idea what that meant. I was at the stage of enlightenment when mules were the ones that looked like horses with big ears and cougars were the big cats with long tails. Karen has built a new house in New Harmony, modest but speaking well of her success at putting strangers in close contact with large cats. The guests stay upstairs in a loft room, sharing it with a stuffed mountain lion crouching on a tree limb fastened to the wall above the double bed. I was surprised at how well I could sleep with a seven-foot-long cat poised over my head, its teeth exposed in a permanent snarl that glimmered in the faint moonlight penetrating the louvered window blinds. A few years ago, in a bed-and-breakfast in Montana, I had shared a bedroom with a life-sized Raggedy Ann doll that sprawled in an easy chair by the window. It was a much more troubling companion than the cat. There was enough glow from the street lamps that I could still see the embroidered staring eyes and the yarn hair after turning off all the lights in the room. I finally got up in the middle of the night and took Raggedy Ann and stuffed her into the clothes closet. The lion, handsomely mounted and in perfect condition, was natural. The doll was eerie.

New Harmony is a quiet town, give or take a pack of coyotes that roamed between Karen's house and the interstate highway four miles to the east, the insomniac howling lion dogs belonging to the other outfitter, and occasional whinnies from Karen's mules. Her dogs, eight of them, chained, sleeping in individual dog-houses out back, made not a sound all night. Over breakfast I asked her why hers were quiet and his weren't, and she thought about it for a minute and then said, "Well, they don't have to howl, do they? I don't yell at them and they don't yell at me."

In another life and at a younger age, I would be tempted to take up mules as a hobby, if not New Harmony as a residence. They are an excellent example of hybrid vigor (a mule is sired by a donkey, born of a mare, and for some reason it doesn't work half as well done the other way around) and have only one defect from the stockman's point of view: they are sterile, and you can't build up a line of mules. Mules just come the way they are, variable. Some mules (there are no general rules about them) are better jumpers than the finest jumping horses but are barred from competing in organized horse shows. Humiliation, to a horseman or horsewoman, is being whipped by a mule. Good riding mules are, for durability, superior to horses. Gen. George Crook, the great Apache conqueror, never rode anything but a mule. He was also an expert at picking, training, and maintaining pack mules. In between Indian campaigns he literally wrote the United States Army manual on the care and use of mules.

People who think mules are unusually stupid or stubborn are not well acquainted with the brain power of the average horse. Karen's mules were as amenable as any other version of horseflesh. One of them avoided the bridle as long as possible, the other had some momentary objection to getting into the trailer, but both were easy to saddle. One thing I was sure of a few days and a few miles later was that mules are self-contained and don't bother with entertaining you or one another. There is something attractive about an animal that doesn't waste energy, a trait that makes house cats interesting companions.

We were headed for a place called the Browse Guard Station, an old Forest Service camp on South Ash Creek, traveling up a road navigable (in dry weather) by truck but, for reasons of safety, restricted to all-terrain vehicles among the array of engine-powered devices. There were a few tread marks here and there, but mostly they had been blown over by dust. There were no boot prints and no horse or mule tracks, except the ones that we were leaving. It was not exactly wilderness, not with the bulldozed road, but it was hardly overused country.

Karen led all the way. This had nothing to do with getting lost; there was only one road to follow. It had to do with the society of mules. My mule was the second-place mule and knew it. That, of course, made me the subordinate person. The argument could be made that the only honorable way to get to a wild place is to walk, but the mule makes a case for muleback just by its mulishness. The animal sets the pace of the journey in a way that no motorized vehicle can. Mules do not have accelerators, and the brake system is marginally effective. Humankind is something of a burden to the earth, and we exaggerate our control over our destiny. It makes sense to travel it on occasion as baggage. Such movement causes reflection.

I noticed after an hour had passed that Karen was spending most of the time looking down at the road as if she had lost something or expected to read some important news scrawled in the dust. She reined in her mule and mine continued ambling on until it got within a few feet of the first-place mule. She had been expecting a message and she had found it. Pressed into the powdery soil was the track of a cat, about the size of my hand but rounder. We were in lion country, and Karen was adding one more animal to the list of potential quarry.

A lion track, whether you are hunting one or not, does concentrate the mind and heighten awareness. The hillside vegetation had evolved from juniper and sage to oak and piñon pine, a simple fact of elevation that I had not noticed before we saw the big cat's sign on the road. After the track I began looking hard at the shaded ground under the trees. It is a different sense of nature than you get from seeing a deer's hoofprint. That just means there are deer around. Having a cougar for a neighbor is a fact that alters the world.

SOUTH ASH CREEK, ALTHOUGH OFTEN OUT OF SIGHT, HIDDEN IN A deep canyon, was never out of earshot. It is one continuous sequence of plunges and pools and makes noise all out of proportion to its size. Where we finally cut its path, just downstream from the Browse Guard Station, it was smaller than I expected, considering the ruckus it made. It appeared to be at summer level, running somewhere around two or three cubic feet per second, which works out to a surprising amount of water, approximately 900 to 1350 gallons a minute (a city fire hydrant, with good pressure in the mains, will spew out about 800 gallons a minute). It's not that hard to guess the flow of a small stream if you can estimate the cross-sectional area with some accuracy. And seconds are time units we have all tried to measure, usually by saying "thousand and one, thousand and two," while counting the seconds between a lightning bolt and a thunderclap. I have no idea why it is so comforting to count those seconds (five to a mile of traveling sound), but it does occupy the mind. In any case, a good guess about the width and depth, and a twig tossed in and timed for four or five feet as it floats down, will get you within a few hundred gallons a minute for any creek you can jump across.

Ms. LeCount, not having any advice to give about fishing or much interest in spectating angling (a sensible and understandable state of mind), had arranged to occupy her mind during the trip by bringing along a friend and neighbor, Kathy Coon, who had a palomino trail horse in training that needed a day's ride to be convinced it was a working animal and not just a cute pet. They could talk horse talk. The palomino, by the way, was the first of us all to realize we were in lion country. It shied at the pug marks in the trail before anyone saw them. It was harder to tell if the mules noticed, but it's always harder to tell what a mule knows.

Little South Ash Creek historically lacked trout. It is a tributary of the Virgin River, which comes into the Colorado much too far south to have Colorado River cutthroats in it. Over the years, because it was there, the Fish and Game Department had stocked it with rainbow trout, a fish that only fitfully reproduced, making for swings in the population from year to year. With its variable flow, high summer temperatures, and tumbling plunge and pool hydrology, it would be a good stream for interior redband rainbow trout *(O. mykiss gairdneri)* if you had to have rainbows, else it would have done better with any of the spectrum of riverine interior cutthroats; but all of these, back when stream stocking was the rage, were unavailable. Hatcheries simply worked with domesticated strains of coastal rainbow *(O. m. irideus)* or with cutthroats from Yellowstone Lake, fish that had evolved a lifestyle dependent on spending their adult years in a large cold lake.

Besides the alien rainbows, the men who used Browse Guard Station and its access road had added another Pacific Coast anomaly. Just uphill from the station rose a magnificent evergreen towering above the ponderosas and oaks. It looked both familiar and unfamiliar and provoked the same puzzlement as does running into an old western acquaintance back East or a New England face across the Missouri. One has more than ordinary difficulty remembering a name when the person is in the wrong place. On examination, the tree had deeply corrugated fibrous bark and carried its needles in small flattened bunches. Someone, for the hell of it, had planted a Giant Sequoia behind the guard station.

The fisheries people, taking advantage of the relative remoteness of the upper reaches of the creek and of the road that made packing in equipment easy, decided to stash some Bonneville cutthroat trout in South Ash Creek after they had "renovated" it. That is one of those useful and necessary euphemisms that fisheries managers have at their disposal. It means poisoned. It took two tries, but they eradicated the alien rainbows in 1986 and moved some Bonneville cutthroats over from the other side of the Pine Mountains.

The usual way to catch fish when you want to study them or relocate them is to use a backpack gasoline-powered electrical generator (about the heft and size of a leaf blower or a weed cutter) to stun them so that they can scooped up in a net and bottled up for the trip. Dale Hepworth, regional state fisheries biologist, tried lugging in the generator and found it was too difficult to calibrate for the small streams. "Kept zapping fish dead the first time," he said, "so, thinking there might be a problem, I'd brought along a little rod and some worms. Now when we're collecting fish to move, I leave the backpack in the office and just use worms." That gives you some idea how easy it is to catch mountain trout. Hepworth has collected hundreds of them with no more equipment than a rod, a monofilament line, a barbless hook, and a few nightcrawlers.

One of the reasons for picking South Ash was its habitat and steady summer flow, two things that are almost always related. Good habitat, as usual, means the absence of cows. "The entire South Ash Creek drainage," the mimeographed report explained, "is ungrazed with domestic livestock and consequently exhibits excellent riparian vegetation and fish habitat." What that means in a canyon creek is very difficult fishing, especially with the artificial fly, an object that needs to be flung around in the air. In most places you couldn't see South Ash Creek if you were more than three feet away; it was completely screened by a mixture of brambles and alders that often dipped down to the surface.

I went bushwhacking while Karen and Kathy sat on the porch of the locked guard station and talked about whatever it is women talk about when they're by themselves. I poked through the brush here and there and caught a few small fish by dapping a fly wherever it was possible, which was not necessarily the same place that a fish wanted to live. A few hundred yards downstream from the guard station, the creek slowed and deepened as it crossed a flat that was densely shaded by large ponderosa pines. With less light reaching the ground, the streamside growth, that "excellent riparian vegetation," thinned considerably.

One moderately large and mildly colorful Bonneville cutthroat snapped at a grasshopper imitation and hung on long enough to find itself on the grass having its picture taken. The most obvious difference between this native fish and the commonly stocked Yellowstone cutthroat was the spotting pattern. The spots were larger, less densely concentrated toward the tail, more evenly distributed along the fish's back and sides. The Lahontan cutthroat *(O. c. henshawi)* also has larger spots more evenly scattered, but its spots are nearly as numerous below the lateral line and along the belly flanks as they are above the line. The Lahontan has spots, to put it another way, rather randomly placed and evenly spaced, as if you had given a schoolchild an outline of a fish and a box of little round black stickers and said, "Put some spots on it, please," while the Bonneville fish has the pattern you would get by saying, "Please put most of the spots on the top sides of this fish."

Someone else had found the fishing was better in the pine-flat section. Wrapped around an alder trunk I saw the top end of a fish stringer, the kind associated with fishing from a boat, a chain-and-clip contraption you hang over the side with live fish wiggling on it. I unwrapped the top end of the chain and pulled the stringer out of the pool. It was about three feet long with a couple of dozen big safety-pin clips. Two well-washed Bonneville cutthroats, the largest more than ten inches long, hung from it, stiff with rigor mortis. The stringer easily outweighed the fish by five to one. The trout were in decent condition, considering they'd been hanging in the cold current for at least twenty-four and probably forty-eight hours, if the all-terrain-vehicle tracks on the road were as old as they looked. (I exclude the possibility that someone who clips trout to a stringer was a hike-in fisherman. It's too long a walk for a person who does things like that.)

All the subtle color, the iridescence, had long since been leached away, but the spots were strong and black against the pale skin. The fish looked much like the ones you see in museum jars of formaldehyde.

That seemed like the end of the day as far as enjoying the esthetics of trout fishing in South Ash Creek. I unsnapped the big brass safety-pin clips and shook the fish onto the grass for whatever critter wanted them and carried the stringer back up to the guard station, hung it over the porch railing in case somebody wanted one, and we all mounted up and headed for the horse trailer at the bottom of the mountain.

Going downhill on a mule is an interesting way to travel. I had not noticed while ascending that mules don't have any shoulders to speak of. (I believe they call them withers.) The saddle goes around the mule at the widest point, and the mule tapers toward the front end. The inexperienced rider begins to wonder about the possibility that the saddle, with its single girth, will also head for the front end. Unease, as I noted in regard to the mountain lion track, increases the powers of perception and deduction. For the first time I noticed that mules are saddled differently than horses. This was late in the day, considering I had just spent an entire morning looking at the downhill ends of a horse and a mule walking side by side ahead of me on the way up to the guard station. Mules have a loop of strap that goes under their tail and back up to the saddle, and this keeps the saddle from sliding forward. It is particularly visible when the mule raises its tail out of the way to do its mule business.

I was a bit downcast myself, having spent all that time and some discomfort to get to a place where people kill trout and then forget to take them home; mule and I slouched downhill. And then, while I was wondering if this day were worth the trouble, Zion appeared. It had been there on the way up, but I had not turned and looked back. Far away, across main Ash Creek, over the invisible interstate, beyond the red sandstone kolob cliffs that line the east side of the valley, rose Zion's great bleached bones like the skyline of a titan's metropolis.

I savored the view from thirty miles distant. For a moment I thought about fishing my binoculars out of the saddlebag and then changed my mind. I had not come so far to see Zion closer up but to see it as it was once—a horizon, not a possession. Over there, the people in automobiles and tour buses were doing Zion. From over here, high on the Pine Mountains, it was still untrammeled, unpaved, uninterpreted.

Farther downhill, as we passed the spot where the big cat had crossed the road, my mule sniffed and then snorted a little harder than usual and rolled its eyes back farther than usual and cocked its ears left and right. It was not my imagination to think that the mule was uneasy; it was better perception. I reached forward and patted it hard on its thin shoulders. In another life, I would try to get to know a mule.

8

Saddlebag Trout

THE SOUTH ASH CUTTHROATS HAD BEEN TRANSFERRED FROM Reservoir Creek over on the western slope of the Pine Mountains, and we had deliberately scheduled that trip for the second day. I wanted to go backward on the time line. It was just a whim, plus an old habit of trying to save the best for last; and a certified federal wilderness area should be a finer, wilder place than one at the end of an all-terrain vehicle track. It was something like eating the layers of cake first and saving the icing till the end.

The shortest way to the Reservoir Creek trailhead was to truck the mules over a dirt road that skirted north of the Pine Mountains and then cut due west to a paved road that links Cedar City with the small settlement of Pine Valley high on the western side of the mountains. We were going only as far as Grass Valley to find the trail. If you keep going past the Pine Valley turnoff you hit Mountain Meadows, site of a ghastly massacre of emigrants by Mormons and not a popular destination for tourists, Mormon or gentile.

We crossed Pinto Creek on the last steep grade up to Grass Valley. Pinto, a stream that heads northwest into the Great Basin, historically would have held Bonneville cutthroats. They were long gone, long since genetically swamped by imported rainbows.

Reservoir Creek, whose headwaters we were seeking, comes into Grass Valley, which is south and west of Pinto Creek across the subcontinental divide in the Virgin River drainage. That puts it in the Colorado watershed, headed for the Gulf of California instead of the Great Salt Lake. It is something of a mystery why Reservoir Creek had a surviving population of absolutely pure Bonneville trout in it. No tributary of the Virgin ever held trout, or not until the settlers arrived.

There are two possible explanations, each in its own way illustrative of the country. A few ranches were established in Grass Valley, and the nearby town of Pine Valley grew up in the late nineteenth century. The settlers came from the Pinto valley, and one of the first things they did was hand-dig a tunnel through the low hills that separated Grass Valley's several creeks—all tributaries of the Virgin River—and Pinto Creek. This shifted water across the biological and geological barrier. The reason for moving the water is that agriculture in the ordinary sense is impossible up in Grass Valley; it's subject to frosts any month of the year at its elevation, over 8000 feet above sea level. It is good mountain-hay country but not amenable to row crops, not even to that hardy item the rutabaga. So they moved water from Main Canyon Creek and lower Reservoir Canyon Creek in Grass Valley over to South Pinto Creek and brought it down main Pinto to where it could irrigate fields in the neighborhood of Newcastle, Utah, out on the fringe of the Escalante desert in the Great Basin. That is a very Mormon thing to do, jiggle things around to improve on nature.

They might have moved the fish, too. The tunnel is shallowly pitched between Grass Valley and Pinto Creek, where a hand-dug reservoir stored up water from Main Canyon Creek (another troutless Virgin River tributary when the Saints arrived) before shipping it down to the basin. The devices controlling the water are upward-lifting headgates, allowing easy passage through the divide for fish when the gates are even slightly open. Alternatively, settlers in Grass Valley might just have missed their trout back over there in the Pinto and hauled some up in milk cans and fixed Eden properly. The Lord's work, as far as the Mormons were concerned, was not finished, and it was up to the Saints to complete the task. Unfortunately, in the same spirit of continuous improvement, rainbow trout were brought into Main Canyon Creek in the 1930s, and now it holds a hybridized population of rainbows crossed with cutthroats.

The Reservoir Canyon fish have a clearer history. In the mid-1980s, while working with Reservoir's Bonneville cutthroats, Utah fisheries manager Dale Hepworth made the acquaintance of a local rancher, Kumen Gardner of Pine Valley, the village just south of Grass Valley. Mr. Gardner related that when he was about twelve years old (which would have been shortly before World War I), he and his brother noticed the parlous absence of trout up in Reservoir Canyon and decided to improve the bioscape. They caught some Bonneville cutthroats in Main Canyon Creek and packed them by horseback to upper Reservoir above some waterfalls, where they have survived pure and unsullied to this very day. You would have to be about twelve to even think of it: the trail from Grass Valley up to the high meadows of Reservoir Canyon is a solid three-hour ride, a long way to pack a milk can full of fish, even on horseback. Nothing is quite so miserable a load as sloshing water.

The meadow around upper Reservoir Creek, when we reached it, seemed worth the trip. In a country where everything you ride through is either cow chewed or solid brush, coming on an open grassy parkland with nothing taller than sedges growing by the stream is a pleasant discovery. It is not exactly virgin territory, although within the boundaries of the designated wilderness area. It is the only sunlit spot on that side of the mountain and a popular destination for campers. Every pack outfit does just what we did, turn out the animals to graze. Karen's two mules and Kathy's pinto spent most of midday in hobbles, chewing on the landscape. Even at that distance from civilization, the meadow was dotted with dandelions.

Wet meadows are natural results of stream flow, rare as they seem to be today. Undisturbed by man and cow, streams want to cut down mountains and make flatlands. A high water table results, and grasses and sedges flourish. Seasonal flooding kills back the trees, and running water undercuts the banks where overhanging grasses shade the water. This creates shelter for trout—or would create it, as soon as Kumen Gardner and his brother provided some fish.

Karen and Kathy found a well-polished pine log to sit on, and I went a-fishing. There were trout, as will happen in high country far away from vehicles and stringers and refrigerated cartons of nightcrawlers, everywhere a fish should be. Although it was almost the end of June, it was still spring and spawning season at 9000 feet. Pairs of fish were waltzing around—the male trying to herd the female toward his own half-dug spawning bed in the gravel at the head of the pool where the current had washed away the fine sediments. Some fish stop feeding while reproducing, salmon notoriously, but mountain cutthroats don't have the luxury of postponing meals. I stopped the first trout in midlust with an artificial grasshopper. He quit following the female, quivered his fins, let the current push him downstream a foot, and then rose to the fly as if he had not eaten for days (which was possible) and had absolutely no interest in sex (clearly improbable).

Bonneville cutthroats are not noted in the literature for their coloration, which Behnke (in *Native Trout of Western North America*) describes as similar to the rather bland brassy shades of typical Yellowstone cutthroats. He suggests they are not at all like Colorado River cutthroats, which have "a disposition to develop brilliant red, orange, and golden-yellow coloration." Take away the adjective "brilliant" and substitute "charming" or "noticeable" or "distinct," and what can be said of Colorado fish can be honestly written of these Pine Mountain Bonnevilles. The cutthroat mark itself was bright orange and, in breeding excess, spread out from the gill opening like smeared lipstick. The flanks were distinctly yellow, golden yellow when you turned the fish to the right angle of light to enhance the iridescence. On the belly, around the roots of the pectoral fins, a rosy red wash was visible even before the trout had been hoisted onto the streamside grass for a photograph. These tints are, with the exception of the narrow cutthroat mark, ephemeral colors and fade after a trout gets through the breeding season, or when you fry one.

Even the trout who weren't participating in the old dance were easy to spot. Cutthroats truly do bask in the sun. I saw eleven fish in an hour (and caught ten of them). I also saw several more swirls and ripples as trout flushed from shallow water and hid themselves under banks and fallen logs. The challenge, such as it was, had nothing to do with getting the fish to eat but everything to do with seeing them first. The creek was perfectly clear and ran slowly with almost no surface turbulence. Once you remember to stay well back or to approach the water on your hands and knees, it is easy angling and should be. Anytime it's hard to catch trout, you are not in the real West; you are on some river stocked with alien trout and freighted with eastern anglers who have taught the fish painful lessons and then put them back.

The only thing missing from the Reservoir Canyon's antique naturalness was Old Crackfoot, the last local grizzly bear. Let me amend that thought: the only thing missing was the distinctive track of a grizzly pressed into the soft ground by the creek. If it was 1897, this Reservoir meadow would have been an excellent place to strike the trail of the big bear, and in late spring's spawning season a likely place to find it fishing or rooting for grubs and roots in the wet soil. It is better to think of than to experience. I have surprised one grizzly and seen bear tracks, and tracks are better.

When the Spanish speakers came to the Southwest, they did not have a word in their language for the wet meadows that surround mountain streams. Neither do anglophones, but we make do with compound constructions. The Spaniards just called them *ciénagas*, the generic word for swamp or water-dwelling vegetation. That is not exactly what they are. Except in flood, the meadows are just places with high subsurface water tables fed by the meandering streams. And as they were good places for trout, they were excellent places for grizzly bears, an omnivore that feeds seasonally on fresh green matter, on roots and berries. Bears will take trout, small a mouthful as they are, when the fish are distracted by spawning and less wary than usual. To newly arrived cattlemen, the sedge and grass meadows were perfect pastures, food and water side by side in an otherwise arid, brushy world.

They could not take the pressure of grazing, these *ciénagas.* They were once common, found everywhere that running water slowed, deposited silt, meandered, and achieved a balance with the land. In flood time they absorbed the flow like great flat sponges; in drought they slowly released it back into the creeks and streams. But cattle broke down the banks, trampled the bottoms, ate away the channel-holding willows and alders, and the water ran faster and cut deeper into the ground, hurrying toward the valley floors and on to the great rivers. We traded the old *ciénagas* for the new washes.

Speaking of these wet meadows, David E. Brown wrote in *The Grizzly in the Southwest*—another of Karen's books in her guest room library—"Now rare, such marshy streamsides were once important foraging sites for grizzlies." And their use as pastures complicated matters, as he noted: "Unfortunately for the bears, these were also the habitat first affected by the white man's exploitation of the southwest—this was to play an important part in the grizzly's extirpation." It seems impossible to imagine now, but the California grizzly bear, the one on the state flag, once roamed down from the Santa Monica and San Gabriel Mountains into the heart of what would become Los Angeles. About the only evidence left is a street name: La Cienega Boulevard, now the avenue of muffler shops.

Perhaps the best (or worst) example of overgrazing in southern Utah is just west, over at the Mountain Meadows massacre site. This shallow bowl on the rim of the Great Basin was heavily grazed by emigrant trains (including the ill-fated one in 1857) even before numbers of cattle were run on it. It is not a mountain meadow anymore but a high and arid plain with deeply eroded washes. Even the springs where emigrants and livestock watered have dried beyond usefulness.

Grass Valley, where the local Mormons diverted Water Canyon Creek and Reservoir Creek over to the Pinto Creek drainage, is obviously dewatered as much by man's hand as by his cattle. Looking at it today, "Grass Valley" is not the first sobriquet that a traveler would think of; "Sagebrush Flat" is likelier.

I walked back upstream watching the trout. In the pool where I had caught the male, the pair were circling again, not quite ready to move on to the spawning bed. At the head of the meadow, where the stream came out of the shadows of the circling pines, a recent meander in the stream had cut back the bank, exposing a sad collection of plastic—plastic sheeting, plastic food packaging, plastic spring-water bottles. It had been buried once in the soft sand near the creek, and now the creek had cut back, as they all do sooner or later, and excavated the packer's dump.

Karen said she had noticed it, and she thought they would have to come up in the summer and pack it out. Things like that gave outfitters a bad name, although she knew it wasn't left there by any of the local hunting guides. "We make a living getting people away from things like that," she said.

The first long shadows of the ponderosas were on the ground, and it was suddenly chilly. I undid the fly rod, stowed it in its short aluminum case, and walked over to my mule and put the case in the rifle scabbard. The mule seemed interested; it took this, I guessed, as a sign we were headed back to the truck, and that meant a ride home, and that meant a feed of oats. Mules do not have a happy expression that I can perceive, but this mule looked like it was good and tired of short mountain grass and had high expectations. I led it over to the pine log Karen and Cathy had been sitting on. This made getting on easier, particularly for someone with low expectations of the next few hours. Riding and running have two things in common: downhill is harder on the knees.

We worked our way down the mountain along Water Canyon Creek, which has only intermittent flow at its seasonal headwaters but picks up two springs just below the boundary of the wilderness area. The springs, to keep cattle out, had exclosure fences, and between them, and below the second one, the creek burbled along. Even from muleback you could see trout resting in dappled sunlight or, if not the trout itself, a shadow on the bright sand. These were Bonneville cutthroats as well, stashed away in this little piece of water just in case something happened to the ones up in Reservoir Creek. Over several years, even when the springs ran low and there was nothing but pools of water in a few deeper holes, they had survived. It is an admirable trait of all the aboriginal interior cutthroats that they can take anything nature hands out except an excess of cows.

Down at Grassy Flat, Water Canyon Creek disappeared into the ground, percolating into the aquifer. My mule either saw or smelled the trailer and started thinking seriously about oats. This caused it to trot, which is an unpleasant gait for the ill-equipped and afflicted tenderfoot, so I reined it in, which was the first time in two days I had done anything but sit. The mule slowed to a walk and then very deliberately turned its head and rolled its eyes back, as if to get a good look at who this was who had suddenly decided to be in charge.

By then we were on a jeep road across the flats, and the tire ruts were windblown, eroded down a foot or more below the scrubby grass and sagebrush. And jutting out of the side of the cutbank—a light gray sandy soil—I saw something warmer-colored and sensed artifact. The mule was still walking but pulling on the bit. Its ears were cocked forward and its eyes focused on the truck and trailer just a hundred yards away. I wanted to look at that piece of stone; it had to be flint. Whether it was a big flake or a tool or an arrowhead, I knew not.

The mule was amenable to reversing direction or, to be more accurate, the direction in which it was looking. By pulling hard on the reins, I could get it to stop and then turn it back toward the flint sticking out of the ground. But it would not go back the way it had come. It was an interesting moment in my mule career. I could stop it, I could turn it, but I could not make it retrace its steps away from the trailer. The mule and I did four sets of 360-degree revolutions (three counterclockwise and then one clockwise to see if that made a difference), and then I gave up, and off to the trailer we went.

Dismounted, I walked back up the tire ruts. The flake of stone was visible from fifty or sixty feet, so distinctly colorful in a bland landscape. I bent over at the waist and very carefully pulled the stone out of the sand, holding it gently by its rounded base. It was long and thin and appeared to be a complete arrow point, the earless, willow-leaf style of the Great Basin archaic people. I think that by extracting it so carefully I was trying to invoke a kind of magic: if I went slowly enough, it would all be there, right down to the fine point. It worked.

THE GUEST ROOM AT KAREN'S HOUSE NOT ONLY HAD A STUFFED MOUN-
tain lion for the visitor's enlightenment; the room also contained
the larger part of her professional library. It is not often that one
gets bedside reading material of such rarefied matter as *The Wolf in
the Southwest*, or *The Ben Lilly Legend*. (Lilly was the great lion and
bear bounty hunter of Arizona and New Mexico.) Odd as the
decor and entertainment might be in an ordinary bed-and-breakfast, it was perfect for guests of Cougar Country Outfitters, Inc.
After I left, the next guests would be a couple celebrating their
wedding anniversary by going lion hunting. This odd choice for
nuptial celebration did not come up because Karen gossips about
her clients but because we had to drive into Cedar City one afternoon to pick up groceries; this included a stop at a bakery to get a
Happy Anniversary cake that the husband had ordered for the occasion.

I was up later than usual, waiting for the pain in my knees to
drain down a little before falling asleep (one begins to understand
why cowpokes are bowlegged), and I started browsing through
these histories of predators in the West. Karen's books produced
an insight, which is more than I can say for typical bedtime reading. It is so perfectly obvious an idea (once conceived) that an un-
generous reader might wonder if it deserved the name of insight,
but I will state it: a person planning a trip to the West in search of
the last remnants of the magic it once held would do well to study
up on the history of both the extermination and the survival of
large predators. Where they are now and where they last roamed
are wondrous places. It would do as well as my way—sticking flags
in the map wherever swam the last remaining native fish. In fact,
if you chose grizzly bears or timber wolves and I stuck with trout,

we would meet on the trail. Mountain lions might do, although they always ranged more widely than trout or grizzlies and have been turning up lately within the city limits of Los Angeles, California, where, I assure you, no trout swim and few birds sing.

The obvious example is Yellowstone Park, where the largest number of native trout in the West still survive in company with, and are preyed upon by, grizzlies. And the wolves are not far behind; there is good reason to believe, at this writing, that timber wolves have managed to make it down to the banks of the Yellowstone from Glacier Park (which is itself the home of a few isolated populations of the rare Westslope cutthroat trout).

Absent living bears—which is fine by me: I prefer the possibility of grizzlies to the reality of white fangs set off by a purple tongue and, as all survivors of close encounters with grizzly bears remember most vividly, horrid breath—it also is the case that going to the last places where grizzly were seen or killed will get you into much the same territory as looking for the wild trout of the West.

In Utah the last grizzly was taken by a state trapper in the late 1920s, a few miles from the Idaho border. It was probably a recent immigrant from Idaho rather than the last surviving native Utah grizzly. Its name, inevitably, was Old Ephraim. That is the usual sobriquet for grizzly bears, an animal discovered in the nineteenth century when everyone, even mountain men, knew their Old Testament. (It is "grizzly" as in "grizzled," not as in "grisly.") In the book of the prophet Hosea, the name "Ephraim" is used by the prophet to personify wayward Israel, in fulfillment of Jacob's prophecy that the son of Joseph (Ephraim) would be fruitful and multiply. The people have become idolators and are scorned by Hosea: "Strangers have devoured his [Ephraim's] strength," Hosea preaches, "and he knoweth it not." Using a metaphor of unacknowledged decline by heedless Ephraim, Hosea rails on: "Yea, gray hairs are sprinkled here and there upon him, yet he knoweth not."

Prior to the slaying of Old Eph (and the records for last bears are much better kept than for penultimate bears), the last native Utah grizzly might have been Old Crackfoot, a bear carrying the visible scar of a trap on one paw who left his signature track all over the Pine Valley Mountains between New Harmony and Grass Valley to the west. Current residents of New Harmony like to think Old Crackfoot was the longest-surviving genuine homegrown Utah grizzly.

The last evening I was in town, Darce Prince, New Harmony's senior male citizen and volunteer oral historian, stopped by for a barbecue that the Coons and Karen were putting on just because it was Friday. Water Canyon was nice country, I said to Darce, a little hard used by pack-in campers but not in too bad a shape. We had seen plenty of deer sign and a little overbrowsing, but it looked like good game country when you got above the parts of the Dixie National Forest that were leased for grazing. Talking about cattle reminded Darce of the last grizzly bear in the county.

Old Crackfoot, Darce thought, became a problem to local ranchers because the Pine Mountains had been sheeped out and cowed out, grazed so hard there wasn't the wild game to feed a bear anymore. There was plenty of game now, but not much when Darce's father was a young man.

"It was in '98," Darce said. "Of course I wasn't there, but I know that's the right date. Back in '44 I was up on the mountain near Reservoir canyon, and right there on a quaking aspen it was carved: 'Mitt Moody Killed Grizzly Bar Today.' The year carved on the tree, it was 1898. I can't remember the month and the day.

"My dad, he and a friend, they ran into Old Crackfoot once, but they decided they didn't want to tackle him. My dad said his gun was run over by a wagon and didn't shoot too straight; and his buddy, he had one of those old 45/70 carbines and that wasn't too powerful. They let that bear be.

"You understand," Darce continued, "that of course these stories get better the more times they're told, but Mitt Moody, he claimed he could reach out and touch that bear before it died."

We chatted on, and the talk turned to the landscape around New Harmony, so typical of the arid West at the base of mountains—sagebrush foothills cut by wide sandy washes where seasonal floods carve channels all out of proportion to their summer flow, if there is any summer flow at all. Darce said it might be the way the West looked now, but it wasn't that way when the settlers came. "My father was very clear about that; he told me that there were no washes in this country when he was a boy. He said it was the cattle did it."

And then, just when my favorite nemesis, the cow, had become part of the conversation, a telephone call interrupted us. It was for me. New Harmony, Utah, is such a small town that when you aren't at your outfitters, when you're over at the neighbors, a telephone call will reach you after a few tries. I will say it again. If you must have a problem far from home, try to have it in Utah.

9

Across
the Great Divide

THE TELEPHONE CALL WAS THE NOT UNEXPECTED BUT UNANTICI-
pated news that my mother had "taken" a heart attack, as she
would have said, and died that morning in San Diego. I excused
myself from the barbecue and went back to my room to pack. For
some reason, while slowly rearranging the contents of the suitcases, I recalled the opening sentence of Camus's *L'Etranger*, that
iconic novel of existentialism: *"Aujourd'hui, maman est morte."*
When you are in college and very wise, you understand that the
stranger of the novel is a classic disaffected twentieth-century
man. And then when you are older and not nearly so full of wisdom, you find yourself looking a stuffed mountain lion in the eye
and saying out loud, "Today, my mother died."

That sense of loss altered my plans. I had thought I was done
with Montana; I had seen it when it was good, and that was
enough. But after I flew to San Diego and while we cleaned up
the usual things one sorts through in times like that, my sisters

and I kept finding one reminder after another of relatives and places—old square-format Brownie photographs of downtown Miles City or Chinook, postcards and address books—most of it as old as we were. Even a photograph of me, age three or so, fell out of a book. I am proudly carrying a dead fish I had found on the shore of Flathead Lake, over west of the Rockies from our home in Miles City. When my mother could afford it, back in the lonely years of World War II while my father was away, she always took us to the water in the summer, across the plains, west through the Rockies, up into the pines. I wanted to go back.

I was suddenly tired of the desert. It is a wonderful setting for pine-covered high mountains, but I needed a turn through well-watered country. One loss can put you in the mood to face another, and that summer she died I went back to Ross's Hole and the East Fork of the Bitterroot and stared hard at it and thought about family and time and the end of things. My favorite uncle, dear Gordon, had always taken me to the East Fork when I was younger. I missed him more than the river, which he would take as a compliment if he could hear it.

The Bitterroot River valley puts a traveler within a few hours of better country, one with fewer ranchettes and no urban sprawl at all. Just over the towering mountains in Idaho is the Lochsa River, and it's fir trees all the way, not a tumbleweed or an alkali flat in sight. I was in the mood for richness after so much rimrock and sagebrush.

Over there in the Lochsa still swam Captain Lewis's cutthroat trout, the singular and original fish, and not a brown trout to be seen. Two tributaries of the Snake on the sundown side of the Bitterroot Mountains have a reputation for cutthroats: the Selway and the Lochsa. A traveler with a sense of history must choose the Lochsa: it was Lewis and Clark's path west, the first tributary of the Columbia (via the Snake) that they were able to descend on their way to the Pacific Ocean.

The Lewis and Clark Trail is fairly well marked from St. Louis, Missouri, through the Dakotas and in Idaho and Oregon. It popped out of the Idaho road map on first glance and settled the question of which river to visit. On the other hand, most road maps of Montana, including the state's own tourism map and one in the reliable *Rand McNally Road Atlas* of the United States, Canada, and Mexico, will not show the Lewis and Clark Trail in that state. This seems odd, to neglect the path in a state with two Clark Fork Rivers, a Lewis and Clark National Forest, a Lewis and Clark County, and the substantial rural trading center of Lewistown smack dab in the middle. There is a reason for this: there isn't room on the map to print the labels for all the Lewis and Clark Trails in Montana.

It is disconcerting to wander across this Big Sky state in any direction and along virtually every major highway and always find yourself back on the Lewis and Clark Trail. If you drive clockwise around the state, from Miles City in the southeast to Dillon in the far southwest, and north to Great Falls and Cutbank, and then back east again along the Highline (the old Great Northern, now Burlington Northern Railroad) to Chinook and Sidney, and then, just to make things more confusing, if you cut straight back west across the middle of the state, through Lewistown to Great Falls and Missoula, and up the Bitterroot River to the Idaho border, you are forever doomed to ride along behind Lewis and Clark.

Depending on which direction you travel, the pensive Sacajawea on the trail's signposts points by turns east and west, north and south. A stylized Clark or Lewis, it is not clear which one, leans on his muzzle-loader and stares off where she points, toward Seattle or Chicago or Los Angeles or Anchorage.

Everywhere else, in every other state they went through from Missouri to Oregon and back again, there's just one Lewis and Clark Trail, a single-minded track out and back. They went up the Missouri to its several Montana headwaters on the way out, and that accounts for some of the confusion. And on the way back, they split the party in two for part of the return journey through Montana. That accounts for more of the confusion; you could call some segments of it the Lewis *or* Clark Trail. Once out of Montana on the way west, they went straight down the Lochsa River to the Snake to the Columbia and beached themselves at the mouth of that true River of the West at Cape Desolation.

They were not exactly lost in Montana; they were just looking for something that didn't exist . . . an easy way through the mountains. Thoroughly discouraged, they stopped near the Great Falls of the Missouri and ate some fish. As a group, they were not fond of fish or adept at angling. Clark seems to have gone down the Yellowstone the following year without noticing how well stocked it was with trout. His journal entries consist entirely of notes on the unbelievable abundance of game animals. I think of him as I watch the tourists in Yellowstone Park gasping at the sight of buffalo and elk. There is a moment in Clark's journal where he apologizes for constantly mentioning animals and promises not to do it again. He sounds very much like a tourist showing slides or camcorder tape to the neighbors . . . *oh, gosh, here's some more buffalo.*

The whole way, except when starving, they ate meat: buffalo, bear, deer, elk, bighorn sheep, antelope, rabbit, partridge, duck, and, when it got worse, their own horses. But at the Great Falls, while they repaired their moccasins and caulked their boats and pulled prickly pear thorns out of their feet, they ate trout. They put one in salt to take back to President Jefferson because it clearly was not a brook trout *(Salvelinus fontinalis)*, and that was the only kind of river trout anyone had ever seen in America. It was a new species of fish, and that was part of their job, bringing back new animals and vegetables and minerals. It was years until anyone back East remembered that Meriwether Lewis had brought home a fish. I think that puts it in perspective.

In 1853, the surgeon of the Pacific Railroad survey party, who knew that an odd trout had been caught at the Great Falls of the Missouri almost fifty years earlier, got out his fly rod and caught several specimens in what biologists like to call the type locality for *Oncorhynchus clarki lewisi.* Better preserved than Lewis's salted fish, they were examined and deemed a new and unknown species of trout and given originally the handle of *Salmo lewisi.* There already was a *Salmo clarki* and had been since 1836, when a British scientist had the courtesy to name a cutthroat trout caught in Washington State after Captain Clark. Among the reasons that Clark was the first to get a fish named after him may be the fact that Lewis had committed suicide in 1809 (he might have been murdered, but that is a modern supposition; at the time, the verdict was suicide), while

Clark lived forty productive years after the trip.

Suicides, putative or real, give off an odor of despair. Persons who spend their life dissecting embalmed fish have it hard enough without being depressed when it comes time to name the thing. The assumed cause of Lewis's mortal melancholy (it was even mentioned in a contemporary issue of *The Boston Review*) is distressing to all authors and should be to readers. He couldn't rewrite the journals of the expedition, and they needed considerable work before they could be published. William Clark, the more consistent daily diarist, was hardly a stylist and couldn't spell "fir tree" unless you spotted him the *i*. If Lewis did take his own life, he was the first American to die of writer's block.

I wish I could make this next part easier: there is no plain old *Salmo clarki* or *Salmo lewisi* anymore. All cutthroat trout are now divided up into subspecies with three names. As you may remember, the generic name, following much discussion and a bow to precedence and genetics, is now *Oncorhynchus* instead of *Salmo*. The species name is *clarki*, and the third name is the subspecies title. So, Lewis's old salted trout is now *O. clarki lewisi*. The one originally named after Clark alone is now *O. c. bouvieri*. And getting the scientific names straight is the easy part.

Unfortunately the Lewis fish, which was caught on the eastern side of the Continental Divide in the Missouri drainage, has the official common name of Westslope cutthroat, although it occupied the headwaters of the Missouri as well as all of the interior headwaters of the Columbia and Salmon Rivers. I have written a little about this earlier, but it should be emphasized, now that we are about to follow Lewis and Clark to the Selway. This diffusion of the Westslope cutthroat created a problem, one not lost on Captains Clark and Lewis. As little as they cared for fish to eat or for angling as sport, they were sensitive to biological indicators. And they could not tell by looking at the local trout whether they were in the Missouri drainage or the Columbia/Salmon drainage. That is, the Westslope trout, *O. c. lewisi*, was no indication of a Continental Divide, and big divides are usually a biological barrier. To find out if they were truly across the Great Divide, they had to find a river with sea-run Pacific salmon in it. Although the interior

West was a mystery, the Columbia (or Oregon, or River of the West) already had been explored thoroughly up to The Dalles by Russian, American, and British seamen and not a few scientists. Clark and Lewis were well aware that it held a population of large, seagoing salmonids, and they were looking for the headwaters of the Columbia by the process of finding a "salmon river." They did not obsess on fish, hard as the going was, but kept an eye out for other biological oddities.

Besides *O. c. lewisi*, the only other animal with the unfortunate explorer's name is Lewis's woodpecker, shot by him not far from where his trout was caught. The very bird he killed and skinned, neatly labeled *Melanerpes lewis*, lies in a tray in a cabinet on the fifth floor of Harvard University's Museum of Comparative Zoology. Harvard, back in the nineteenth century, acquired the contents of Charles Willson Peale's museum in Philadelphia, getting various souvenirs of the expedition, including Indian artifacts, the captains' very own clothing, medicines, plants, and stuffed birds. Peale, an excellent painter himself, is perhaps better remembered for naming his children after famous artists than for his career as pay-per-view museum entrepreneur. Sons Rembrandt and Titian Peale are best known for their portraits and for illustrations of birds and plants from the family museum.

For many years the Harvard/Peale museum specimen was the only one known to science. Titian Peale, on a trip west, shot a breeding pair of Lewis's woodpeckers, and they are at Harvard as well. The original is easily to spot, even though it shares the museum tray with dozens of specimens of Lewis's woodpecker. All the others are lying neatly on their backs with their beaks pointing straight ahead and their feet tucked down in the classic museum-specimen style. Lewis's own *Melanerpes lewis* has feet askew and sticking up, dried in a clasping grip; its beak points forward and up. It was once mounted on a slab of bark in Peale's museum and served as the model painted by Alexander Wilson for his multivolume *American Ornithology* (1808–1814).

Wilson, an immigrant from Scotland, was a sort of John James Audubon with modesty and attainable goals. Not a flamboyant painter, Wilson created stiff portraits but excellent representations—better, in fact, than some in many a modern bird book. One would have the devil's own time trying to identify a Lewis's woodpecker using the *Macmillan Guide to Birds of North America,* which represents the bird's main color in a bilious green. Its body is truly black (*melanerpes* combines two Greek words, one for "black" and one for "creeper," a typical movement of most wood-peckers); there is only the slightest green iridescence in certain angles of light.

In their era, Lewis and Clark were less appreciated than one would imagine today driving by their names blazoned along the trail from St. Louis to Portland, Oregon. (Or from Lewis County and Clark County and the villages of Clark and Lewistown—all in Missouri—to Lewis and Clark College in Oregon via the twin cities of Lewiston, Idaho, and Clarkston, across the Snake River in Washington.) It was not until the settlers came out on the Oregon Trail that the captains achieved mythic status. Of their contempo-raries, it was only Alexander Wilson, in his *American Ornithology,* who would write a truly sorrowful obituary for the unfortunate Meriwether Lewis.

The solitary stuffed specimen that Lewis brought back, Wilson explained in his discussion of Lewis's woodpecker, was

discovered, and preserved, amidst a thousand difficul-ties, by those two enterprising travellers, whose intre-pidity was only equalled by their discretion, and by their active and laborious pursuit of whatever might tend to render their journey useful to Science and to their country. It was the request and particular wish of Captain Lewis, made to me in person, that I should make drawings of such of the feathered tribes as had been preserved and were new [to science]. That brave soldier, that amiable and excellent man, over whose solitary grave in the wilderness I have since shed tears of affection, having been cut off in the prime of his life, I hope I shall be pardoned for consecrating this humble note to his memory, until a more able pen shall do better justice to the subject.

After a fish, and before a bird, the best-known souvenir from the expedition that has Lewis's name on it is a handsome alpine flower, and even that has a distinctly morbid and ghostly quality. A few years after Lewis's death, a certain Mr. M'Mahon of Philadelphia noticed that the tuberous root of one of the dried and pressed specimens brought back by the expedition seemed to be healthily plump. On the chance that it might grow, he planted it, and it grew, although it died by "some accident" before flowering. (This was a disappointment, as the blossom parts were critical to scientific description.) The plant was the bitterroot, now the state flower of Montana, a showy spring bloomer with cupped petals that range from electric rose through pink to solid white. In good years, it carpets the unplowed prairies and hills from Wyoming to Washington. Bitterroot's scientific name is *Lewisia rediviva,* "Lewis come back to life."

The plant was collected on July 1, 1806, as the expedition was retracing its steps back to Missoula from Oregon. Lewis found the plant growing on gravelly ground just where Lolo Creek enters the Bitterroot River. It was too late for it to be in bloom at that elevation, even though the winter of 1805–6 had started early and ended late. The party had been caught in snowstorms crossing the Lolo Pass in September 1805 and barred from returning over it by deep snows until late June of 1806.

*Lewisia*s (the whole genus) are notoriously fussy if highly rewarding plants for alpine garden hobbyists. In Britain, where they appreciate these things, there are several ornamental hybrids of *Lewisia rediviva.* The British are especially fond of growing wildflowers from their former colonies. This has the aspect, one imagines, of lost empire preserved.

There are, however, no cutthroat trout *(bouvieri* or *lewisi)* in Britain outside of museum jars. There could be. Another western trout—the rainbow—is stocked in rivers and reservoirs throughout Britain and in Europe, India, Australia, New Zealand, Africa, and Japan as well. No, if you want a cutthroat, you have to go where they always have been, although you cannot expect them everywhere they were. There are no more cutthroat trout at the Great Falls of the Missouri (and no more falls, for that matter: the water makes electricity now, not fish).

* * *

The Bitterroot Mountains that Lewis and Clark crossed to get to the Pacific are quickly found on a national map. Their peaks and high ridges make up the squiggled line that is the north-south Idaho-Montana border along the eastern edge of the panhandle of Idaho. This is an almost-continental divide that separates the two great tributaries of the Columbia River. The Clark Fork of the Columbia, fed by the eastern slopes of the Bitterroots and the western side of the Rockies, flows north and only decides at the last moment to swing west to the Pacific through Idaho's Lake Pend Oreille. The western waters of the Bitterroots drain into the Snake and run properly on westward until they meet the Columbia at Pasco, Washington.

The actual Continental Divide, marching down from Glacier Park to Yellowstone Park, is impossible to find on a political map for all of its passage through interior Montana. Not even counties or national forests pay attention to it. We are wrong to think too much of the Great Divide. It is flat enough in places that a man with a shovel could change the course of waters from the Pacific to the Atlantic drainages.

But just where the Idaho-Montana border begins to swing east below the Idaho panhandle, starting at the place where U.S. Highway 93 crosses from Salmon, Idaho, on the way north to Missoula, Montana, via Sula Meadows, that meandering line of the Atlantic and Pacific watersheds becomes political again. From Route 93 east to Yellowstone Park and Wyoming, the border of Idaho and Montana is the true continental divide, parting two states and two oceans along the high ground of the Beaverhead and Centennial Mountains.

It was through the Beaverheads that Lewis and Clark first crossed the divide. They had run out of water on the Beaverhead River (their last hope for a tributary of the Missouri that would bring them to the edge of the Pacific slope), and they crossed an open and treeless high plain to the Lewis River in what is now Idaho, and came down it to the Salmon River. They were across the divide and in the wrong place. Yes, the Indians called it the

Salmon River because it had salmon in it. And though it ran to the Pacific, the Indians told them it was not to be boated. No one ever did that. The Salmon was, as it still says on tourist maps, the river of no return as it beats through the great canyon between the towns of Shoup and Joseph, Idaho. It is much boated by outfitters now, this Middle Fork of the Salmon, but the Indians were right: it is still only floated in the downstream direction, and only in high-technology rafts manned by expert oarsmen.

It was already September of 1805 when they got this last bit of discouraging news, and winter was coming. Lewis and Clark's party wended its way back over the divide to the Big Hole valley in the Jefferson-Missouri drainage and marched up it looking for a pass. They named this stream that we now know as the Big Hole River for one of President Jefferson's three virtues . . . the Wisdom River. They named what are now the Beaverhead and the Ruby Rivers—the other two main tributaries of the Jefferson—the Philosophy and Philanthropy Rivers. You have to admire them; they were lost, cold, half starved, worried sick about hostile Indians, and they were still able to make gallant gestures in the direction of Monticello.

It is hard to imagine, now going on two hundred years since Thomas Jefferson sent them out to find a route to the Pacific, exactly what Lewis and Clark expected. Some kind of interior northwest passage was surely their dream.

In America, it was in those years almost possible to paddle from Montreal or Manhattan to New Orleans, and engineers were already drawing the plans for the canals that would make that potential actual. Jefferson and Lewis and Clark were well aware of those Rocky Mountains out there, but there could be, indeed there ought to be, a water route to the Pacific with just a portage here and there. The Rhine and Danube nearly met at a low pass over the Alps. Why shouldn't the Missouri and the great River of the West skirt the high Rockies and approach each other?

As late as 1776, maps of North America showed the River of the West (the Columbia) rising far to the east, most often in Lake Winipigon (Lake Winnepeg) in Manitoba, Canada, and flowing through a gap in the Stony (now Rocky) Mountains at about the

45th parallel. But by the time Lewis and Clark set forth in 1803, Lake Winipigon was more accurately charted and its outlet was known to be Hudson's Bay, not the Pacific Ocean.

The Louisiana Purchase was something of a pig in a poke, for its northwestern boundary was the uncharted Continental Divide between the Missouri drainage and the Oregon territory (jointly claimed by the United States and Great Britain) in the Columbia River drainage north of Spanish California.

A. Arrowsmith, a London mapmaker, relied on reports by the employees of the British Hudson Bay Company for his understanding of the Canadian Stony (Rocky) Mountains and on Spanish sources (particularly the then-recent expedition of Fathers Dominguez and Velez de Escalante) for the Rockies north of Santa Fe, New Mexico. His edition of 1796, the last one before negotiations to purchase Louisiana began, shows the Canadian Stony Mountains stopping on almost exactly the 48th parallel, with a gap south to the 42nd parallel near the Great Salt Lake, where they rose again, continuing south to present-day Arizona. When you think about it, in an era when the land that would become the states of Washington and Oregon was still in dispute between Britain and the United States—there was a serious question whether the 48th parallel would be the boundary all the way to the Pacific—the Hudson's Bay men would be chary to tell all they knew about the land south of the unagreed-upon de facto boundary line.

Absent information from Hudson's Bay travelers for land south of the border-to-be and with no help from Spanish explorers and missionaries for the country north of Utah, Mr. Arrowsmith declined to speculate and drew no mountains at all in that *terra incognita* between the Great Salt Lake and Canada. With rivers he was equally chary of guesswork: his Columbia mapping stopped abruptly near The Dalles, Oregon (the rocky rapids that were the head of navigation); his Missouri is traced no farther upstream than western North Dakota. All responsible contemporary maps, from 1796 until just before Lewis and Clark went west, resembled Arrowsmith's.

Almost simultaneously with the 1803 Louisiana Purchase, Arrowsmith produced a new North American map with "additions to 1802." Jefferson, from Monticello, wrote away for one in the summer of 1803, specifying the London edition, for he knew the quality of the engraving would be superior to the inevitable American-made plagiarized chart. Arrowsmith's 1803 map showed the entire Rocky Mountain chain from the Yukon down to New Mexico, a skinny barrier between the Louisiana Territory and the Oregon country. A few mountains in the Rockies even have acquired names. The map shows Battle Hills in the approximate location of the Absarokas, and just south and west, the Pap. That would be a polite, if folksy, translation of "Grand Teton." The 1803 map has one additional piece of wonderful information: the Missouri is phonetically spelled out—Missesourie River. I am sorry we have elided the second vowel. Try saying "Mississippi and Missesourie Rivers." We have lost some musicality out West.

After being warned off the Salmon River and returning to the Missouri headwaters, Lewis and Clark recrossed the Continental Divide to the Columbia drainage for the second time. They traversed what we now call the Chief Joseph Pass and met up with a band of Flathead Indians camped in Sula Meadow. It was September 4, 1805, when Clark (the most consistent daily diarist; Lewis specialized in cartography) recorded that

> we met a part of the Flat head nation of 33 Lodges about 80 men 400 Total and at least 500 horses, those people recved us friendly, threw white robes over our Sholders & Smoked in the pipes of peace, we Encamped with them & found the[m] friendly but nothing but berries to eate a part of which they gave us, those Indians are well dressed with Skin Shirts & robes, they Stout & light complected more So than Common for Indians, The Chiefs harangued untill late at night, Smoked our pipe and appeared Satisfied. I was the first white man who ever were on the waters of this river.

That would be the East Fork of the Bitterroot, and the Bitterroot flows north into the Clark Fork of the Columbia, and the

Flatheads told Lewis and Clark that the Clark Fork ran down to the Pacific. For Lewis and Clark, and for the modern motorist, this is another U-turn on the trail; the explorers, having first crossed the Continental Divide heading south from the Beaverhead to the Salmon River and having recrossed it from east to west, from the Big Hole to the Bitterroot, now turned north toward Missoula, Montana.

THERE WAS A PROBLEM WITH THE CLARK FORK, WHICH EITHER THE Indians at Sula did not bother to mention in their harangue or Lewis and Clark forgot to ask about. Conversations with other Flatheads when the explorers reached the junction of the Bitterroot and the Clark Fork produced the unpleasant news that spawning salmon never came anywhere near Missoula. Lewis and Clark knew a bad sign when they saw one. Either the river didn't go to the Pacific or somewhere it was impassable to migrating fish. Something—horrid rapids or vast waterfalls—lay across this possible path to the western ocean.

But the Flatheads at Missoula knew where the salmon could be found. Other Indians, Nez Perce as the French Canadian trappers called them, caught salmon in a river just over the mountains, dried them, and brought them to Missoula to trade for buffalo meat and hides. If Lewis and Clark would turn around again (you can see how Sacajawea ends up pointing in every direction), go back up the Bitterroot (south) until they came to a warmish tributary stream (Lolo Creek) fed by hot springs flowing from the west, then follow it, they would find the Nez Perce trail over the mountains to the salmon-bearing river (the Lochsa), and that one would take them to the Pacific Ocean.

This particular Lewis and Clark Trail, from Missoula to Lolo Creek and over the hill to Idaho, was the last and the true way out of Montana. Today, until you reach the Lolo, it is a depressing trip—Montana urban planning at its very, very worst. An endless strip of junk-food restaurants and chain motels and shopping malls line the highway out of downtown Missoula until you reach the Bitterroot River valley. After that, it is semirural, which in Montana means shabby aluminum trailers next to mansions next to llama-raising ranchettes, log-cabin-home manufactories, and the occasional surviving alfalfa field that is just waiting for the right price and the wrong idea. The road up Lolo Creek to the pass and the old Nez Perce trail is a little less eye watering and altogether country once you get past the barren new buildings at the hot springs resort, a group of varnished log-slab-imitation garrisons set in a dusty, treeless lot. You can fish in Lolo Creek, both above and below the hot springs; they only temper, they do not scald, the water. Lolo has brown trout in it, for people who like that sort of thing.

Except at the pass, where the headwaters—of Lolo Creek on the Clark Fork side and of the Lochsa on the Columbia side—are insignificant brooklets, the highway between the Bitterroot valley in Montana and the Snake River drainage in Idaho follows the moving water. It is always next to and just a few feet above the streams, first up Lolo Creek and then down the Lochsa to the Snake River and on to the town of Kooskia and the twin cities, one on each bank, of Lewiston, Idaho, and Clarkston, Washington. It is a gentle road today, with no steep grades and no emergency truck escapes. A few hundred vehicles traverse it in each direction daily, including more truckloads of wheat than carloads of tourists. It is an illogical route for most travelers. They will stick to the interstate between Missoula and Spokane if headed west or to U.S. 93 between Salmon and Missoula when headed south. Those are scenic roads too, and unless you are hauling pulp wood to the mills in Lewiston or grain to the barges (Lewiston/Clarkston mark the head of navigation on the Columbia system), there is not much reason, when you are leaving Montana, to go to Lewiston in the first place.

IN OUR TIME IT SEEMS REASONABLE TO US TO TRAVEL NEXT TO RIVERS. Floodplains and stream banks appear to be natural places to build highways and railroad beds. It was not always so, particularly in mountainous country like the Lochsa. River valleys were, before modern forestry and river management, great accumulators of God's trash, of fallen trees and landslides; the land grew up into brambled green hells along the banks. Stream beds so encumbered were prone to flooding, something not allowable when they run next to asphalt cement. The old Nez Perce trail over the Bitterroots kept to the near-summit of the mountains because, high and cold as it might be, the ridgeline was not barricaded by millennia of rockslides, fallen logs, and well-watered brushy undergrowth.

The Indian trail was easy to see, if difficult to traverse, once Lewis and Clark struck it at the head of Lolo Creek. The packs on the Indians' horses had worn smooth spots on the trunks of the densely growing trees that pinched in the narrow path along the ridgeline, far above the stream. On occasion, the explorers dropped down from the high trail to the creek below, hoping to find some salmon. They were hungry enough by then to consider eating fish.

By an accident of civil engineering and geography, the highway down the Lochsa (or the Crooked Fork of the Lochsa, to be too precise) hits the river just upstream from the first point where Lewis and Clark descended from the Nez Perce trail to the river below. That is at the junction of White Sand Creek and the Crooked Fork, the place where the main Lochsa officially begins. They found evidence of an abandoned Nez Perce fishing station, not described in their journals but very likely a netting and spearing stand built out over the creek. Finding no fish, Clark wrote: "here we were compelled to kill a Colt for our men & Selves to eat for the want of meat & we named the South fork [now White Sand Creek] Colt killed Creek."

In the next two days they would kill and eat three more horses. Any dream of an easy passage to the Pacific was then dead and buried, and you can almost hear the disappointment in the diarist's entry. Describing the country just west of "Colt killed Creek," Clark wrote: "The Mountains which we passed to day much worst than yesterday the last excessively bad and Thickly Strowed with falling timber & Pine Spruc fur Hackmatc & Tamerack, Steep & Stoney our men and horse much fatigued, the rain . . . " At that point, the entry trails off into a blank and melancholic space in the journal.

It would have been much better trout habitat in those days when the Lochsa and its tributaries tumbled through a tangle of living ancient forest and fallen logs. One of the first rules of fishery restoration is to stop cleaning up the mess and let the river gouge its way under and over the debris. The Lochsa runs unimpeded by trash now, sliding gently over a clean rocky bottom, and the roadway is safe from flooding. Man has done considerable housekeeping in the valley.

The only section of trail where the explorers and the automobilists travel the same route is from the junction of the two creeks downstream to a modern improvement, the White House campground. There the explorers left the river bottom and went back up on the high trail, not to return until they were far enough downstream to build boats and paddle away to the far Pacific shore. They struck the river again and built their *bateaux* near what is now a large state of Idaho rest stop just upstream from the town of Kooskia, Idaho, and an easy landmark for the modern traveler. Style is not everything. I like Clark's description of that trek:

> We set out early. the morning Cloudy and proceeded on Down the right Side of River over Steep points rockey & buschey as usial for 4 miles to an old Indian fishing place, here the road leaves the river to the left and assends a *mountain* widnding in every direction get up the Steep assents & to pass the emence quantity of falling timber which had falling from dift. causes i.e. fire & wind and has deprived the Greater part of the Southerley Sides of this mountain of its gren timber . . . [We] encamped on the top of the mountain near a Bank of old Snow about 3 feet deep lying on the Northern side of the mountain and in Small banks on the top leavel parts of the mountain, we melted the Snow to drink, and Cook our horse flesh to eat.

The Lochsa (and the Selway) once hosted great spawning runs of Pacific salmon, a fishery almost entirely destroyed by dams on the Columbia and its tributaries. The few fish that do make it up to the headwaters are now the subject of great concern, and several side streams of the Lochsa are marked with government signs indicating that they are being restored to their original condition. They are small streams, now deliberately left clogged with snags that create, by making turbulent the flow, the sand and gravel beds that all salmonids need for spawning ground. In the otherwise logged and reforested land adjacent to the highway, only these natural riparian areas, as the signage calls them, look exactly like they did for Lewis and Clark—they are deliberately recreated patches of that "emence quantity of falling timber."

The cutthroat trout of the Lochsa were, one can be certain, once both more numerous and larger than they are today. The cutthroat, like the coastal rainbow trout, thrives in rivers frequented by spawning salmon. They gorge directly on salmon eggs that escape from the spawning redd. The bodies of the dying salmon (and they all die) provide nutrients and encourage the growth of invertebrates (the basic diet of cutthroats) for months after the spawning season. And then in the early spring, when the water begins to warm, the swimming-up salmon fry with their pendulous yolk sacks are devoured by cutthroats. By and large, that feast is no longer available.

WHEN I WAS ON THE LOCHSA, JUST FOR A DAY, IT COULD NOT HAVE been less encouraging for a fisherman. The summer had been hot and dry in the Bitterroots from the beginning of July, and by the middle of August the river was low, clear, and warm enough to swim in. I did not swim, but that is not an offhand estimate of water temperature. While rounding a curve on the road, I caught a glimpse of what appeared to be a short slim female person. She was swimming, almost out of sight behind some riverside trees, without benefit of a bathing suit. I realize nonangling readers will have some difficulty understanding this, but the sight was not titillating or amusing or charming; it was depressing. Water warm enough for skinny-dipping is not good trout water. The fish may survive in it, but they are put off their feed when the temperature gets anywhere above 60 to 65 degrees.

The river, from the Powell Ranger Station (near Killed Colt Creek) down to the junction of the Lochsa and the Selway, is under a special regulation—trout are there to catch and then release, and that, along with the heat, may have accounted for the fact that not a solitary soul was fishing. I have never seen as many pullout parking spaces by such a lovely piece of water so completely deserted. After many years, one recognizes trouble on the river: one car parked in a dozen miles, and that one's driver is seeking relief from the heat by stripping and backstroking gracefully across a nice-looking trout pool.

There was nothing to be done but have faith in the good nature of cutthroat trout, and so, a discreet distance downstream from the young lady in the altogether, I pulled over in the first parking area that had some tree shade and geared up to go fishing. Ordinarily, that means pulling on hip boots or waders, but that didn't seem like a good idea. It was 90 in the shade, and the water didn't look promising enough to make a really serious effort. I strung up the rod and took one box of trout flies out of the fishing vest and stuck them in my hip pocket, locked the car, and scrambled down the granite riprap to a long gentle glide of the river. Nothing moved. Across the river, on the south bank, a Steller's jay *(Cyanocitta stelleri)* stood motionless by the water, its feathers puffed out in the style that birds adopt to allow heat to dissipate. It looked more like a blue-black fuzzy football than a jaybird.

The box of flies was the one I always take out first: it has a mixture of imitation grasshoppers and some caddis flies (a group of aquatic insects that have a buzzy, mothlike flight) and a half dozen other hair-winged artificials, ones that fall in the general category of "attractors." These latter flies look buggy, but they don't resemble any particular insect. Having no better idea of what to do, I tied on a large caddis imitation and started casting.

There is a moment at the beginning of ordinary sloppy fly casting when all you are trying to do is get some line off the reel and through the guides and onto the water so that you can do something more artistic with it. Barring obstacles, the easiest way to do this is to let the current carry it downstream while you hand-feed some line off the reel and let it slip through the guides on the rod.

I was doing this, and the line was in loose loops on the river directly below me (I had, in cowboy boots, scrambled out onto a large rock), and the fly was half drowned and dragging across the surface somewhat upstream from, and toward the middle of the river from, the farthest away loop of fly line.

I remember it rather vividly because I was looking at the line to see if enough was payed out to start casting, and while I was estimating the length of the line, a very decent cutthroat trout came up and tried to eat the fly. It was unsuccessful: just as it reached the general area of the fly, the tug of the line going downstream pulled the lure away in a kind of snap-the-whip motion. The fish really did try. It chased the fly for four or five feet before giving up. This seemed promising.

And it was. Although nothing in the natural fly field was hatching or laying eggs or even doing enough recreational flying to fall in the water and interest the fish, trout would come up and look at any artificial fly I put in the right place. There is a certain charm about cutthroat trout on a hot August afternoon when they really aren't hungry (and the water temperature surely has slowed their metabolism to a crawl). They appear from nowhere (they are lying near the bottom where the water is coolest, often under a shelf of rock to stay out of the bright sun), and they drift up under the fly; and, tailing backward downstream, carried along by the current with their head upstream and just under the fly, they follow it for a few feet. Sometimes they take the fly; sometimes, less often than than is good for them, they refuse it.

Fish do not have expressions; they lack both emotional lives and facial muscles. But cutthroats do an excellent imitation of a foolish, sentient being. You can imagine them thinking: "Oh, that really isn't something I should eat. Or maybe it is. I shouldn't. I really shouldn't. Oh hell, I will."

Being in an experimental mood, I caught cutthroats on caddis flies, grasshopper imitations, and one attractor pattern. They were not large trout, at most twelve or thirteen inches long. Whether there were larger fish but with more sense, I know not. If there were bigger ones, they could have been caught, I would guess, by putting some small imitation of underwater aquatic life on the end of the leader and fishing deep. But deep is out of sight, and I am too old now to care about size for its own sake. It is nice to catch a large fish (or as large an animal as the river can produce), but it does not matter anymore. All that matters is to bring the fish up to the threshold between our two worlds and watch it take the fly down into the darkness.

An occasional car or truck went by while I was fishing. I thought about the tourists, headed over the hill to Missoula or down the river to Lewiston. Would they even notice an angler? If they did, would they have time to see that he was actually catching fish? That is not something you see every time you drive by a fisherman. I think I did not want an audience as much as I wanted to share the fish. I really hoped that someone would stop and walk over and ask what I was doing. I wanted to say, "Watch this." I could have shown them the most interesting thing that a river can do: give a person a trout for a minute, lift the fish up to the surface and make it take the fly and help it struggle for a few moments, and, when it is released, take the trout back into the stream's obscure heart. But no one stopped.

It was time to go, and somewhere downstream waited the Three Rivers Motel, a modest establishment of affordable price near the junction of the Lochsa and the Selway. (The third river is the Snake, which begins at that point.) The room turned out to be a small cabin on the edge of the river with a few resident mosquitos and a well-used mattress hiding under new and clean sheets. Sleep came slowly, in part because of the motel's large sign shining through the window. It not surprisingly said MOTEL in large incandescent letters, and an accompanying sign announced CAFE in blinking lights. It could have added SALOON: there was a good one next to the cafe, but that is more or less understood out West. If you can eat and sleep somewhere, you can almost certainly drink too.

Dreams are seldom wholly spontaneous. Sometime in the night (I did not fully waken) I had the only dream of my life which had both trout and women in it. They are not all that compatible a paired fantasy. Like most dreams, it started with a recent real experience and then elaborated the image. In the dream, an attractive black-haired woman appeared in the river, dog-paddling, head up, swimming upstream in the slow back eddy below the rock I was standing on, keeping her hair dry above the surface of the water. And then I caught a fish and she waved it toward herself with one hand and held the other hand, her left, palm up and out toward me as if to say, "Give it to me. I will take care of it." It was a small fish, ten inches or a little bit more, and I led it toward her, and she lifted it with one hand, cradling it against her—I blush to remember it—entirely naked breast and deftly unhooked it with the other hand, and she laughed when it splashed and fled into the deep water that swirled around her.

That was all. I was puzzled, recalling it in the morning, bemused that it had taken so long, so many years and trout and dreams, to have a dream with both a woman and a fish. But then, I suppose someone who has chased women for many years with as much purpose as I have followed trout (nine states, four countries, two continents) would be as confused as I was if a trout should show up, uninvited, in *his* dream.

10

Mud Volcanos

WHEN THE LEWIS AND CLARK PARTY RETURNED FROM THE PACIFIC shore, they retraced their steps to Missoula, went up the Clark Fork of the Columbia to the Big Blackfoot River, and took the Indians' buffalo trail over to the Missouri by the Great Falls. That is still one of the major routes across the Continental Divide, although the highway sticks closer to the Blackfoot than did the trail. They split into two groups. Lewis wanted to explore the Marias River, a major tributary of the Missouri near Glacier Park. He was still looking for a portage across the Rockies. The Arrowsmith map of 1803 (with revisions to 1802) that they had studied at Monticello had one anomaly in the long barrier of the Rocky Mountains. At around the 48th parallel, a major tributary of the Missouri was shown to rise well west of the Rockies in the same country as the headwaters of the Columbia (the "River Oregon" on the map). The only possibility was the Marias, which they had not had time to explore on the way west. Lewis would not go home without trying it.

Clark would explore the Yellowstone River, and they would rendezvous at the junction of the Missouri and the Yellowstone, over on the modern Montana–North Dakota border. Clark's route took him back up the Missouri to Three Forks (where the Gallatin, Madison, and Jefferson Rivers meet to make the Missouri). After floundering through a huge beaver-chewed marsh at Three Forks, Clark headed east over the Bozeman Pass. He hit the Yellowstone River where it exits the Absaroka Mountains and becomes a plains river, near modern Livingston, and rafted on down to the Missouri. Trout being of no interest at all, he ignored them and kept notes on the game animals. He was not the last traveler in Montana to remark on the incredible abundance of buffalo and elk and ignore the fish. When it comes to tourism dollars, one herd of buffalo is worth more than all the trout in the Rocky Mountains.

But for anglers (the least numerous fraction of all tourists in the West) the Yellowstone River up in the national park is a mecca. For some forty years I've been telling all who asked and many who didn't that they had to see the park. I never mentioned the fishing as a reason: if you haven't seen Yellowstone, I would say, you haven't seen America. Everyone who took the advice came back pleased, which began to trouble me just a little. People tell me how much they like San Diego, California, for instance, and I can't bear the place anymore. It is plagued with the usual problem, too many people. I hadn't been in the park since I was fourteen, and I thought it was time to go back and see for myself if it was still true. I did, five years after the big fire of 1988, and it's better than it was. Try and think of a place in America that's better now than it was in the 1950s. It is a short list.

Oh, more people come to the park now than when I was a lad and inexpensive automobiles had eight-cylinder engines, but three million tourists aren't going home every year and telling their friends to forget it. Those visitors—and many will never get out of their vehicles except to go to the bathroom, look at the geysers, and take pictures of buffalo—make it America. In some national parks people want to be alone or have the illusion of solitude. In Yellowstone they want to share. For most of us it is more like America's national street fair than a wilderness—a sociable place.

Established in 1872, carved out of what is now Wyoming and a thin sliver of Montana and Idaho, Yellowstone was a giant theme park, a natural Walt Disney World, for the first century of its federal life. The 1970s brought a new vision, and now it is an international biosphere preserve, and preservationism is the religion of the hour. This can take extreme forms, some meaningful, some silly. One recalls watching a female park ranger accost a male bicyclist who was taking a rest at the Lewis Lake picnic area by the road between Old Faithful and the south entrance. He was juggling three rocks, and she told him, "That's government property, fella." He suggested that she might like to, as they say these days, "get a life," a thought that brought audible murmurs of assent from a few interested spectators. On the other hand, the park is spotlessly clean, the concessions are fair and well managed, the humans are well behaved, and there is wilderness enough. The bears own everything but a few hundred square miles of accommodations, parking lots, and near-road walking trails. Unfortunately, in the eyes of preservationists, the park is imperfect. Among other faults, it has too many people and not enough wolves.

If you entered a substantial computerized database and typed in the command to search for Yellowstone Park, you should be prepared for the greatest printout of partisan screeds and righteous outrage since the inevitably simultaneous invention of movable type and the Protestant Reformation. Only the visitors who traverse it by the millions without much caring whether the fires could have been put out, whether the timber wolves should be reintroduced, whether the buffalo should be called bison or not go home gruntled. Yes, they would like to see the wolves restored (a straw poll of visitors ran 97 percent in favor of wolves in 1982, and you can bet the other 3 percent were locals), but if you offered them a choice of wolves or flush toilets, I'd put my money on the plumbers, not the Sierra Clubbers. Nature, on the other hand, has its money on the wolves. They're coming down from Glacier and they're within a couple of hundred miles, if not already inside the park. The odds that wolves won't find the largest collection of elk steaks and buffalo burgers in North America is a very long shot.

What journalists and activists forget is that Yellowstone is essentially a monstrous practical joke played out in the midst of spectacular scenery. If you think the master of the universe couldn't possibly have a sense of humor, you haven't been to the park. It is mostly the fault of the geysers. Anything that spits up is funny; that is a common human reaction that all the soy-based ink on recycled paper in the world won't change. I have seen the original Geysir, the one in Iceland from which all others take their name, and it too makes people laugh.

If water geysers are amusing (except for Old Faithful, which would be funny if people hadn't been standing in the hot sun for at least an hour waiting for it to go off), mud geysers, or mud volcanos, are hilarious. Yellowstone has mud volcanos to spare, especially along the two most popular fishing rivers in the park, the Yellowstone itself, downstream from Yellowstone Lake, and the Firehole River, which runs from the area around Old Faithful down through a swarm of small and large intermittent geysers and quite faithfully bubbling mud volcanos. The crowd favorite is a small pool of hot mud near the road in the Lower Geyser Basin in the Firehole valley, a boardwalked visitors' site just south of Madison Junction on the way to Old Faithful. This little mud geyser spits out baseball- and golf-ball-size gobs of brown goo from one side of the crater, and they arc across the roiled pool and land with a splat near the farther wall. People simply cannot watch it without smiling, pointing, giggling, and clapping. There is a scatological overtone to the humor; the sight of the flying ejecta is enhanced by a distinct odor of hydrogen sulfide, a noisome component of all sewer gases.

If YELLOWSTONE'S GEYSERS SEEM IMMORTAL (ALTHOUGH OLD FAITHful, after several earthquakes, is Old Semi-Faithful, with a periodicity ranging from half an hour to an hour and a half), there are changes in the park. The greatest in my lifetime is the best known and most obvious one—the utter disappearance of begging bears along the roadside and roistering bears among the cabins and up on the porches of the big lodges. I miss them just a little, I'll confess. It got the day off on the right foot to open up the door to go to breakfast and find yourself staring at a 300-pound black bear

with a nose for syrup and, one imagined, small boys. No one, I suspect, misses the nightly shows at the park's several hotel dumps,
where visitors got incandescent-lit views of grizzly and black bears
squabbling over that day's garbage.

The absence of bears, to these old eyes, is even more startling
than the scars of the great fire of 1988. Yes, in the nineties we
drive past mile after mile of dead lodgepole pine. Skinny bare
trunks march endlessly back from the roadside; a few scraggly
burned branches at the top gesture to an indifferent heaven. But if
you take an honest look at the intact and unburnt lodgepole forest,
you also see skinny bare trunks topped with a short flurry of green
branches. In either forest, burned or green, you can see for a mile
back into the woods. This is going to change, and change dramatically. Amid the still-standing dead trees, a riotous growth of new
lodgepole pine is coming up. It was only a foot high five years after
germinating in the ashes of the big burn, but there was a new
lodgepole every square yard or less. In a few more years, the burn
is going to be a solid green mass of young pine branched down to
the ground, and you won't be able to see ten feet into the new forest. It will be decades before the trees start losing lower branches,
shading out the weak ones, opening up the views. The first half of
the twenty-first century will pass before you can take long views
in most of the park, and coming on open valleys and old forest will
be like exiting a tunnel. Every geyser basin, every alpine prairie,
will be even more beautiful.

Less obvious than the bear reforms or the new forest is the
change in trout fishing inside the park. It is better now than it has
been since World War II, although angling remains a minor activity compared to buffalo watching or geyser spectating. In 1982
(just to put fishing in its proper perspective in the world of
tourism), 3,187,000 recreational visitors entered Yellowstone, and
only 162,000 picked up the free fishing permit. For every angler
that year there were at least three visitors who walked out onto
Fishing Bridge on the Yellowstone River by the lake (a place
where fishing is no longer allowed) to watch the spawning rites of
cutthroat trout. That is a new world, indeed: passive spectating of
fish. It is like watching out-of-focus public television film of the

biological imperative. On the other hand, if fishing is less popular than voyeurism, it is far ahead of hiking, something you would not guess reading the environmental press, which assumes all of America wants to be alone. A mere 6575 folks got a back-country permit and left the sanctuary of pavement, boardwalk, or trout pool for the deeper mysteries of high country trekking and a chance in the annual lottery to become grizzly munchies.

Most of the park's rivers, even in this world heritage site and international biosphere preserve, are contaminated with one or another species of imported trout. At the beginning of the century, fisheries management at the park was in the hands of the U.S. Fish and Wildlife Service, an agency devoted to propagating and disseminating fish, not one interested in maintaining a natural ecosystem. The Madison has European browns and coastal California rainbows (it should have Westslope cutthroats and grayling); the Gibbon has both brown and eastern brook trout; the Lamar's cutthroats are much altered by the addition of rainbow genes; and the Firehole, which drains a huge basin filled with fumaroles, geysers, and hot springs, had no fish at all when the park was established. The geyser basins, powerful as they seem to visitors today, must pale in comparison to the millennia when they stifled fish life. The Firehole can still get too warm to fish, in a combination of August heat and geyser and hot-spring drainage, but it is not lethal today. Now the Firehole is brown trout country, with rainbows mingled in.

But most of the Yellowstone River in the park was protected from invading aliens by a series of waterfalls and remains a pure fishery from the genetic point of view. Park policy is now dead set against stocking and in favor, when the opportunity arises, of restoring the native fishery.

The authenticity of the Yellowstone River is more good luck than intelligent planning. From time to time early in this century, the Fish and Wildlife Service tried to introduce rainbow trout and landlocked salmon *(Salmo salar sebago)* to the Yellowstone, and not once but twice, in a real fit of imagination, the service tried to establish a population of whitefish in the river above the Great Falls. There is nothing wrong with whitefish—they do rise to a fly—but they are not very sporting, and ugly to boot. Below the Undine Falls, about twenty miles before the Yellowstone River exits the park, there are enough whitefish to annoy trout anglers to near distraction. But above Undine, for sixty miles, it is bank-to-bank trout, most of whom never see an angler or a lure as they swim undisturbed in the Grand Canyon of the Yellowstone.

The trout you do see in the easily accessible part of the river above the Great Falls—between Canyon Village and Lake Village—are, except for tiny baby fry, all big fish. They come in two sizes in the tributaries into and out of Yellowstone Lake: large and extralarge. The absence of medium and small in the river below the lake and the inlet streams is simply explained. The outlet's cutthroats are allacustrine in biology-speak. That means that they go down the outlet river for spawning and then return to the big lake. In the tributaries to Yellowstone Lake, the identical fish would be called lacustrine-adfluvial, a lake dweller that goes up streams to spawn. In both cases, after the next generation hatches, all the youngsters migrate back upstream or downstream to Yellowstone Lake to do their growing up.

When hormones dictate, usually at four years of age, the big adult trout start to leave the lake for their natal river, moving leisurely toward their ancestral spawning grounds. The large fish are four-year-old first-time spawners, the extra large are repeat spawners, usually six years of age or older. It takes most of them a full two years to get reorganized internally for another spawning run. Stream anglers are pleased to be assured that the average fish caught will be sixteen or seventeen inches long and the odd fish will go over twenty-two inches. Curiously, scores of millions of Yellowstone Lake cutthroat trout eggs were taken and distributed across America and Europe, although almost never into ecosystems that were suitable. Absent a great freshwater sea to grow up in, the lake strain of cutthroats are paltry fish.

There are several nineteenth-century photographs of famous anglers in Yellowstone, including one of Lt. Col. George Armstrong Custer, posed with strings of Yellowstone cutthroat trout, taken the year before the Little Bighorn. It was the same then as it is now, all handsome big fish plus a few whoppers. Good as the angling is, and it is easily the best native trout fishery in North America, only 5 percent of the park's three million annual visitors goes fishing. Still, the number of angling hours is up dramatically. This is proof that diffident anglers have been supplanted by obsessive ones. They are mostly fly fishermen practicing catch-and-release and are visible along the shores of lakes and banks of rivers, but they are less frequently seen than buffalo, taken as a group. One reason for the low volume of anglers is that casual fishing, particularly fishing for food, is discouraged throughout much of the park and forbidden in many streams, including the Yellowstone.

Indeed, anglers in Yellowstone have been banned entirely since 1965 from perhaps the finest stretch of wild trout water in the world—nine miles of the meandering Yellowstone River downstream from the mud volcanos that bubble away at the south (and upper) end of Hayden Valley. The signs on the road note that fishing is prohibited for the next six miles, but that is six miles of rather straight road. Hayden Valley is prime wildlife viewing country, a treeless plain, a high prairie on the ancient lake bed of a greater Yellowstone Lake, with broad vistas of running water, flying ospreys and eagles, grazing buffalo, and the occasional elk or bear. The reason for banning fishermen is simple enough: three million visitors come to the park to look at wild animals, not at men in rubber pants. And while animals can be dangerous and aggressive, they are basically shy and the large numbers of anglers drove them out of Hayden Valley. This prohibition was a good deal for everyone: the undisturbed spawning beds and loitering pools in the Hayden Valley assure a reservoir of very large fish that will amble upstream and down into fishable waters for the amusement of fly fishers.

The most popular fishing hole on the Yellowstone River, to use that inappropriate jargon for a braided channel with rising fish in it, is Buffalo Ford, just a few miles upstream from the Hayden country toward Yellowstone Lake. What buffalo can walk across (they will swim if they need to), anglers can wade comfortably. The ford, which is still used by buffalo to the consternation of fishermen who do not pay attention to what's catching up on them from behind, is often overrun with anglers. A mile or so downstream, at the beginning of the swarm of mud volcanos, a parking pullout on the river side of the road is less crowded with rental cars and offers the same fishing opportunity. The Mud Volcano Hole, to make up a name for it, is marked at its downstream end by two small mud volcanos on the far (east) side of the river and along its length upstream by a narrow island that divides the river into two channels of approximately the same volume. Of a summer afternoon you can expect to find two or three anglers in the area, compared to the scores of fly casters upstream at Buffalo Ford. And just downstream from the Volcano Hole is a large backwater that always attracts the attention of anglers who do come to that area: big fish cruise in the nearly still water, poking their noses up to eat the aquatic and terrestrial insects that get caught in the eddy.

It is an easy drive from West Yellowstone over to the river, about forty-five miles, which at the park's speed limits would take just over an hour to travel if it weren't for the 95 percent of the visitors who have come to look at wildlife, not to fish. Buffalo frequent the valley of the Madison River just upstream from West Yellowstone, and since they are the buffalo closest to that entrance and the first that visitors see, they get immediate attention and traffic backs up as everyone stops in the middle of the road for a better look. Farther along, the Gibbon River flats between Madison and Norris Junctions are sure to produce an elk or two and another herd of buffalo. On an ordinary day, you can count on an hour's extra travel time caused by animal incidents, and perhaps another half hour caused by perpetual summer road repairs and resulting one-lane traffic. If I remember the begging-bear traffic accurately, I would say that in the decades when they were posted along the road, they added another thirty minutes' delay to the same trip.

There is probably no worse place in North America to build a paved road than Yellowstone Park. Winter temperatures fall to 40 and 50 degrees below zero, and patches of ground below the pavement, warmed by geothermal activity, will remain at the boiling point. Much of the soil is fluffy volcanic ash or, worse, the same ash saturated with water and transformed into jellylike clay.

Sometimes nature in its whimsical way takes a more active hand in destroying the roadbed. As I drove through the designated mud volcano viewing area along the Yellowstone, I noticed a set of temporary barriers in the road shoulder parking lot at Sulphur Cauldron, an abyss of hot mud right next to the road. The black-and-yellow striped sawhorses appeared to be fencing off a pothole the size of a card table. On inspection, it turned out to be a brand-new mud volcano, yet unnamed, that had melted the asphalt pavement and was burbling away just a few inches below the parking lot surface. This is not a good omen for the road between Canyon Village and Yellowstone Lake: it is already pinched in between the Sulphur Cauldron on the east and the Dragon's Mouth on the west side of the highway. We will see. If the volcanos want the road, they will take it.

Up by the Mud Volcano Hole, to continue to give it a name, a single vehicle was parked, a pickup-camper with distinctive black-and-white Missouri license plates. The walk to the river was a mixture of wilderness and civilization. Just by the foot trail out of the parking lot a paper sign stapled to a post informed the visiting anglers that several trout in the river had been supplied with radio transmitters, and should we be so fortunate as to catch one, we would notice a small four-stitch surgical scar in the belly of the fish, and having found that fish, would we be so kind as to return it to the river and notify the authorities, that is, the park rangers or a fisheries biologist, of its exact location? The only other request to notify the authorities is the park's standing invitation to report all bear encounters of the mildly to incredibly unpleasant sort. A bear that does not shun human beings is a bear that makes the park service very nervous.

Aside from offering a gateway to cooperative field-research opportunities, the path to the river held deeper mysteries. In case the angler had forgotten that the buffalo own the park, the short grass was well spotted with buffalo chips. Many of them were as fresh as could be. I am not sure of the right word for a pile of buffalo doo that has not dried to the chip stage, but it closely resembled ordinary cow flop. Several bare trampled areas, each the size of a generous automobile parking space, indicated where buffalo had been dusting themselves, rolling in the powdery dried clay. I recalled the warnings not to approach buffalo and wondered what one should do when approached *by* buffalo.

Persons of sagacity and most young readers are probably wondering why I insist on saying "buffalo" for the animal properly called "bison," indeed whose scientific name is *Bison bison*. It is simple enough: "buffalo" is the true American-language name, and no one ever heard of Bison Bill Cody. The National Park Service, when producing its prodigious amounts of reading material, properly calls the animal a bison when communicating serious biological data. However, when they demand the undivided attention of ordinary people, they call it a buffalo, as on the bright yellow handbill given to every tourist at the entrances: "WARNING. Many Visitors Have Been Gored by Buffalo!" So do we all. No one ever says, "Look, Alice, it's a bison!" or relates "I saw some bison at Buffalo Ford."

Down at the river's edge, I discovered a solitary angler, hidden from view by the cutbank of the river until I was close upon him. (Farther up- and downstream, no nearer than a third of a mile, more fishermen were distantly visible.) It was the man from Missouri, fishing intently in the channel closest to the road, casting carefully. While I watched, he took a fish, a fine fish, a jealous-making fish.

He appeared to be using a dry fly, or so I assumed from the way he cast and mended his line. But the fly was invisible to me, standing behind and above him on the cutbank of the river. I walked downstream and forded the river at the lower end of the island and came back upstream and watched him some more. He took another fish, while I was doing nothing that worked. After he landed it and unhooked it and turned it loose, I called across and asked him what fly was working. A number 18 mosquito was the answer. He added that, the day before, he had used a number 20 (which is a size smaller) with greater success, but it was too much trouble tying one on the leader. A number 18 mosquito is a bit of feathers on a hook that would rest comfortably on any adult's little fingernail and not lap over the edges. A number 20 is ridiculously small.

I tried a variety of dinky flies, all of which were impossible for me to see and none of which interested any of the fish on my side of the run. An occasional trout rose to some hatching aquatic insect, but nothing I showed those fish was deemed fit to eat. The September afternoon sun lowering in the southwest glared across the water at me, obscuring any natural flies and all my own poor imitations of life. When the man from Missouri decided to leave, I crossed back and started walking up the high bank to the place where he had been fishing with such success and where the sun would be behind me. On the way upstream I happened to glance down at the edge of the river in time to see an enormous trout, frightened by my long shadow, slip away from the bank into deeper water. This gave me pause, and I recalled the general rule of fish behavior that states that a disturbed trout will return to business in five to seven minutes, absent further harassment.

I marked the spot mentally, and since I had the river to myself, I went upstream to fish while the big trout made up its mind to come back to the spot from which I had flushed it. (One could say with assurance, *his* mind. It was a colorful fish, yellow and red on the flanks, and male trout are brighter than females the world over. Also, most extralarge spawning cutthroats are males; they grow better than females at mature ages, possibly because they surrender less body mass in the act of spawning than do the egg-heavy hen fish.) After clambering down to the river, I cast a few times, but even with the advantage of light behind me rather than in my eyes, I could barely see my artificial fly. It was not a number 18 mosquito, but it was equally minute. I began to think that the Missourian was something of an expert.

Every once in a while, on the order of every two or three minutes, I heard the distinctive sound of a trout rising and taking a fly, a slushy *thluck* noise that all angling readers will hear in their mind's ear. It is a complicated sound, caused in part by the trout's body breaking the surface of the water and in part by the suction created when the fish opens its mouth to ingest an insect. It was downstream but nearby. So, treading softly on the very edge of the river, I walked down to the source. Human ears, if not on the level of owl ears, are rather good at range finding, and I was quite sure I knew where the fish would be. The sensible thing to do is not to cast blindly but to walk down, stop and watch and wait, and cast directly to the fish when you see the rise. As I did the proper thing, I heard the sound again. It was not in the river; it was behind me. Halfway up the high bank, at my shoulder height, a small vent in the earth leaked a vapor. Below the vent, spilling down the bank for a few feet, was a smear of white mud. As I watched, the vent ejected a blob of mud the size of a golf ball, and as it did, it went *thluck*. I was more charmed than embarrassed. Given the small amount of white mud on the bank and the average size of the glop coming out of the vent, this little tiny mud volcano couldn't have been more than a day or two old. The sensation was that of being present at the creation, or perhaps the Cretaceous. The scene, although miniaturized, reminded me of dinosaur dioramas in museums, the ones where a volcano always fumes in the background.

THERE IS NOTHING LIKE WATCHING A MUD VOLCANO, EVEN IF IT IS NO larger across than your hand, to remind you that you are not in Kansas (or Missouri) anymore. I think it was that realization, that I was not just fishing but that I was fishing in Yellowstone, that took my brain out of neutral and engaged some gears. Occasionally even anglers stop and think for a minute. I was trying to catch a Yellowstone cutthroat trout, and that is not a fish with a great deal of inherent wariness or selectivity in what it will eat. Yes, they were eating something tiny, but that was because minute insects were all they had to chase. Who was I or the Missourian to say that they wanted nothing else?

Yellowstone cutthroats are so catchable, in fact, that Bob Gresswell, the U.S. Fish and Wildlife Service biologist in the park for many years, used to give a speech about the local cutthroat trout with the title "Preserving the Dumb Gene in Yellowstone." He refers to the eponymous trout's "naïveté" (not a word one comes across often in fisheries literature) and describes it as "extremely gullible"—so much so that in spite of its "ease of capture and large average size . . . some anglers feel that there is little challenge to fishing for cutthroat and prefer the more selective brown trout to test their angling abilities."

The adjective "selective" might be misunderstood by nonangling readers. It does not mean that the brown trout is selective about whom it will allow itself to be caught by, although dedicated brown-trout anglers often make that assumption in stories they insist on telling you about their angling prowess. It simply describes a behavior in trout: when they start eating one species of aquatic life, some hatching insect or drifting nymphal form, they stop eating all the others that may be simultaneously available and feed "selectively." Cutthroats, Mr. Gressley was saying indirectly, were not selective. Why fancy anglers regard narrow-minded obsessive behavior (in fish) as a form of intelligence is a mystery. I suppose the man from Missouri could have gone off to find something harder to catch, although he seemed perfectly happy. Naïveté, when you regard the concept thoughtfully, is exactly what we are seeking in the West. We like buffalo that regard our automobiles as some sort of bad-smelling cousin and mingle with us. We appreciate naïve grizzly bears who are not so sophisticated as to realize that we are (1) probably carrying food (they tend to find us unappealing fare after a few bites) and (2) unarmed, like all law-abiding park visitors.

Having pondered the situation—a river full of large trout that I knew could be caught by expert anglers using very small flies—I decided not to test my angling ability at all. I took a good look at the bank again, now that the vented mud had attracted my full attention. The bank was only a half dozen feet back from the river's edge and fully eight or ten feet above the river's surface, and it was from the high bank that I had been able to see the enormous fish, the one that was still waiting for me downstream. The added elevation, if I chose to cast from the high ground, would make up for any greater distance from the fish, much like an elevated tee will make for longer drives on a golf course. Why, I wondered, was I standing ankle deep in the water when it wasn't at all necessary?

It was also hot, and I was basking in the sun completely covered from chest to foot in three millimeters of air- and watertight dark green solar-radiation-adsorbing neoprene waders. I was, to put it mildly, humid. There was something wrong with the whole picture, and it was me. I had brought the advanced technology of eastern fishing with me; I was a dude, a tenderfoot, a pilgrim. Filled with mild but easily cured self-loathing, I scrambled up the bank, walked back to the car, wrenched off my chest waders, pulled on my semi–cowboy boots (round roper toes, low walking heels), and fished around in my suitcase for a box of very large flies. I bit off the fine tippet on the end of the leader, cutting it back to where it was quite strong, and tied on the biggest imitation grasshopper in the box. If nothing else, this would improve the scenery. Any tourist glancing casually in my direction would not see a man in rubber pants. It would be a western character in Wrangler jeans and cowboy boots and a Stetson who just happened to be holding a fly rod. Walking back to the river, I thought the boots and jeans a more appropriate dress than chest waders for sashaying across a prairie speckled with buffalo flop and punctuated with buffalo dust baths. The afternoon breeze was also cooling, while before it had been impalpable to the flesh below the armpits and a slight annoyance while fly casting.

Standing on the high bank I tried a cast and saw, as expected, that I could reach as much or more of the water than when wading in the shallow edge of the river. I considered going after the big fish waiting downstream and thought, almost aloud, Why spoil it by hurrying? I love fishing down at a river, although it is not always the best way to proceed. On the second cast, which floated over the dark bottom across the run, a lovely extralarge trout in full spawning regalia came up from the darkness and drifted along with the ersatz grasshopper for a few feet and then opened wide and ate it. Naturally (for me it is an old habit), I pulled the fly away before the fish could close its mouth. I will do this once a day, given the opportunity. It is particularly likely to happen if you are standing high above the water; you get much too good a view of what's going on and have several seconds to panic.

There is no point in bragging on my fishing, given Mr. Gresswell's comments on "ease of capture." But it was simply the case that about half the fish I could locate in the water would take the improbably large hopper when I put it over them, including the

huge one I had flushed earlier. It took a while to catch him because, just as I planned to go back, two women came walking over
from the roadside parking to take a picture of the river. They
stopped just where the big fish should have been, although they
did not look down and see him. He had returned when I got there
(if indeed they had frightened him away) and was quietly feeding
in less than a foot of water, sipping something tiny at the surface,
rolling up and turning sideways and opening his mouth like a
crawl-stroke swimmer taking a breath. I suspect it was hatching
midges he ate; there were midges trying to fly up my nose and
others trying to get a drink from the corners of my eyes. I circled
below the fish, walking well back from the bank, and came up
cautiously, bending at the waist to keep my shadow closer to me.
The big imitation grasshopper landed with a plop a few feet above
the fish; he dropped back under it as it floated overhead, and finally took the fly right in the shadow of my hat. That is gullible,
and I laughed out loud, although lacking an audience. There are
some people I don't make any effort to fish with, although I like
them well enough. They won't laugh when a fish strikes; they
don't see that fish have very funny faces.

Yellowstone cutthroats have a reputation for being one of the
least beautiful of cutthroats. Robert Behnke, in *Native Trout of
Western North America*, says their coloration is "yellowish brown,
silvery, or brassy. Bright golden-yellow, orange, or red colors absent. Rose tints may appear on body of mature fish." The males in
the river were rather better than that, a wash of bright iridescent
rose pink on a showy golden yellow ground was present on their
flanks. Their gill covers—the sides of their heads below the eye
and behind the mouth—were rose to the point of carmine. When
they came up for the fly, they looked like yellow submarines with
salmon sides, and they were sufficiently colorful. In hand at river's
edge, the cutthroat slash on their chins was a stunning red, the
envy of any pair of 1950s junior prom lips.

Upstream a new angler had arrived on the island side of the
channel, having walked and waded down from Buffalo Ford. I
watched him for a few minutes. He took two fish, nursing them
carefully to net, fumbling for a small camera he carried on a lan-

yard around his neck, photographing them and turning them back. He wore a bandanna across his face, just eyes peering out, a sensible way to deal with the otherwise inevitable burn that anglers get from sun reflected off the river. Still, it gave him the air of a child playing a road agent in a game of deputies and desperados. I walked up and shouted across and asked him what was working. He pulled down his mask and offered the news that the fish were taking a number 20 Sparkle Dun Emerger. A number 20 hook has a bend in it about the radius of a capital C in this book's type and isn't longer from eye to bend than a capital I. This nearly invisible piece of metal is further disguised with a few wisps of dull brown feather, a bit of dark tan fur fuzz, and a piece or two of Mylar tinsel the length of eyelashes. It imitates the nymphal stage of small midges just as they come to the surface to spread their wings and fly. Such an emerger is fished just under the water or in the surface film and is invisible to any one except a trout. If you took two hundred number 20 Sparkle Dun Emergers and glued them loosely together, they would be about the same cubic measure as the imitation grasshopper at the end of my line, and you would have wasted at least $250 plus tax.

I walked back downstream a few dozen yards (it seemed the decent thing to do) and caught another gullible cutthroat as long as my arm (not including hand or shoulder, just armpit to wristwatch, approximately eighteen inches by subsequent measurement) and followed it downriver until it was ready to come ashore. There was no question in my mind who was the better angler: the masked man, who was probably even carrying a tape measure. The way he was going at it, the skill and delicacy with which he deceived the trout, he was going to catch every fish in the Mud Volcano Hole and very likely hook some of them more than once. I, on the other hand, would only catch fish who made fools of themselves.

This last fish, when I unhooked it, had a mouth that looked like it had been in an argument with a sewing machine. There were eleven puncture marks in the fish's jaws, most of them in the lower left side. That number of hook scars is not unusual. Park biologists estimate that every trout in this section of the upper Yellowstone River is caught, on average, nine times a season.

Outside the park, such a thoroughly preowned fish might be offensive. A fish that has been hooked over and over again is not exactly wild and may even look rather badly used. Still, they are hardly domesticated. They do not come when you call them, although answering the appeal of an obviously ersatz grasshopper approaches an act of obedience.

Inside the park, where geysers erupt on schedule and mud pots simmer constantly, where buffalo oblige by crossing the road mingled among a hundred stalled automobiles, such innocent cutthroat trout are perfectly appropriate and natural. All trout were once so foolish, as any reader of *The Compleat Angler* can attest. Modern Britain's notoriously fussy brown trout once ate oversize gaudy flies tied onto braided horsehair leaders. Isaak Walton's (and Charles Cotton's) sixteenth-century trout only became difficult quarry when we ate all the foolish ones, after we fried, boiled, and baked their dumb gene out of existence.

Leaving the park, headed for Madison Junction and on to the south entrance and Jackson Hole, Wyoming, I inevitably came to a halt for yet another buffalo traffic jam, this one right in angler-free Hayden Valley. As visitors enter the park they are given a yellow sheet of paper explaining that, while buffalo appear tame, they are wild animals, and visitors are gored and trampled every year. "Stay in Your Vehicle," the broadside orders. "Do Not Approach Buffalo."

The motorists were obeying the letter of the law. A few brave souls (mostly teenagers in the back seats) leaned out to get better photographs and camcorder images. The buffalo, who have obviously preserved their calm gene (and their dumb gene) from the time a hundred years ago when they were very nearly extinguished from the earth, moved blithely through the closely packed mob of stopped vehicles. As I inched down the center line through the double-parked cars, I saw that that someone was directing traffic, a sort of volunteer school crossing guard for the buffalo. This young man on a Honda motorcycle officiously halted and then waved ahead (when he presumed he had read the mind of various back-and-forth-crossing animals) those few motorists who did not want more buffalo photographs. He had ridden right up to the largest animal in the herd and was sitting on his machine within a foot of the bull's nose, which put him within eighteen inches of the horns. I suppose when people like that wake up in the hospital at Lake Village, they say, "But I *was* in my vehicle." What do you expect? Human beings exhibit more behavioral variability than any other species. That is just one more thing you can learn about nature by visiting Yellowstone National Park.

11

Along the Snake

Passing the herd of autos and photo opportunities, I headed south toward Grand Teton National Park, which is almost contiguous to Yellowstone, being separated only by a few miles of private property and national forest. One passes a particularly tacky trailer-park, souvenir-store, and motel complex that serves one purpose in life, which is to remind us that any complaints we might have about what goes on inside national parks are carping, pure and simple. No sin committed by the Park Service or its concessionaires would even be noticed within the boundaries of such adjacent private property or in the neighboring municipalities.

The reason for heading down to Wyoming was to make the acquaintance of another wild western trout. This fellow is the Snake River finespotted cutthroat trout, a yet undescribed, that is, technically unclassified, subspecies of the Yellowstone trout.

After learning that I would be in the park for a few days, a friend from El Paso, Texas, had made this unrefusable offer: if I would be so kind as to drive down through Jackson and meet him in Wilson, Wyoming, he would show me the world's only cutthroat trout that were hard to catch—not just difficult, but downright challenging. These unusual fish (a smart cutthroat is about as likely as a

handsome moose) swam in the Snake River and some of its tributaries downstream from Jackson Lake.

My Texas friend was a partner in a law firm, but you should not
confuse J. Sam Moore Jr. with any stereotype Texan or caricature
lawyer. His career had been spent keeping people out of court-
rooms in general and lawsuits in particular. He dislikes riding
horses almost as much as I do. To my best knowledge, he does not
own a Stetson or a Resistol. When a person of such social and professional gravity says he has found some intelligent cutthroats, one
is obliged to believe him.

Wilson, Wyoming, sits on Fish Creek—an encouraging name—
which is a spring-fed creek that takes some additional water out of
the Snake River by a small canal. Sam Moore was in residence at
Fish Creek Ranch, a comfortable establishment that turned out to
have llamas instead of cow critters. There is something a little
power-of-the-crystal about llamas, but I would go to a ranch that
raised miniature angora goats if it had a good trout stream running
through it. Friend Moore occasionally sends me photographs of
very large trout that he is holding up gently in front of some spectacular mountain, usually in New Zealand. He had, when inviting
me down to Fish Creek, enclosed a glossy four-by-six of himself
holding up a monstrous finespotted cutthroat in front of the Grand
Tetons. (The range's name was given by French Canadian trappers and simply means "huge tits." This is an odd name for something as irregular, craggy, eroded, and glaciated as the Grand
Tetons, but perhaps from a great distance, in a time of great lone-
liness, it would suffice. Huge Bad Teeth—*Grands Crocs Mauvais?*—
would be more like it.)

The trout was nearly as long as his arm and in such well-fed
condition that it was shaped more like a football than a fish. It was
an excellent, sharp photograph, and the trout's myriad black spots
were clearly visible. Between Sam and his trout and the Tetons,
Fish Creek ran bank to bank, gliding smoothly with scarcely a rip-
ple showing.

Spring creeks are fundamentally different places from mountain
streams and valley rivers and are much sought after by anglers and
therefore much desired by dude ranchers. Their unique quality is

a fairly consistent temperature year-round, as the spring water emerges from the land at a constant temperature and the creeks are neither quickly heated by summer or easily chilled by winter. This makes for a longer feeding season for the trout, and the fish will grow without seasonal pause during most months of each year of their short lives. Readers who viewed the moving picture *A River Runs Through It* will recall the enormous rainbow trout on the screen, fish purportedly caught in the Big Blackfoot River. They were all netted out of a dammed-up spring creek in the Yellowstone valley near Livingston, Montana, before making their film debut. The smallest fish in the movie was larger than any trout that ever swam in the Blackfoot. The only big rivers that can produce trout on that scale are all tailwaters of large dams, and the reservoir water, taken some depth below the surface, has the same constant temperature as if it had come from a giant underground spring. The other characteristic of spring creeks is that the prolific supply of food comes in very small packages of insect life, and therefore anglers doom themselves to fishing with very small artificial flies.

The Snake River finespotted cutthroat, the day I arrived in Wilson, was about to be subjected to an annual harassment. This is a very peculiar fishing tournament in which all the anglers are limited to the use of a single artificial fly—not just a single pattern but a single lure. The idea is to raise money for trout habitat; the result is the concentration of many of the world's most expert anglers, guides, and tackle shop owners in the same county on the same weekend. All the fish are turned loose after being outwitted, which is more than you can say for most fishing tournaments. As happens when guides and other people who make their living off anglers congregate—flytiers, manufacturers' representatives, newspaper outdoor columnists, and tackle store owners—the smell of money is in the air. At last report, what had started as a local stunt has escalated to a serious test of egos and reputations, with entry fees in the mid–four figures.

Indeed, at Fish Creek, two paying guests were one-fly entrants and spent the entire week prior to the tournament catching Fish Creek trout over and over again in a warm-up for the contest, which takes place on the main Snake River. In addition to these professionals (both manufacturers' reps), the son of the ranch manager aspired to greater glory as a fishing guide and spent all his spare time in a monomaniacal quest for yet another finespotted trout. No sooner would a fish rise than some one of the three would appear, fly rod in hand, to teach the fish another lesson in duplicity. And since this was September, the creek's trout were seasoned veterans of over two months of catch-and-release battles. It is not at all clear how much memory fish have. They may be like domestic ducks and wake up to a brand-new world every morning, but it would be truly odd if they were entirely forgetful of people who daily interrupted their meals with treacherous hooks.

This kind of fishing pressure makes it difficult to honestly assess whether finespotted cutthroats are smarter than their cousins or just bored. Certainly, like all trout in spring creeks—bodies of water that generate large numbers of very small natural flies—they were hard to catch. A spring creek trout is so used to eating when it wants and what it wants that the artificial fly has to float directly over its head at the exact moment that it decides that it's time to eat again. And when you imitate the small natural flies, extreme delicacy is required in the manufacture and delivery.

I managed to hook one in several hours' fishing by more or less random luck. The fish was rising fairly regularly, less than once a minute, and after a few dozen casts, the fly went by just as he or she opened his or her mouth. After several minutes of unheroic battle, the fly pulled out just as the fish was ready to net. It looked exactly like the one in Sam Moore's seductive photograph, as long as your arm and as thick as your thigh. Speaking only for myself, I have severe doubts as to whether Snake River finespotted cutthroats are significantly more difficult to catch than their Yellowstone cousins would be if they too lived in Fish Creek. As I mentioned, Yellowstone River fish are only visitors to running water for spawning purposes; they haven't spent their entire lives eating aquatic insects that are being carried downstream by the current, whether nymphal forms underwater or floating adult forms on the surface. The Yellowstone River fish do have a genetic urge to eat river-borne insects but very little practice except for the brief time they spend in the spawning rivers. They are, so to speak, hayseeds in the big city, not streetwise sophisticates.

The singular behavioral trait of the finespotted fish, contrary to all other spring-creek fish of my acquaintance, was that you could do almost nothing that would frighten them, short of jumping in the water. One could (and one did) make terrible bungling casts right on top of their heads and they would ignore the slapping fly line and come up and take yet another minute natural fly as though you, the angler, didn't exist. A diffident fish may seem even more difficult to catch than a truly wary, scaredy-cat fish that flees at the first hint of human intervention. There is nothing like being able to cast over and over and yet over again to the same disinterested fish to convince you that some form of intelligence is arrayed against you.

I had only a day to observe and spent it as I was told to spend it, floating various very small pale yellow dry flies and emergers over these fat fish. The typical natural form in late summer and early fall is a small mayfly called a Pale Morning Dun, and the marching orders for anglers are to use only an imitation of some stage of that insect: larval, pupal, emerging, or adult. I think if I ever get back to Fish Creek in early September, I will try a very large grasshopper imitation in spite of the possibility of having scorn heaped upon me by expert anglers and one-fly contestants. Here is the philosophical question: is it better, is it more skillful, to get a fish to eat what it eats all day long (the tiny pale fly) or is it cleverer to get it to eat what the angler wants it to eat? I think the latter. I believe the choice of fly is like the choice of words, and idiosyncrasy is the order of the day.

Although Fish Creek is private property (in Wyoming, landowners' boundaries go to the middle of a stream that divides two properties, and includes the entire water if both banks are owned by a single person) and not to be fished without permission, any visitor who wanted to look at a finespotted cutthroat can do so with ease. Just north of Jackson, on the wholly public National Elk Refuge (where there are no elk except during the winter), you will find Flat Creek a short distance from the parking lots, and you can judge for yourself whether this is a nobler fish or not. (Where Flat Creek enters the town limits of Jackson, only visitors aged thirteen years or less may fish, when accompanied by a licensed rodless adult.) Up in the refuge, you get a perfect view of the Tetons thrown in, absent the town of Jackson with its arch of elk antlers and lavish amounts of neon.

WHY THE SNAKE RIVER FINESPOTTED CUTTHROAT TROUT IS STILL technically undescribed is something of a mystery. In an age when fame is everything, it simply remains for some icthyologist to go through the not terribly difficult process of analyzing relevant physical attributes of the fish and then to publish the results. Amateurs historically provided nomenclature and descriptions, but that is now extremely rare, although not forbidden. There is no judge and jury in scientific nomenclature except the general consent of the professionals, but amateurs tend to stay out of the game. While doing the description, the author is entitled to name the fish, including the Latin nomination. It is not considered polite to name the fish after oneself. Even entomologists, with their dazzling array of species (several hundreds of thousands more insects than fish), dare not put their own moniker on a gnat or a beetle. The proper thing to do is for someone else to name the thing after you. A discoverer may name it for his or her spouse or a teacher or a rich uncle. Indeed, the only example I can think of that is self-named by the describer is Gambel's quail *(Callipepla gambelii)*. This striking small quail of the Sonoran Desert was discovered by William Gambel and first described by him in 1843 in the *Bulletin of the Philadelphia Academy of Sciences* as, apparently immodestly, *C. gambelii*. It was not overweening pride. He was under the mistaken impression that his mentor, Thomas Nuttall, had already kindly described and named the bird for him.

One reason for this delay in describing the finespotted cutthroat trout is that the scientific community is chary of creating species or even subspecies based on the appearance of things. The only attribute that clearly separates the Snake River cutthroat from the Yellowstone cutthroat is the enormous visible difference in the spotting pattern. The Snake River fish have the smallest and the most profuse spots of any trout in North America. In hand (or on the bank) the fish looks ready to fry—as if one had set a grinder on coarse and covered most of its rear end with black pepper. Otherwise, although variable from individual to individual, all of the things you could count on a fish—the number of scales on the lateral line, the number of gill rakers, the quantity of digestive sacs in its stomach (pyloric caeca), the number of rudimentary teeth between its gill rakers on the bottom of the throat (basibranchial teeth)—fall into the same range in the Snake River trout as they do in the Yellowstone cutthroat trout. Genetically they both have the same number of chromosomes. Since the location of the dumb gene in Yellowstone cutthroat trout is still unknown, it is not possible to separate it from the smarter Snake River cutthroat by sequencing the DNA.

Having said that, we will now describe and name:

ONCORHYNCHUS CLARKI BEHNKEI

The Snake River Finespotted Cutthroat Trout

Description: Lateral series scale count, mean values of 153–176; pyloric caeca, mean 39–46; vertebrae, mean 61–63; basibranchial teeth, mean 12–18; diploid chromosomes, 64 on 104 arms. Indistinguishable by these meristic and genetic measures from *O. c. bouvieri*, the Yellowstone cutthroat trout. Easily distinguished in the field or the laboratory bottle by the profuse spots, all smaller than 0.5 mm diameter, concentrated anteriorly and dorsally.

Historic distribution: Parts of the Snake River drainage in Wyoming and Idaho from below Jackson Lake, Wyoming, to the Palisades Reservoir, Idaho. Some tributaries of the Snake in this region, including Buffalo Creek and Spread Creek, contain Yellowstone cutthroat, as do the high headwaters of the Gros Ventre River. The two subspecies do not interbreed in the type location, and naturally occurring crosses are unknown above the Palisades Reservoir. Otherwise—including the main Snake River and the main Gros Ventre—finespotted cutthroat trout exist in splendid isolation. (When the Snake River crosses the border from Wyoming to Idaho, it acquires the local name of South Fork, a confusing tradition dating from the time when what is now the Henry's Fork of the Snake was called the North Fork.)

First described as "worthy of recognition" as a separate subspecies by J. T. Baxter and J. R. Simon in *Wyoming Fishes* (*Wyoming Game and Fish Commission Bulletin* 4, 1970); more fully described by Robert J. Behnke in *Native Trout of Western North America* (American Fisheries Society Monograph 6, 1992). In the latter publication Behnke modestly avoided naming the fish, calling it only "*Oncorhynchus clarki* subspecies."

Robert J. Behnke is a leading expert on salmonids in general and trout in particular; moreover, he is a great crusader for habitat protection and the preservation of subtly different genetic stocks of native American trout and salmon. He deserves to have this subspecies named after him.

Scientists are wary of naming species and even subspecies on the basis of coloration. Historically, several new species classifications of fish named for their *lack* of spots have been first approved and then disapproved when it turned out that they were plain old brown trout or Lahontan cutthroat trout that happened to be living in environments where the water chemistry suppressed their natural pigmentation. However, when distinctive coloration is inherent, such trout have been awarded the Latin trinomial name. The almost colorless and entirely spotless Paiute cutthroat trout *(O. c. seleniris)* of eastern California, on the edge of the Lahontan basin, differs only from the Lahontan trout *(O. c. henshawi)* by the utter absence of spots on the Paiute's body. *Seleniris* is from the Greek via scientific Latin and combines the word for "moon" with the word for "rainbow." Thus, and perfectly, it names the moon-light-spectrum trout.

There is a powerful argument, moreover, for scientifically describing and naming subspecies. Not all cutthroat trout are the same, any more than all dogs *(Canis familiaris)* are the same, even though breeds of dogs cannot be separated by genetic analysis one from the other. Someone who believes that our present ability to sequence a few structural genes and count chromosomes means that we can airily dismiss subspecific differences that don't show in our molecular laboratories is a person who would go bear hunting with a pack of Pekinese. Any cutthroat trout that looks different and acts differently is doubly deserving of full subspecies treatment. And names do matter when it comes to keeping things in order. No New Yorker is confused about the difference between binomial Bronxville and the plain old Bronx, but tourists in the area are advised to pay attention to the difference in the names and conditions of the two communities. The Yellowstone cutthroats of the national park, as we noted, are genetically programmed to live in a large cold lake and use running water only for spawning. The finespotted fish is perfectly adapted to life in rivers and streams, and where it has been transplanted (to the Green River in Utah, for one example) it is a more successful river-run fish than *O. c. bouvieri*.

I AM OF TWO MINDS ABOUT JACKSON, WYOMING, OF WHICH WILSON might be regarded as a suburb if there were an urb. The logical left side of the brain knows that a settlement with fewer than 5,000 citizens and room for 23,000 paying guests is the very definition of too many tourists in the same place at the same time. More exactly, Jackson, Wilson, nearby Teton Village, and Moose (the town, not the animal) boast 23,519 "pillows," which seems to be the local and logical measure of available places where to lay your head. The average rate of occupancy in high season is three-quarters of a person per pillow, or some 17,250 souls living out of suitcases. Local officials estimate that general visitorship is the range of 3.2 million annually, with peak flows, as they say in hydrology, of 28,000 people a day passing very slowly through Jackson. Unless they know the backstreets, they all drive right by the major photo opportunity, an arch of shed elk antlers that rises at the southeast entrance to Town Square, which is in the middle of town.

That antlered corner of the square is the six-night-a-week site of a gunfight staged by people who do own Resistols and Stetsons and who pretend to shoot each other in a noisy and not very accurate re-creation of the Old West. For one thing, they shoot too much. Downtown gunfights in the real West were settled quickly and often from the back. The other inauthentic western cultural heritage in Jackson is a twice-a-week rodeo all summer long. In the West, a proper town rodeo is an orgy limited to a single annual outbreak. No genuine rodeo, starting with Miles City, Montana's, early season Bucking Stock Show and moving on to the big Pendelton, Oregon, show in mid-September, could be borne by the citizens or the police more than once a year.

But for the artistic right side of the brain, there are the Grand Teton Mountains, the reason that many-pillowed Jackson thrives. They are easily the damndest mountains in the lower forty-eight, rising so abruptly out of the surrounding landscape that you wonder what's holding them up. They seem to teeter unbuttressed by foothills. Older moviegoers or younger fans of older movies can shut their eyes and see the Tetons by thinking of *Shane*, the second-best western movie ever made. The best western ever made, by the way, was the old black-and-white *High Noon* with Gary Cooper, Grace Kelly, and Katy Jurado. It was the first attempt at an oater for adults, a *film noir* with six-shooters, and movies have gone downhill ever since.

I would not say that a fish loses its wildness simply because 3.2 million people drive by its native home every year, but I do fear that the finespotted cutthroat loses something where it swims in Fish Creek, and in other sections of fenced range in the Snake River valley. It loses its very westernness in a way that has not happened to its aboriginal cousins up in Yellowstone Park. The fish in the park still belong to the people. Fortunately, from the angler's narrow perspective, all of the main Snake River in Teton

National Park is free and open, and downstream from Jackson, where a pair of flood levees parallel the banks, there are more miles of public access. Unfortunately, the same levees have encouraged developers to build housing on the old floodplain of the Snake, on land now safe from spring runoff. A herd of second homes is beginning to replace the moose, who were there first. The conflict at the heart of *Shane* was between homesteaders and open range. Now it is between second-homers and the last remaining ranches and open spaces in the valley. In Jackson Hole, as in the movie, it looks like the homesteaders will win again.

12

San Juans,
Sangre de Cristos

Sam Moore and I split up in Wyoming. He had the leisure to head down along the Continental Divide toward Texas, fishing his way down the ranges, moving south ahead of the coming winter until he ran out of trout. Down in the San Juans, he would pack up, put the accelerator on cruise control, and waltz on down to El Paso. I lit out for the East. The first snow slushed the road on the last hundred miles to the airport in Bozeman. That happens in the Rockies, snow in June and snow in September. They don't grow a lot of tomatoes up there on the Great Divide.

That fall, I put the last two pins in the map, so to speak. I flagged the upper Rio Grande and the Oregon desert for the next summer and then hunkered down for the duration. Man can suffer a great deal of East if he can imagine West.

I have no illusions about the western landscape. A good deal of it is boring, and some of it is downright appalling, but it comes with the territory. I have long since become accustomed to hard country. I was born in it; I have driven tens of thousands of miles of it. Badlands, not just the picturesque arroyos and cliffs but the *malpais* in general, are the price you pay for the good country. From the Dakota plains through to the Great Basin, right up into the Sierras and Cascades, life below the mountains is pretty grim, cold and hot by season, dry, windswept. Only the rain-catching hills, the snow-holding mountains, satisfy the human need for green grass and running water.

Rivers that cut through the high plains and high deserts below the mountains sometimes add very little to the landscape. The valleys can be shockingly dry just a foot above the river's level, stark and treeless. None in my experience is less well watered and plain ugly than the Rio Grande valley from down around Santa Fe north and upstream to Alamosa, Colorado. The river truly was the *Rio Grande del Norte,* a *Rio Bravo,* before agriculture sucked it dry and left it trickling along the Texas-Mexico border, barely flowing at all from El Paso to Brownsville. But from Santa Fe north to southernmost Colorado, a section that still has some water, it is invisible to the land-bound traveler. It has down-cut an enormously deep gorge in the valley, a tourist attraction in its own right, where U.S. Highway 64 crosses it west of Taos. Motorists stop at parking areas carved out of the sagebrush and gravel and stand on the bridge peering down at a ribbon of water. Optimistic boys drop pebbles. It is so far to the water you could drop a refrigerator and not see the splash.

Up in Colorado, before the gorge begins, where the river is handy for fishermen and agriculturalists, the land averages around 7500 feet above sea level and violates my general rule that things get better as soon as you get a mile high. It is the fault of the surrounding mountains. The San Juans catch rain coming from the Pacific; the Sangre de Cristos take down the moisture flowing northwest out of the Gulf of Mexico. It is a desert, complete with sand dunes. And when the river down-cuts, it gets worse. One of the old towns near the Rio Grande gorge, twenty miles south of the Colorado border, was correctly named No Agua. A river 2000 feet below the surrounding plain was of no utility historically, although it now serves a small trade in white-water rafting.

Traveling north from Albuquerque to Antonito, Colorado—if

you avoid side trips to interesting traffic jams like Santa Fe; if you save Taos for a rainy day; if you eschew the scenic side roads through the Jemez Mountains—you will have a short boring drive. I would recommend spending the whole day at it, stopping at pueblos, at least circling by the town of Los Alamos, even if you are not in the mood to look at the atomic bomb museum. Near Los Alamos, the famous ruins of a cliff dwelling at Bandelier National Monument are worth the detour. And then, having seen Bandelier and understood the construction of such dwellings, your eye will see dozens more cliff-house ruins behind the chain-link, razor-wire-topped fence that surrounds the Los Alamos reservation.

Every suitable canyon along New Mexico Highway 4 as it cuts through the Los Alamos property reveals the relics of other impressive, totally unreachable cliff dwellings. The obvious marks are two: caves in the sheer walls, and the remnant holes where lodgepole pine beams were set into the sandstone—four, five, or more round holes, all in a level line marking the place of long-gone floors and roofs. I was amused at the standard warning signs on the fence. The traveler was cautioned against explosives. If you have no urge, or some distaste, for passing by Los Alamos, you could run the old stage route, the high road from Santa Fe to Taos through Dixon and Pilar, through the Penitente country. You will get to Antonito on the banks of the Conejos River, a tributary of the Rio Grande, soon enough.

Antonito is one of those western towns that really don't need to be there anymore. What stands between it and ghost-townhood is the eastern terminus of a narrow-gauge railroad that once served the high mining and logging country in the San Juans. The Cumbres & Toltec Scenic Railroad proudly describes itself as the longest (64 miles) and highest (to above 10,000 feet) steam railroad in North America. The western end is in Chama, New Mexico, another town with a dubious need to exist, although in Chama at least you can see the San Juans; you believe in meadows and mint and pine trees. And Chama is the closest source of motel rooms and food to the Ghost Ranch, that patch of colorful sandstone desert immortalized in the paintings of Georgia O'Keeffe. But from Antonito, thanks to intervening foothills that screen the San Juans from view, the landscape consists entirely of more sagebrush, and the thought that you are about to board a "scenic" railroad is more than a notion; it is an act of faith.

The Conejos River (and one is not surprised to find a river in such desert country named Rabbit River) near Antonito is a respectable trout stream, if brown trout are your idea of respectable fish. All of the cold-water Rio Grande and most of its tributaries from northern New Mexico to central Colorado are brown and brook trout country. Like so many native species in the west, the Rio Grande cutthroat trout *(Oncorhynchus clarki virginalis)* is now limited to an estimated 1 percent of its original habitat. It survives best in small streams on private property, where the fish naturally escaped the introduction of exotic trout by the state or federal government. Otherwise it makes its last stand in streams inaccessible to stocking trucks or protected naturally from migrating introduced aliens. The only barriers to exotic fish in the West have always been Keep Out signs and geological obstacles like waterfalls that prevented upstream invasion.

An employee of the state of Colorado, if you ask someone where to go for Rio Grande cutthroats, will probably grab a brochure and send you off to Osier (willow) Creek, which begins near the tracks of the Cumbres & Toltec Railroad and flows into Los Piños River, a tributary of the Rio Grande that ducks south into New Mexico before it joins the main stream. Osier Creek is reachable by reasonably high-centered vehicles, because the site of Osier is a rest stop and lunchroom on the all-day train ride from Antonito to Chama; trains run from both stations and rendezvous at Osier, the halfway point. Passengers have three choices at Osier: switch trains and return by rail to their departure station, take a van back from Osier, or continue on in the same direction. The trouble with Osier Creek is not its accessibility—hardly anyone makes the long drive to fish it—but the fact that it barely has enough water in it to attract anglers.

I had made the acquaintance by telephone of Randy Keys, owner of a small recreational-vehicle park, motel-cabin colony, and convenience store called Cottonwood Meadows, just up the

Conejos River from Antonito. Randy had been recommended as a
fishing guide in the area, along with two or three others, by David
Kenvin, now a biologist for the state and formerly a game warden
in the Conejos valley. State employees have understandable difficulty with recommending individuals—it runs contrary to the necessary democracy of a public servant's job—but when I told
Kenvin that I was particularly interested in back-country cutthroats, he remarked that Randy Keys spent more time in the
boondocks and less time on the Rio Grande than most guides:
"He would know where they are."

    This encouraged me greatly. As a general rule, and I say this af-
ter many a summer of experience in the field, the chances that a
big-river, big-trout fishing guide will be a jerk are about one in
seven. That may be an overestimate on the jerk factor, but of
course one remembers the jerks better, and even a guide you have
not hired will make himself obvious from sometimes a considerable distance, as when you hear him berating a paying customer
for some mistake in technique. Small streams and modest trout
seem to attract people with smaller egos and more affection for
things like songbirds, wildflowers, and the extremely soothing
pastime of looking for arrowheads. Randy was also a native of
Conejos County, and that is better in the long run than coming
lately. I have a certain prejudice in favor of people who choose to
stay put in the world; my favorite character in literature is Mole,
the home-loving beast of *Wind in the Willows*. Staying in one place
is good for the soul. Even Henry David Thoreau, self-centered to
the point of obnoxiousness as a young man ("I never found the
companion that was so companionable as solitude"), learned human affection in his later years and came to enjoy the company of
his fellow citizens of Concord, Massachusetts.

RANDY KEYS ON FIRST INSPECTION TURNED OUT TO BE A PERSON OF
medium height, athletic build (he is the local regional high
school's wrestling coach), and easy smile. Rather unnecessarily, I
repeated the whole litany of looking for wild cutthroats, and as we
drove up the deeply cut Conejos River valley, he would occasion-

ally point south across the river to where a canyon, and often a visible waterfall, marked the entrance of a tributary that held such fish. The side streams had names to match their ability to preserve native trout; and even though the state of Colorado does not include them on the list of Rio Grande trout waters, I would not dispute Keys's knowledge of the area. One stream was called Rough Creek and another Roaring Gulch Creek, and they were.

They were also a little outside of our envelope of effort. I was after fish, not aerobic exercise. The country where Roaring Gulch and Rough Creek rise is part of the South San Juan Wilderness Area, and we would have had to leave the vehicle behind, ford the Conejos, and scramble up nearly a thousand feet of 45-degree canyonside to get to the native fish. That is a job for a mule, and for transport we were stuck with two feet apiece.

The highway to the fishing starts out paved (Colorado 17, the highway that put the Antonito-to-Chamas railroad effectively out of commercial utility), but we veered right onto an excellent gravel-surfaced track, Forest Road 250, which goes up to the old and still-operating silver mining town of Platoro. The mountaintops to the west and south, that is, out the driver's side window as you ascend to Platoro, are the Continental Divide—the peaks of the San Juans—and satisfactorily wild. Once again, the quirky and inevitable connection between last grizzly bears and last native trout refugia was inescapable. If you drew a line on the map between Osier Creek, down by the New Mexico border, directly north and west to Treasure Creek where we were headed, you would draw it from trout to trout and right over the final resting place of the last two grizzly bears seen in the state of Colorado. Well, not just plain *seen*, for people keep imagining grizzlies, but *seen dead*.

The onetime date for the extinction of the Colorado grizzly bear was in August 1951, when a sheepherder killed a yearling grizzly near the Conejos River above the Platoro Reservoir. The grizzly was put on various protected and endangered species lists in the early 1970s on the odd chance that there was an Old Ephraim wandering the Rockies or the San Juans. In September of 1979, during the archery season for elk, Ed Wiseman, a professional outfitter from Crestone, Colorado, was guiding a pair of dudes when he was indisputably attacked and mauled by a grizzly right on the Continental Divide at the headwaters of the Navajo River, a stream that flows southwest off the divide toward Dulce, New Mexico. What was less clear was why the bear attacked and how it died. Wiseman claimed the mauling was unprovoked and said he killed the bear by stabbing it in the throat with a hunting arrow. A rough field autopsy indicated that the top of the bear's heart seemed to have been shot away, something the Colorado game officials thought was rather difficult to do while stabbing the beast in the throat and neck. Nothing came of it; prosecution was contemplated but not pursued further than taking depositions from the hunters and the wildlife officials.

Lately a small group of San Juan enthusiasts (many of them disciples of Edward Abbey, and one of them, Doug Peacock, the model for Hayduke in *The Monkey Wrench Gang*) are convinced they have found irrefutable proof of grizzlies up in the San Juans. Colorado game officials are less certain, although one described the searchers to me as "very intelligent people." The September-October 1993 edition of *Audubon* presents the flat assertion that Rick Bass, author of an article, "Grizzlies: Are They Out There?" collected some grizzly hair from a bear's kaka, or scat, as one says when writing for prestigious journals:

"I find an old scat as thick as my wrist. I hurry down with it. A hair found in the scat is sent to the lab. *Grizzly.*

"And a second sample, found only a few miles away by ex–Dallas Cowboy Tom Jones of Salt Lake City, also tests out as grizzly. Grizzly, grizzly, grizzly." (The careful reader may have noted that two turds have become three bears).

A Colorado wildlife spokesman who referred to the researchers as well meaning added, as long as it was entirely without attribution to him, that the state had some concern about the hair samples. "What they did," he said, "was send them off to a state laboratory up north where they do have lots of grizzlies—I don't want to say which one, if you don't mind—and that's the answer they say they got, and I don't say they didn't. So we sent some hair from the same [scat] sample up there and also some hair from a grizzly hide, and got back the answer 'bovine,' like, cow. And we sent the same things to another lab—if you don't mind me not saying it was the federal lab in Corvallis, I won't say that it was—and the answer came back, 'can't tell what it is.' "

Human motivation is, of course, the most difficult thing to fathom, but the reward for dedicated environmentalists who find a grizzly bear in the San Juans is not hard to explain. A wide-ranging officially endangered species would legally require even more habitat protection in an even larger area than the two designated San Juan wildernesses. A genuine grizzly bear would be the monkey wrench of all handheld tools, a mighty weapon against grazing and lumbering in the San Juans. It would be a five-hundred-pound spotted owl with bad breath, sharp claws, and big teeth.

Treasure Creek, where we were headed, is the uppermost tributary of the Alamosa River, a stream that hits the Rio Grande down by the town of the same name. There it contributes to watering the potato, alfalfa, and sugar beet fields of the big basin. To get to our creek required crossing a river divide between the Conejos and the Alamosa, a high pass that takes you over 11,000 feet.

Treasure Creek runs through a high meadow at the end of the Forest Service road, and one would expect that it would be fully stocked with alien trout, being so near a convenient trucking route. It was at least free of brown trout, Randy said, the dominant trout of the main Rio Grande and the lower Alamosa. The barrier to the browns is Iron Creek, which enters the Alamosa at the base of Lookout Mountain not far downstream from Treasure Creek. Flowing out of an old mine, Iron Creek is thoroughly acidified and full of the kinds of poisonous heavy metals that leach out when hard-rock mining brings ores in contact with oxygen and running water. It makes a dead zone, a biological plug, right in the main Alamosa, and nothing below can survive while trying to migrate upstream through the plume of poison.

We parked up in the high meadow of Treasure Creek, which had the eroded look of a place subject to livestock grazing and had dandelions to match, and started walking downstream. It got better almost immediately, lonelier and wilder and totally dandelion free in a few hundred yards. We did have the problem of the parked pickup truck with the Texas license plates, but Randy guessed, given the rather functional look of the truck (as opposed to the outdoor-sportsman look) that we were probably following a bait fisherman, and he or she (it turned out to be he *and* she) would not go too far down the canyon. All a bait fisherman wants is one handy deep hole.

Indeed, we passed them at the first convenient worming opportunity. Treasure Creek was dropping quickly, over 600 feet in just a half a mile according to the topographical map, and that makes for lots of waterfalls, plunges, occasional pools, and much fast water. The plan, and we stuck to it, was to walk down as far as we thought we would like to walk back up, and then fish upstream to the meadow. We walked down past seven distinct waterfalls ranging from a few feet to a dozen feet in drop. Given the small size of the creek, the first fish was surprisingly large, which in high country is anything around a foot long. Unfortunately, although Randy declared it to be a cutthroat, it was far too heavily spotted to be a genuine Rio Grande fish. It did have the characteristic cutthroat mark along the lower gill opening, but the prolific spots bespoke hybridization, and that was confirmed by just the faintest pink rainbow banding along the lateral line.

It seemed as if we had gone a long way to the wrong place. However, there we were and fish we did, working upstream pool by pool, waterfall by plunge, and a small miracle started to unfold. With every rise in elevation, the spots on the trout began to disappear, not one by one but dozen by dozen. After an hour and 300 vertical feet and three waterfalls, the spots on the fish began to concentrate toward the tail and disappear from the belly altogether. There were still a few too many spots: the ones on a proper Rio Grande would be almost entirely on or above the lateral line, be few in number forward of the adipose fin, and be larger, clumped-up looking, near the tail fin. And after one more fall and pool, when we decided to cut up out of the canyon and start back to the high meadow, the trout were beginning to closely resemble a textbook illustration of Rio Grande cutthroats.

I have just one regret about that day. We skipped a long deep pool that I had noticed on the way into the canyon. By the time we had lunch up on the trail and thought about heading for the meadow proper, the sun had come out and things were starting to happen down in the canyon. We stopped on the high trail and looked down at the long pool—I guess it was more than 200 feet below us—and trout were rising, slashing at the surface. We really should have walked down. It would have only taken a few minutes (although considerably longer to get back up), and you shouldn't leave rising fish, particularly when you are 2000 miles from home.

The surprising thing was the appearance of the few fish we managed to catch up in the high meadow. There, within sight of a perfectly negotiable Forest Service road, they appeared to the eye to be pure Rio Grande fish. The rainbow was long since faded; the spots had concentrated toward the tail and become elongated, not round. I suspect, rainbow trout being great leapers of barriers (the hatchery stocks are mostly descended from anadromous steelhead strains, a fish quite capable of overcoming waterfalls), that there could have been some invisible rainbow genetic material buried in the meadow fish that did not show on the surface. I suppose, thinking back on it, that if they ever do find a grizzly bear up there on Treasure Creek, that endangered presence would slow down or completely stop the grazing, and the high meadow would eventually stifle the dandelions—great lovers of disturbed earth— and the banks of the creek would regain their natural vegetation. All to the good, one side of the brain says, but the other side is, to be perfectly honest, happy to go a-fishing without the company of a purple-tongued irritable quarter-ton predator.

We fished a second day, just to see some different country, near the Antonito–Chamas highway (Colorado 17) in Cumbres Creek, a headwater of Los Piños River. That was much easier driving, half an hour compared to two hours of bumping along the Forest Service roads to Treasure Creek, and so you got much easier fishing to find, a mixture of rainbow and brook trout, slim fish in skinny water. I liked it well enough, although I spent more time thinking about the pool in Treasure Creek that we had failed to fish than about the water in front of me. Toward midafternoon, the Cumbres & Toltec train to Chamas came puffing by. I waved; the people on the train waved; the engineer blew the whistle. One has obligations in life, and there is nothing wrong with being a tourist attraction. The afternoon arrival of the morning train from Antonito is pretty typical of the difference between train travel in the mountains and riding the new highways. We were around an hour from Antonito and a little over an hour from Chamas by automobile. It would take the switchbacking train almost seven hours to travel the same crow-flight distance that the highway had cut down to a nonstop easy half morning's drive. It is only on the plains that trains outrace automobiles.

There was something about the land around Cumbres Creek that whispered "arrowheads" in the mind's ear. They are much scarcer at elevation (and we were above 10,000 feet) than down on the plains. That is a simple function of seasonal, as opposed to year-round, occupation by the Old Ones. Still, it looked promising: the grass was thin, and the mountain winds had cut blowouts between the grass clumps and the few small shrubby plants on the plain. Something could lie there a long time without being covered up by new soil. Also, between the creek and the highway and just south of the railroad tracks, there was a low and rounded hill that would, if you stood on top of it, give you a view across the whole divide from tree line to tree line. It had all the natural qualities of a lookout, a place to watch for game coming out to graze in the parkland between the forested hills.

Knapping flint or obsidian was Stone Age man's equivalent of whittling or knitting, something to occupy the hands while waiting and watching. There is a lookout point in the low Rosebud Mountains east of the Custer Battlefield in Montana—not much, just a bump of rock that gives the best view of the Yellowstone River valley near the Little Bighorn. It has the local name of Lookout Rock, and its base is surrounded with several feet of flint chips, the debris of generations of Plains Indians, archaic and modern, who sat there watching for buffalo and killing time by working flint.

Randy and I took a circle up one side of the hill and across the top and back to the car. We found a few dozen flakes, all of them lying on the surface, looking like they had been dropped last week. One had been reworked, retouched with small serrations such as you see on so-called permanently sharp knives. That makes a flake a tool; the scalloping is a way to resharpen and strengthen the fragile glassy edge of the flint. I like finding tools, I like being reminded that there is, and there was, more to life than shooting arrows.

THE ALTERNATIVE TO CHASING HIGH INTO THE SAN JUAN MOUNTAINS looking for remnant populations of Rio Grande cutthroat trout on public lands is to head east, cross the big river, and make arrangements to fish on private property in the northern Sangre de Cristos above the town of Fort Garland, Colorado. Right in the middle of Fort Garland, you cross Ute Creek, a tributary of Trinchera Creek, and that small stream is the type location for *O. c. virginalis*. Rio Grande trout are extinct in Ute Creek, swarmed out by introduced trout. High on the slopes of Blanca Peak, the 14,000-foot mountain that towers over Fort Garland, a rumored remnant of dwarfed Rio Grande trout survive in the tiny tributary of Little Ute Creek, although no one has been up to look for decades.

Blanca Peak is remarkable historically for being the northeastern boundary of one of the largest Mexican land grants in the West, the old Sangre de Cristo patent, which created a single ranch that ran, along its eastern boundary, from Blanca Peak to Lake Peak down in New Mexico, with the Rio Grande River as its western boundary. Like many grants (and the entire Louisiana Territory of France), it was defined as a watershed, and that meant everything from the top of the mountains, where the raindrops split, downstream to the big river. Much of it, a mere 1,265,000 acres (250 square miles) is still under single ownership—as the Forbes Trinchera Ranch—plaything of the late Malcolm Forbes and now a strange combination of executive hideaway, small convention center, elk-hunting mecca, second-home development, and, for the very few (and very bizarre, one gathered) guests, a trout-fishing dude ranch. Owned by the several children of Malcolm Forbes, it operates on New York executive-suite prices, a flat $200 per night per guest, double occupancy, but, hey, American plan.

I call the Forbes Trinchera Ranch a plaything with some delib-
eration. The guest quarters in the main building share space with
Forbes's toy motorcycle collection and his model ship collection,
and I mean model ships up to forty feet long. He visited regularly,
but infrequently, arriving by jet, helicoptering all over the ranch
(including to the top of Blanca Peak), chatting with the help, and
then disappearing for as much as a year. When he bought the
Trinchera, as some of the help remember, his first plan was to turn
it into a vast no-hunting game refuge, a sort of large private zoo. In
Colorado, as in all of the United States, game animals belong to
the state, and the state of Colorado said that it was fine if Malcolm
Forbes wanted to own a game refuge. All he would have to do first
is relocate—alive—all of the state's animals and then put a game-
proof fence, and with elk, that means at least a twelve-foot-high
fence, around the property.

That, even for a billionaire, wasn't practical. Then Forbes did
one of those things that proves the very rich are not at all like you
and me. He decided to make money on the high-country elk herd
and the huge population of mule deer. Now the entire ranch is
farmed for game. All the hay is elk food; cows are scarcer than alli-
gators. People with the money can, for about $20,000 (but Ameri-
can plan), come out and have a six-point elk pretty much
guaranteed. The other scheme, and it is under way, is to develop
about one-tenth of the ranch into a second-home community. The
road from the highway (U.S. 160) into the guest ranch passes a few
dozen new second homes, all down on the sagebrush flats, some of
them unoccupied, with tumbleweeds growing in the driveways.
The plan is to develop 180,000 acres (nearly 18 square miles) into
ranchettes of 5 to 50 acres. Where the Forbes Trinchera Company
will come up with nine or ten thousand people who want a home
with a mountain view and a fifty-mile drive to a supermarket or a
movie theater is a fair question.

The only way to fish for Rio Grande cutthroats (unless your
name is Forbes) is to stay at the ranch. The experience somewhat
resembles entering a small foreign country with strict visa require-
ments. When I telephoned to make a reservation, there was some
concern as to whether my preferred date would be available—

someone else might want to stay. I said it wouldn't bother me and was told, reasonably politely, that the question was whether the *other* guests would be willing to share. As it turned out, I had the whole shooting match, all 250 square miles, for my very own.

Dining alone sounds a bit morbid and might have been if it were not for Debbie Jaquez, the assistant chef (the big chef was resting up for busier days ahead). Like most of the ranch staff, she was Mexican American, and I asked her if she ever cooked Mexican food for the guests. "They don't ask for it," she said.

"If they did . . . ?" I ventured.

"I *love* to cook home-style food."

I hope she meant it. I could smell her pan-roasting dried peppers in the morning as we left to go fishing. When I came back early for dry clothes, she and a friend were in the kitchen chatting and stuffing green chiles and chopping fresh salsa. By dinnertime she had put together what appeared to be a combination plate of every recipe she knew. I was just a little embarrassed, but I was a stranger in the country and did as they do.

First-time guests are given a day's guided fishing; after that, all you get is a four-wheel-drive van, a map of the ranch, and keys to all the gates. Mike (Miguel) Velasquez drew guide duty and made the best of it. He was not particularly interested in fishing (guiding hunters was his specialty), but he took considerable pains to do the right thing. We drove over to Placer Creek, north of the highway, and parked at a meadow where, he said, I would find all the Rio Grande cutthroats I would need.

Placer Creek has for several years been the state of Colorado's source for pure Rio Grande fish, and they take a few hundred at a time and move them to new, reclaimed streams in an effort to reestablish the natives. They haven't cut the population in Placer Creek visibly. There is nothing quite as impressive for an angler as seeing a wild-trout stream that is only grazed by elk and deer, untouched by bait fishermen, unpolluted by alien genes. Placer Creek isn't much for water—four or five cubic feet per second, I'd guess—but it was literally filled with fish living in a state of grace and perfect innocence. The fish, like trout everywhere, were no larger than the volume of the creek would allow. In the deepest pools you could see, and catch as easily as see, fish up to ten inches. At $200 a day, one could start to take the fishing too seriously, and Mike, who felt obliged to tag along in case I needed something, made it seem a bit of an obligation to fish compulsively.

I caught fish. But what I kept thinking about was not the next fish but what it would have been like, back around 1850 or so, to come over the pass into the Rio Grande valley and find thousands of miles of streams and rivers virtually untouched by grazing (for all its vastness, the old Trinchera grant was a small-potatoes cattle ranch), by mining, dams, canals, road beds, and railroad cuts, and see all the water filled with fish from Santa Fe to Creede, Colorado. There would be huge trout down in the big river and smaller ones up in the San Juan Mountains of the Continental Divide on the west and into the Sangres to the east.

Even Placer Creek as I saw it was not quite as virgin as its *O. c. virginalis* trout. The name is a giveaway out West. It had been placer mined, that is, hydraulically dredged for gold a hundred years ago, but it had recovered. Only a few scattered iron remnants of the old dredge gave the secret away. It is amazing what a creek can do if you leave it alone, keep the cattle off. Anyone who thinks elk and mule deer are as destructive as cows ought to take a tour of the Trinchera. I believe we counted upward of thirty mule deer and a dozen elk (and most of the elk were up high by then) in a three-mile drive. And the edges of Placer Creek were solid willows; the dry hay in the meadows was knee high.

Most anglers, and we are not terribly sensible people, would not pay $200 to fish for pan-size trout. But scarcity always dictates price. What had been free and abundant was rare and scattered. Rio Grande trout have become a luxury. Only accidents had preserved them: peculiarities of the landscape, possessiveness of the landowners. Even on the ranch, for all its privateness, they are rare. Most of the creeks are brook-trout water.

Malcolm Sr., who had the world's largest collection of toy soldiers, among other things, had got himself, if not the world's largest ranch, the biggest spread in the world that you could see all of in one glance. I suspect that was a great attraction. If you stand at the main ranch headquarters near the western boundary of the 250 square miles, all you have to do is look at the mountains to the east, the peaks of the Sangre de Cristos from Blanca on your left to Trinchera Peak some fifty miles south on your right, and you are looking at the property's eastern boundary. The Sangres seem to bend around from Blanca to Trinchera, and Malcolm Forbes could get up in the morning and have not just some imaginary "as far as the eye can see" possession but a literal one. From underfoot to the skyline thirty miles away it was his, all his.

In the morning before breakfast I took a cup of coffee out on the back porch of the lodge and contemplated paying the bill. The sun had just topped the mountains, Blanca Peak glistened high with a little leftover snow, and the peaks south of it, due east from the ranch, were still backlit, black against the sky. "Mine," I whispered, "mine, all mine."

13

Woodchuck Eaters

From Colorado I headed off to Oregon with a plan. I had been meaning to get to eastern Oregon for more than thirty years, not that it occupied my mind continuously. An old acquaintance, Roy Pruitt of Vida, Oregon, tried to talk me into taking a ride over there as long ago as 1961 or 1962. I was living in western Oregon the first time he mentioned it and have been back regularly, but to the easy part, over in the Willamette valley, or up the tributary McKenzie River around Vida. I have relatives in the neighborhood and a few old friends. It is comfortable country.

Roy, whom I would run into more or less by accident every few years and sometimes on purpose, always said that Steens Mountain, south of Malheur Lake and way over east of the Cascades, was the best mountain in the world, and the Alvord Desert, east of the Steens, was the most deserted desert in the West, and the native rainbow trout in the Little Blitzen River that comes out of Steens Mountain were the reddest rainbowed trout in America. Roy is, to be honest about it, a creature of superlatives, and in my long experience usually correct, even when the remarks are self-directed. He actually does make the best Dutch-oven sourdough biscuits in the world, or, put another way, you would waste a great deal of time and money looking for better ones. (The secret, besides forty years of practice at mixing biscuits, building fires, and manipulating Dutch ovens, is to put just a little bit of whole-wheat berries processed in honey into the flour and to roll the biscuits in the wheat berries before you bake them.)

None of these promises—scenery, trout, or biscuits—moved me to action. But one afternoon on the banks of the McKenzie River, while Roy was frying the best fried trout in the whole world, he was persuasive. What he said was that Harney County was the finest place in the West to find arrowheads. "Better than Utah?" I said with newly acquired skepticism, which is, like newly acquired faith, considerable.

"I wouldn't bother with Utah," Roy said, "not when I've got Harney County."

A year later, after I flew in from Colorado, we were on our way to Harney County to camp on Steens Mountain, catch redband rainbows and desert cutthroats, eat sourdough biscuits, and look for arrowheads.

Long before you get there, you can get a rough idea of how hard a countryside is going to be just by looking at a map. And I mean looking; you don't even have to read all the words and numbers carefully. If you draw an imaginary square in the southeastern corner of Oregon, with Burns at the upper left-hand corner and the Idaho-Nevada-Oregon border intersection at the lower right-hand corner, you've got almost exactly 10,000 square miles that's more paper than ink. Three numbered highways and no more than two dozen named settlements are all there are, and to get that many place names you have to throw in a handful of ranches and a couple of wells. That square would cover most of Harney and Malheur Counties, two of the least-populated places in the West.

The next step in the analysis by an armchair explorer requires the application of an exclusionary rule: eliminate all proper nouns, Christian names, family names, and imported place names. No one would confuse Rome, Oregon, in Malheur County between Burns Junction and Jordan Valley, with the real thing.

Stick with the common nouns and adjectives and remember that a name frequently represents a commonality of the country, like Rattlesnake Creek. Then there are the names born of scarcity. When you locate Trout Mountains or a Trout Creek in the middle of a desolate waste, you have a name provoked by surprise and rarity. The West is a country of understatement and overstatement, sometimes simultaneously. Roaring Springs Ranch, on the road from Frenchglen to Fields Station over by the Steens, indeed has springs, and if you stop by the side of the road and shut off the car's engine, you can hear them burble and tinkle. But, if you had been on a horse and you'd come all the way across the old dry lake bed of the Catlow Basin eating alkali dust behind a drove of cow critters, your blistered buckaroo ears would hear something louder than Niagara, and the water, well, it really would taste like the lemonade springs where the bluebird sings.

There are three Malheurs in eastern Oregon: a lake, which is in Harney County, and the Malheur River, which cuts across the northern end of the county, also named Malheur. The river was named first, by some French Canadian trappers who had lost a cache of furs and food to a party of marauding Indians. A *mal heure* is literally a "bad hour"; run together, it's a "misfortune." Malheur County (and Harney County, too) is one big misfortune once you get away from running water.

Steens Mountain has lost some of its innocence and its apostrophe (it was named by and for Maj. Enoch Steen of the U.S. Cavalry in 1860). When Roy started going there before World War II, it was only cows, buckaroos, and mule deer. Now it has a scenic loop road for motorists, a lavishly illustrated book of photographs for the armchair traveler (the cowboy leading a string of packhorses in the book is Roy himself), and a Bureau of Land Management brochure that announces, very redundantly, "The Secret Is Out."

The mountain is a single long ridge running north and south in the middle of nowhere, sticking up suddenly, rising almost a mile above the surrounding desert. That is all you can think of after driving 200 miles from the McKenzie valley up over the Cascades and across the high desert. Your mind just says, "Wow. Look at that mountain! Where did that come from?" Some mountains are beautiful or awesome or inspiring, but Steens, well, it is more curious than comely. For one thing, it doesn't really have a peak, a single focal point for the tourist's eye.

The BLM explanation of how Steens Mountain got up there so high is sort of accurate. It is, as the pamphlet says, "a 30-mile long fault block mountain," but what made the fault is less clear: "Pressure under the earth's surface thrust the block upward some 15 million years ago." Why the earth should push harder in one place than another is left to the taxpayer's imagination.

This is what happened: it just popped up, like a cork held underwater in a washbasin. The crust of the earth floats on molten matter, and when the solid stuff gets thicker in one place than another, it presses down into the magma. What is now Steens Mountain, back when it was lying in the earth minding its own business, kept getting thicker and thicker as lava flows poured out and settled down like so much cooling boiled icing, pressing down and down. If you would imagine a whole bunch of wine corks very closely packed across the top of a bucket of water, we'll agree to call that the crust of the earth. Now, if you start packing down more corks on top of the first layer, putting thicker and thicker icing on your cake, as it were, you can mash some of the ones in the bottom layer down into the water, but only up to a point. Sooner or later the buoyancy of the cork is going to overcome the friction that's holding all the corks together as they are pressed in by the sides of the bucket. Where the layer of cork is thickest, where the ones underneath are pushed the farthest into the water, that place will pop up to relieve the pressure.

That is what makes a block-fault mountain range like the Steens. When one pops, it can stretch out the solid ground around it in a kind of rebound effect, and you get a depression in the surrounding surface. The low ground on the west side of the Steens contains Malheur and Harney Lakes, two dead-end water collectors. On the east side of the mountain are the Alvord and Whitehorse basins, a pair of sinks that are miniatures of the Great Salt Lake's Bonneville basin over in Utah, complete with salt flats in the Alvord that rival Bonneville's racetrack.

The country around the Steens has been hard going for thousands of years. The Bannock (or Paiute) Indians of the high desert were never populous and scratched out a living with more ingenuity than success. They were as fixated on their next meal as any people who ever lived. The Bannock nation was divided into small bands, and each one was named after food. A band member, for example, would be a crawfish eater, a seedeater, a salmon eater, a tuber eater, or a wild onion eater. The Bannock diet consisted of everything imaginable that grew in the desert or swam in the rivers. L. S. Cressman, the University of Oregon anthropologist who was probably more famous for being Margaret Mead's first husband than for his profound knowledge of the prehistory of Oregon, wrote: "It is known that their diet included 36 kinds of animals, about 40 varieties of birds, seven kinds of insects and their larvae and some 40 kinds of seeds—in short, anything edible." They were also cannibals and in hard winters killed the weaker and ate them.

The amount of desert it took to support human life without agriculture or animal husbandry is heartbreaking. One band, the woodchuck eaters, who never numbered more than 200, defended a foraging territory of over 5000 square miles. Cressman estimated that the entire Bannock population of eastern Oregon never amounted to more than 2.45 persons per 100 square kilometers (38 square miles). The miserable clan of woodchuck eaters averaged just about two-thirds of a person per 100 square kilometers, or not quite two-tenths of a person to the square mile. Roy's assertion that Harney County was fairly littered with arrowheads seems hard to believe when you're talking about a county whose modern boundary lines would have included no more than 650 Bannock-Paiutes at a time. But remember that we're talking about nearly two thousand years of arrowhead-losing by the Bannocks and maybe another ten thousand years of archaic Indians scattering an arrowhead or a lance point here and there across the county; and there were times, as the old dry lake beds prove, when the high desert was lusher. Twelve centuries of litter, no matter how stingily deposited, is a considerable amount of chipped stone.

As far as population goes, things haven't changed all that much. Harney County has 26 persons per 100 square kilometers, which is ten times the density of the Bannock population but still works out to less than one warm body per square mile, and half of them live in two towns—Burns, the county seat, and Hines, the town next door. If you subtract the citizens of Burns and Hines and every Bureau of Land Management employee in Harney County (and subtracting all the federal employees would tickle many of the natives), you start to get down to Bannock population densities. It is not crowded yet, and runs to fifty or sixty miles between pay phones. This sparse settlement also reduces the modern litter. A few yards off the road, a tin can is an object of surprise. Even better, human scarcity cuts down on the number of fishermen.

The rainbow trout of the Oregon desert *(Oncorhynchus mykiss gairdneri)* have the proper common name of redband rainbow trout, which does seem redundant. But most anglers who stay on the western slopes of the Cascades haven't much opportunity to catch a really colorful rainbow trout, and to their eyes the interior fish would be obviously more vivid. The native rainbows *(O. m. irideus)* of the rivers west of the Cascades are late-winter, early-spring spawners and have lost much of their breeding color by the time fishing season comes. Also, in Oregon's popular rivers, anglers catch many more hatchery trout than natives, and the hand-reared product's rainbows are hardly vivid—pale, watery, and bland is the *irido* of the hatchery trout. Hatchery trout, although they are a biological abomination, are pretty tasty. Roy's world-best fried trout are always stocked fish from the McKenzie River; the rare natives are too much fun to catch and ought not be fed to tourists.

Redband rainbows are the typical interior rainbows of the West; one form or another is scattered from northern California to the Frazer River country in British Columbia. They are an older form genetically than the later-developing coastal rainbows, and where the two mingle, as with so many related species of trout, the coastal stock wins the genetic battle and extirpates the redband rainbows. This happened historically in rivers connected to the ocean via the Columbia, long before man of any band arrived in the intermountain West. Recent government-issue hatchery rainbows, unfortunately, were modified forms of coastal rainbows and programmed to genetically annihilate all members of their genus, be they redband rainbows or cutthroat trout (*O. clarki* subspecies).

The trout in Harney County got cut off the Columbia River (and naturally invading coastal rainbows) millennia ago when lava flows made a subtle barricade around the Malheur basin. The other interior rainbows live in streams that are still connected to the ocean, but they survive above waterfalls that isolate them from invading coastal rainbows.

If it weren't for the mountains, the Steens to the southeast and the Blue Mountains to the north, the Malheur basin would be as dry as the rest of eastern Oregon. These desert ranges wring out the last bit of Pacific moisture that has gotten past the rain-making Cascades and then send it down to the marshes of Malheur and Harney Lakes. East of the Steens in the rainless shadow of the mountain, over in the Alvord basin, it is as arid as any place in America. The last native trout—rainbows on the west slope of the Steens, even rarer desert cutthroats on the east side—survive in the small dead-end rivers and brooks.

THE ROAD TO HARNEY COUNTY, WHETHER FOR AN ANGLER OR A SIGHT-seer (the overlap between those two avocations is small), is extremely contrary to the cliche that getting there is a large fraction of the fun. From Bend, in the foothills of the Cascades, to around Narrows, south of Burns, you traverse 150 miles of rolling desert punctuated with an occasional small conical mountain in the distance and no hint of any salvation over the horizon. What pretend to be towns on the road map turn out to be truck stops with a zip code. Millican, Oregon, is even smaller. It hasn't had a post office since 1953 but is still remarkable for a few things: a store, a semi-perpetual flea market on the roadside, and an abandoned house turned into a cattery. One of the flea market vendors claimed to have counted eighty-five different cats coming in and out of the windowless shack. Apparently they belonged to the storekeeper, but I did not inquire further. I avoid squalor and don't want to know any details; I dislike it even more than I do most cats.

About sixty miles east of Eighty-five Cats, U.S. 20 makes a jog around a prominent mountain, Glass Buttes, a twin-peaked saddle just south of the highway. In this case, the glass is obsidian, which the volcano of the Glass Buttes ejected in quantity and in convenient packages. If you pull over on the side of the road and slip through the barbwire fence, rounded lumps of obsidian are scattered amid the sagebrush, some on the surface, some half buried. Their exposed skins are pitted from a millennium of ultraviolet radiation and winter freezing and summer sandstorms, and the hardened globules look like desiccated cantaloupes. If you turn one over, it will almost glow with a black light. That would have been some fireworks show, blobs of red-hot molten glass from the size of golf balls to the size of soccer balls being shot so high in the air out of a volcano that they had time to cool and harden before they dropped back down to earth. I doubt anyone or anything got to see it. When Glass Buttes was earning its name, the whole countryside was exploding.

The Ancient Ones collected Glass Buttes obsidian and traded it all over the high desert. It was (and is) particularly suitable for making arrowheads and scrapers and knives; something about its formation, deposition, and cooling made it easier to work than similar stone from other places. It is mostly black but with frequent caramel brown streaks and whorls in it. The change in color implies no change at all in the physics of the material; it fractures neatly right through the bands of color. Mottled brown and black points and tools (and of course, much more frequently, chips from their manufacture) turn up hundreds of miles from Glass Buttes.

There is nothing like driving by an archaic arrowhead-material mining district to raise the spirits of a perpetually down-looking but optimistic collector. And a few miles east of Glass Buttes, when Squaw Butte off to the southeast slides out of the way, Steens Mountain starts to rise on the horizon, a low oblong rectangle in the heat haze. And this too is heartening; mountains are always oases in the desert.

Harney and Malheur Lakes, which one drives between to get to the Steens, are in a national wildlife refuge now. Harney Lake, an alkaline salt lake, is more apt to draw down toward its center in dry cycles and was a major source for arrowhead hunters before the federal government decided that hobbyists should be regulated out of existence. Picking up Indian artifacts on federal property is now universally banned. Until the 1970s, arrowhead dredging was a popular vacation activity on the lake. People would wade out into the shallows towing an inner tube or a wooden box with a piece of quarter-inch screen on the bottom. They'd shovel muck into the float and wash it down to the gravel and the arrowheads. They looked like bay scallopers with a resident's permit on Cape Cod, towing their catch behind them. There would be a difference in the speed and intensity of the raking motion—scallops have eyes and can flee; the arrowheads, though scalloped on the edges, are immobile.

There still are roads by Harney Lake where you can see arrowheads out of your car window, especially in the dry years when more lake bed is exposed. It is against the law to even stop and get out of your vehicle on these roads because the number of people who can look at an arrowhead and not pick it up is a very small fraction of the population. The arrowheads are in the lake beds for the same reason that the lakes are in a national wildlife refuge now: spring and fall, the water is a great concentrator of wildfowl, not just ducks and geese and swans but also on the margins the extremely tasty sandhill cranes. Ten thousand years of lake-lost arrows makes a noticeable sprinkle of obsidian points.

The federal government essentially owns southeastern Oregon. Private ranches, always concentrated at the few places with reliable water, have fallen one by one into the hands of the feds—the only people in the high desert who always have cash in the bank. The lakes—Malheur, Harney, and Mud—of the national wildlife refuge were taken by the government in 1908 as bird refuges to stop market gunning for flesh and feathers. Then in the Great Depression they bought the remnants of the old P Ranch from the Swift Packing Company and started taking smaller ranches in the Blitzen valley by eminent domain and by purchase at sheriff's bankruptcy auctions, adding the uplands and the waterways to the protected environment. The Malheur Refuge is about as big as it's going to be, but acquisitions by the Bureau of Land Management continue to the east and the south of the refuge.

Bit by bit, piece by piece, the Bureau of Land Management has taken almost all of Steens Mountain itself and still picks up property as it becomes available. Generally speaking, "BLM" is a swearword in eastern Oregon. When a ranch comes up for sale, it's usually because of a bankruptcy, or else it's being sold by an old rancher who hasn't made a nickel for years. Getting a bank loan to buy a ranch is a long shot out in the high desert. And, of course, the government has the cash; they get it the old-fashioned way— they print it. It got so bad that the Oregon congressional delegation jawboned a moratorium on BLM ranch purchases in Oregon—an outraged citizenry, though small in number and widely scattered, demanded it. It was not just the economics—the loss of jobs and retail sales implied by shifting from a cow economy to a tourist and bureaucrat economy—it was morality. Ranches are the secular shrines of the West; old cattle brands are the icons.

The BLM, which historically paid little attention to wildlife considerations, whether it was wild horses or desert bighorn sheep or trout, is slowly being forced into line with other agencies and now is obliged to reduce livestock damage on its property. Even the smallest amount of attention means keeping cattle out of the creek, and keeping one cow out of one creek has been regarded, in eastern Oregon, as treason.

The summer Roy Pruitt and I went to the Steens to examine the redbandedness of the local rainbow trout and the spottedness of the native cutthroats, we came down to Frenchglen from Narrows, the cut of water that links Malheur and Harney Lakes. We both noticed that the barbwire fence on the west side of the highway south of Narrows was in a state of considerable disrepair. In fact, we realized, it had been ripped up for several miles where the highway borders Diamond Valley. This was odd, because while you may occasionally see an old barbwire fence going back to ground—posts rotted and wire broken—hardly anyone ever makes an effort to demolish a fence. We speculated that the BLM had bought some more property and was removing fences between the federal holdings.

Well, we couldn't have been more wrong. The fence turned out to be the talk of Frenchglen when we got there, which means all eleven citizens knew about it. The three-wire fence was a brand-new BLM project, intended to make it easier to manage the number of cows allowed on the federal land west of Oregon 205, cattle coming out of Diamond Valley ranches. And so a couple of buckaroos (everyone knew who they were) had stolen a BLM backhoe in the middle of a moonlit night and started down the fence line, pulling up posts and knocking down the occasional rock-ringed strong backs that keep a fence good and taut. They only quit when they had so much barbed wire wrapped around the backhoe's tires that it couldn't move. The de-fence project was generally regarded as likely to make trouble but worth the effort. It was something like a barroom brawl where you punch out the deputy sheriff: not smart but temporarily satisfying.

There are only two commercial establishments in Frenchglen, a historic hotel that sleeps a dozen and a general store with a slight bias toward western souvenirs. If you drive all the way around Steens Mountain from Frenchglen to Fields Station (population also 11), there's a motel with four rooms, a cafe, a store with a gas station, and an automotive repair garage. Throw in a couple of bed-and-breakfast ranchettes and another historic hotel over in Happy Valley on the east side of the Malheur Refuge and you can see that the total tourist-oriented business environment of Steens Mountain runs to less than fifty pillows for paying guests in about 3200 square miles, which means, on any given night, tourists and bird watchers are scarcer than woodchuck-eating Paiutes ever were.

The major activity in Frenchglen is sitting on the hotel screen porch and watching the chickens cross the road. The house across the street has chickens, and the store next to the hotel has chickens, and it is in the nature of chickens to be sociable, or, if you don't like ascribing emotions to fowl, it is their nature to interact. The reading library at the Frenchglen Hotel has several field-guide bird books, and they, much to my surprise, turned out to be useful for watching chickens. Between the hotel and the store next door there is a dusty lawn used by momma chickens and baby chickens. One hen, with a brood of six chicks, was doing what mother hens are supposed to do, scratching up bugs and letting the babies eat them. She had five mottled brown-and-gray chicks and one extremely handsome black chick, with a bright yellow head and neck, that was following right behind her and snapping up small crickets and other lawn fauna. On very close inspection and upon reference to one of the field guides, the colorful chick turned out to be an adult male yellow-headed blackbird (*Xanthocephalus xanthocephalus,* which is Latinized Greek for yellow-headed yellowhead) that knew a good thing when it saw one.

The road through town, Oregon 205, averages a car every forty-five minutes during the day, but the chickens are hardly in danger. Almost no one drives through Frenchglen without stopping; it is an oasis of beer, soda pop, gasoline, and, most important, has the only pay telephone on the highway between Burns and Fields Station, a distance of a little over a hundred miles. All evening, into June's late twilight, cars and pickups arrived with young people who had a thirst for long conversations with other young people; giggles mingled with the undulating whistles of California quail hiding in the tall weeds by the old corral behind the telephone. One of the benefits of life in Harney and Malheur counties is that the entire area, save only from within the abutting towns of Burns and Hines, is regarded as a local call by the telephone company, although it could be 180 miles from phone to phone.

Before we got to Frenchglen, we stopped at a pull-off across the road from the Malheur Refuge. Roy Pruitt, who has driven trucks all over the West when he wasn't guiding fishermen and hunters and who worked on the Alaska pipeline to get his time in for a Teamsters' pension, pulls on and off roads very carefully. You can drink coffee when Roy's driving and never spill a drop. "We might find you your arrowhead," he said. "I've found them here." In fact, the location fairly smelled like arrowheads. The pull-off was at a proper ambush site. Across the road was the aboriginal marsh, and deer and antelope would have come down off the lava-rock bench above the parking spot, moving from the daytime shade of the junipers to the rich sedges along the floodplain of the Blitzen River in the cool of the evening. Game trails cut through the juniper trees on the slope between the rim-rocked bench above the highway and the marsh across the road. There is reason to think they have been there for hundreds of years.

Roy got out the driver's side and I got out mine, and then, through the side windows, I saw him bend over and disappear and then straighten up back into view. He walked around the front of the Chevrolet Suburban and held out his hand. "Like this one," he said, and passed me an arrowhead—not perfect, a little lop-sided, but made of excellent brown and black Glass Buttes obsidian. It was broadly triangular and deeply notched where it would have been tied to the arrow shaft—the typical shape of all arrowheads in logos and signage—making it a Paiute/Bannock artifact. The archaic Indian arrowhead, when we found it, would be long and narrow without ears; it would be lanceolate or leaf shaped. One finds a lot of arrowheads like the one Roy had picked up, points that don't look quite right, slightly ill-made as opposed to broken. Flint and obsidian are obstinate materials, and, one supposes, even Indians had to practice.

"Roy," I told him, "I admire a man who can drive a hundred miles and pull over at the first arrowhead."

14

Veltie's Camp

The Frenchglen Hotel is very small. You might not notice how small it is if you stay there sometime in the future, but the night Roy and I checked in it was filling up with a touring group of five couples from up around Portland, all of whom seemed to be involved in the human relations profession, employed by large corporations located in Portland and Beaverton, Oregon. I am sorry not to be more specific, but neither Roy nor I had a conversation with any of them. As a group, they were intensely bonded and continuously reinforcing the bond during the (for them, nonalcoholic) cocktail hour, the dinner hour (family style), and on into the postprandial blue hours of twilight.

Dinner is served at two long tables with benches, which ordinarily provides opportunity for conversation. Somehow, "Pass the salt, please" did not lead to further, as the other guests would put it, interpersonal communication. The interior common space at the hotel, besides the two dining tables, offered one couch and two easy chairs that they had captured before dinner and that they retook with alacrity afterward. This left the screen porch, half of which they also occupied by taking over the thousand-piece jigsaw-puzzle table and chairs, although they were not interested in continuing work on the puzzle. They were interested in their group dynamics. They were not motivated to converse with strangers.

To be fair about their appalling lack of ordinary western howdy-ness, they were in a crisis. (And there was something about the exclusiveness of the Frenchglen Historic Hotel that may have encouraged them to insularity. I do not think they could have gotten away with it at the larger and less precious Howdy Hotel in Forsythe, Montana.) They had bicycles and two rented vans, and they were taking a tour of the high desert with designated drivers and riders for each segment, with long-planned customized schedules for those who wanted to go this way and those who wanted to go that way (the number of choices is small, which apparently had made them even more significant), and one of the vans had broken down and was in Burns waiting for parts and wouldn't be ready for forty-eight hours. They kept splitting up into focus groups—in the living room, on the porch, sometimes down the road out of hearing distance of the others. The groups had volunteer mediators to help them plan how to manage a two-day, one-van safari, which would require them to, as we heard more than one of them say, reassess their recreational values and rethink their concern for the needs (not the mere wishes) of other members of the group.

Roy and I left them to their processes and drove down along the Malheur Refuge and watched the deer that had come down off the benches and out into the marsh now that the sun was almost set. There were two mule-deer bucks the size of small horses. Their antlers were in velvet, still growing but already verging on trophy size. A small flock of sandhill cranes took what amounted to a recreational flight, purling their odd call as they wheeled twice and then settled back down onto one of the mowed hay fields on the high marsh. It is a most uncranelike call, more musical than you would expect from a large and ungainly bird. It sounds more like a xylophone than a wind instrument. I have decided that if dinosaurs could sing, some of them might sound like sandhill cranes, but I have a high opinion of dinosaurs.

When we got back to the hotel and headed upstairs to bed, the tourers still hadn't managed to decide who was going to drive the van the next day, let alone to where. One began to admire the chickens in the yard, who had established a pecking order and who had a plan for the morning: they were going to cross the road and scratch for bugs.

We had our plan: drive up into the Steens to Roy's camp, which would get us about 5000 feet above the sea of mediation, facilitation, modification, and amelioration that had washed over Frenchglen. We left them at the breakfast table, still working through the problem. I believe the last words I heard as I went through the screen door were these: "We all agree we have a consensus on the process for responding to Marilyn's concerns about today's route . . . " One of the reasons that some of us become fascinated with birds, their migrations and nestings and courtships, even if we are watching nothing more exotic than chickens and blackbirds, is that we admire creatures with a sense of purpose.

THE BUREAU OF LAND MANAGEMENT HAS PENETRATED THE STEENS with a gravel scenic-loop road that attracts a few hundred automobiles a day in high season. It is a peculiar scenery: the Steens range is the only forested western mountain I know of with no pine trees. You begin in sagebrush, rise through junipers, reach aspen groves, and the next thing is tree line. We turned off the loop road near the summit of the ridge and motored across an alpine moor of short grasses and tall thistles. Although the weather was calm, you could feel the winds of yesteryear when you looked at the ground-hugging native perennial grasses and forbs punctuated only by upstart and alien thistles. The Pruitts' old hunting camp is about two miles off the loop, on the north side of Little Blitzen gorge at the end of a two-wheel track that wobbles back and forth across the fall line of the mountain, skirting outcrops of rock. Though the camp is not far, it is almost an hour's drive from the loop road to camp if you want to arrive with all the automotive underpinnings with which you started.

There were cattle in the high country, grouped in a shallow bowl north of the jeep trail where the grass, somewhat sheltered, was lusher. It was the usual modern herd, all mixed crossbreeds of the new ox-type European stock—Simmentals and Charolais and Limousin—mingled with more familiar Herefords and Black Angus. Stockmen used to pride themselves on having cows and calves that all looked exactly alike. Increasingly, hybrid vigor is preferred to purebred similarity, and a herd of range cattle is varicolored, dappled, splotched. The conformation has changed, too. Cattle are heavier in the legs and lighter in the ribs and rump than they used to be, and that translates into more pounds of low-fat hamburger and fewer pounds of marbled steaks. The antipodal forces of fast-food restaurants and low-cholesterol home cooking, working together like the opposed fields of a magnet, have combined to change the scenic qualities of a herd of cows.

I am not sure it is an improvement. A purebred herd—even if it was something as painted looking as white-faced, red-bodied Herefords or as Daumier-stark as tar black Angus—somehow looked less intrusive when you encountered them on a wild range than do these piebald bands of hybrid cattle. Although refined by man's choice, the conformity of purebreds mimicked that of nature's herds of deer or elk. The monotype cattle seemed evolved and perfected, like wild animals. One understood perfectly what their future was as individuals, but one regarded them as a species with a communal immortality. All the steak dinners in the world wouldn't drive the Hereford race into extinction. But hybrids are individuals, the result of deliberate and recent tinkering, and the killing floor will be the end of them.

The endless replication of wild things is a large measure of their fascination to human beings. If you stand in downtown West Yellowstone, Montana, there is nothing that greets your eye as it once greeted Jim Bridger's or George Custer's or your own eye of forty years ago. But cross into Yellowstone Park and the first buffalo you see will be exactly like the last one Bill Cody killed. For those few of us who fish, the same thing happens, only sometimes we also eat what Isaak Walton ate. I am as fond of Jersey cows, soft brown with a characteristic dark stripe down their back, as I am of elk. I milked Jerseys once. We are all fond of things that have not changed and will not.

As if summoned to illustrate that point, a buck antelope appeared on the crest of the hill in front of us, looking exactly like every other buck antelope in North America, save only the inevitable variation in size. And for all the talk of trophies that hunters make, that difference is a few pounds in weight and an inch or two in the length of the animal's horns. The buck moved calmly, as game animals will do when it's not hunting season, watching our automobile but not letting us hurry it, even pausing to scratch the side of its head with a rear hoof, like a dog. This is normal for antelope (and their cousins, domestic goats). Then it did something that Roy, who has been watching antelope for more than fifty years, had never seen. It stepped up to one of the tall (and exotic) thistles that had managed, like thistles everywhere, to grow on the disturbed ground where the ruts of the road had cut through the alpine sod, and very slowly and very delicately the buck used the spiny seed head to scratch himself under his chin. "I'll be darned," Roy said. "I didn't know thistles were good for anything. Usually, I see one growing right by the road, I'll run over it and mash it down. I think I'll stop doing that, what with them having some use in life."

Roy's camp is hidden in an aspen grove on the very edge of Little Blitzen gorge, and the Bureau of Land Management now owns the property. Roy's father, Veltie Pruitt, began trekking from the McKenzie River to the Steens in 1936. Veltie was a minister, and, borne down by the troubles in his congregation (the Depression was a great breaker of spirits), he suffered a brief psychological and physical collapse, gave up the ministry, and turned to full-time guiding: boating and fishing in the spring and summer, hunting in the fall. It was a living. One of the things about the guide business is you always feed off customers who live near the top of the economic pyramid, and depressions and recessions tend to chew at the bottom first and longest.

Roy ran a camp for teenage girls in the Steens for a score of summers ("Girls and horseback riding, that's the easiest camp to run and the happiest campers in the world") in the 1960s and 1970s. Now his trips back to the Steens are largely to put things in order; the old cookhouse has been torn down and burnt, the barbed-wire horse corral has been dismantled and bundled up to be hauled away. He hopes the BLM will save the cabin, but he doesn't know.

So, lest everyone forget, he arranged to have a plaque installed on a boulder that fronts the rim of the gorge. It reads:

IN MEMORY OF
VELTIE AND INA PRUITT
STEENS MOUNTAIN 1936–1980

Veltie's camps, pack trips and hunting parties provided exciting opportunities for hundreds to experience the making of memories of the Steens. Ina, with the stroke of her brush, captured God's wonders and made it possible for many to bring the beauty of the area into their homes.

This overlook, which Veltie called "The Lookout," was their favorite place to bring first-time visitors for a view of the area. Ina painted several canvases at this spot.

In April, 1991, they died in Eugene, Ore., at the ages of 91 and 85. Their ashes have been scattered by horseback from this point over the ridges and aspen draws to the Northwest.

Their love for this mountain, with its birds, fish, game and flora and with its breathtaking beauty and solitude, prompted family and friends to place this plaque in their honor.

Placed in cooperation with Bureau of Land Management.

Roy had blocked off the tire-rutted trail to the plaque by rolling some big lava boulders across it. Since last he was there, someone had pushed them out of the way, making it possible to drive up and read the plaque and look at the view through the windshield without getting out of the vehicle. We spent a few minutes humping the rocks back in place.

The Little Blitzen gorge, from the Lookout, is almost 4000 feet straight down, a wide, arc-sided gouge with all the classic features of a glacial valley. At the very bottom, Little Blitzen River has barely deepened it at all; the gorge is the work of ice, back there in the Pleistocene when woolly mammoths roamed Harney County and the dry lakes were full of water and the trout swam in the lakes and spawned in the glacial runoff streams. Across the gorge and toward its head are cross-valleys that stop abruptly, hanging valleys where the big glacier had cut across the smaller tributary ice. We talked and read the words and watched a golden eagle soaring up the far side of the gorge, catching the updraft of the hot desert air bubbling toward the sky. Ina Pruitt's paintings are better than photographs for capturing the immensity of the bowl-shaped gorge; something gets lost in the best of cameras when the three dimensions are optically flattened into the negative.

Older Westerners will remember the Lee Riders magazine advertisements of the fifties and sixties, realist paintings of small-town rodeos, chuck-wagon meals, branding crews, and broncobusters in working corrals. Everyone, of course, wore a pair of Lee blue jeans. Those were Ina's paintings, and quite fine down to every last authentic detail, as good for cowboys as Catlin was for Indians, but not intended to be art. The Steens Mountain paintings, well, they are no mere representations; they could not be painted from photographs any more than a Monet haystack or a Cézanne Mont Sainte-Victoire could be. They look (I have seen two) like Little Blitzen gorge feels; you can hear the aspen leaves rustle and the eagle scream. That may not be art back East, but it'll do out here.

THE LITTLE BLITZEN RIVER WAS BARELY VISIBLE THREE-QUARTERS OF a mile downhill, which raised the question of fishing in my mind. I reminded Roy that we had come to take a look at the redband rainbow trout of the Blitzen drainage and it looked like a long walk to the fishing. Not only long but one-way. There was no possibility that I could make it down the trail and back up in the afternoon that lay in front of us. I should have known; he had a plan. That afternoon we would hike over to Fish Creek (an inspiring piece of nomenclature) and fish that small stream where it made up out of some springs by an old homestead. The next day we'd finish the loop road and stop at the Riddle Ranch and fish the Little Blitzen at the bottom of the gorge. As a matter of fact, we had an appointment to be at the Riddle Ranch gate at 11 A.M., and someone would be there to unlock it and let us in.

Fish Creek, Roy thought, had the purest and reddest of rainbows. It was so high in the Steens, so far above any possible influence of stocked trout, that its fish would be perfectly pure. The redbanded trout in the Blitzen River, he said, got purer and brighter as you went upstream; they were redder in the tributary Little Blitzen than the main stream, and as you hiked into the Little Blitzen gorge, he added, pointing down from the lookout, they got brighter still.

A mountain-stream fishing expedition requires little in the way of equipment. We set off for Fish Creek with one tapered monofilament fly leader, a pocket knife, and a small box of trout flies. When we got there, we were going to cut a willow branch, strip the leaves, lash the leader on the thin end, tie on a fly, and catch a trout. Imagine how that would translate into a fly-fishing article in one of the sporting journals:

> We were perfectly equipped with a seven-and-one-half-foot Cortland 4X knotless tapered leader, our trusty Buck model 525 single-bladed self-locking stainless steel pocket knife, a handcrafted one-piece osier-wood rod of recent manufacture, and a careful selection of terrestrial- and aquatic-insect imitative dry flies, including two Joe's Hopper on no. 12, two extra-long model perfect hooks, three elk-hair caddis, size 16. . . .

What we had was sufficient unto the trout.

We also had cows when we got to the creek. It is very important, in eastern Oregon, to speak well of cows. "That's what this country's all about," Roy said with a proprietary wave at the muley-looking bunch that was drifting away from us, headed downstream. They were confirmed range cows and they well understood that things on two feet were not friends. Cattle don't know much, but they remember branding, dehorning, and castrating, all deeds that are perpetrated by people that looked like us—bipeds in blue jeans.

The creek, which was picking up some little spring flows as we went down the canyon, wasn't big enough to fish until we came out of the aspens into a clearing. The reason for the clearing had something to do with the soil changing, I suppose, and something to do with the beaver dam. It was a low and narrow dam with a small pool above it, much too small to build a lodge in. It was more of a beaver lunch stop than a beaver colony.

I cut the ceremonial willow stick and stripped the leaves off it, wrapped the butt end of the leader around the tip a few times, and threw some hitches over the whole mess. A trout rose a couple of times while we rigged up, and I said I would catch that one, and Roy said he would walk down the creek and scout out a bigger hole and a bigger fish. We picked out a fly, I tied it on, and he went off downstream saying he would stop at the next good place to fish and wait for me.

This fishing with a willow stick was, to be honest, just one more way that fly fishermen have to show off. It would have been a lot easier with a store-bought outfit, because with a line to cast you can stand back from a beaver pond—below the dam is the best place—and be completely out of sight and, to the extent they have one, out of mind of the fish. A floppy willow stem and a short leader limits casts to somewhere around ten feet, so you become a stalker of fish, creeping around, skulking in the willows, less of a gentleman, more of a guerrilla.

Not that there isn't skill to it. I crept up to the dam, and the trout was still rising every few minutes to something too small to see (too small for me to see), probably midges, maybe floating mosquito larvae. That would be a problem if you were fishing for trout in the flatland world of rich rivers and fat fish. Down on the plains, when a trout eats midges, it eats them all the time, and you have to put on a midge-size fly about the size and shape of the next capital letter in this book. Up in the mountains, where the growing season is brief and the pure water is short of nutrients to feed invertebrates, trout eat whatever they see, and so I tossed it a medium-size elk-hair caddis-fly imitation. It would have worked the first time except that I forgot how floppy willow rods are, and when I stopped the forward motion of the cast, the willow kept on bending and slapped into the water. There is a limit to what even a mountain trout will stand for, and I had gone over it.

One of the appealing qualities of trout everywhere is that they have very brief anxiety attacks. On average, as I have mentioned, between five and ten minutes after you scare the living slime off a trout it will come back to the same place and start feeding again. This one, being young and foolish and naive and very likely never fished for in its life, came back down near the dam in less than five minutes and rose again, and I slapped the water with the rod the second time, which reminded me that some anglers have memories as short as some fish. Twice frightened, the trout took the full five minutes to return and then ate the caddis fly as soon as I managed to flip it gently onto the surface of the pool. It was true, the Steens had the reddest rainbowed trout in the whole world of my experience. I took its picture and put it back in the pool and started on downstream.

The creek below the beaver dam looked awful. The herd of critters had fled away from us, but you didn't need a degree in wildlife biology to tell there had been cattle in the area. The banks were mashed; the willows were chewed; the water was dirty. I met Roy coming back upstream. "Damn cows," he explained. Roy hardly ever swears.

"Things," Roy promised, "will be better down at the Riddle Ranch."

The sad thing about it all is this: if ranchers hired buckaroos and moved those cattle out of the creek and got them up and grazing in the high meadows and took them to water when they needed it, they'd do better, put on more weight, sell for more money. But beef is cheap and help is hard to find and harder to keep.

What we were looking at, Roy and I, was a little corner of the process of extinction. There are enough redband rainbow trout around that the species won't go belly-up, but here was a whole drainage that was down to one lonely trout in one small pond behind one low beaver dam. If the cows chew on the riverbank for a few more years, that's the end of it.

We went back to camp and baked the best sourdough biscuits in North America and fried some steaks and browned some potatoes. All of this was made much easier because Shelly Pruitt, Roy's calm and amicable wife, had spent the day getting the camp in apple pie order. Indeed, while Roy and I were basking in the charms of the Frenchglen Hotel, she had driven up and stayed overnight alone, partly for the fun of it and partly to have everything up and running when we arrived.

I have no tendencies at all in the vegetarian direction and try to avoid all feelings of vengeance while eating; it does nothing for the digestion. The only thing I regretted about the steaks was that they hadn't been cut off one of the cows we'd seen earlier. "But," I hear the chiding voice of the vegetarian reader argue, "if we would all stop eating meat, we wouldn't have cattle in our trout streams." Sure, and when ifs and buts are candy and nuts we'll all have a hell of a Christmas.

It was just another piece of federal running water that needed some cowboys to go with the cows, but those cattle had been driven up there as soon as the snow melted and wouldn't see a man on horseback until the fall. They were going to sit on that stream like flies on flop and eat it down to the mud. They weren't going to overgraze the range, just gobble up the good part.

I was glad we only planned to spend one night on the mountain. I'd already caught the last handy trout on top, and it had to be better down on the Little Blitzen. The one thing I had noticed while we were at the overlook glassing the canyon, looking for birds and game animals, was the blessed lack of livestock down in the gorge.

15

Wild Horses

Aꜰᴛᴇʀ ʙʀᴇᴀᴋɪɴɢ ᴄᴀᴍᴘ ɪɴ ᴛʜᴇ ᴍᴏʀɴɪɴɢ, ᴡᴇ ᴄᴏɴᴛɪɴᴜᴇᴅ ꜱᴏᴜᴛʜ and west along the Steens loop road, skirting the upper edge of Little Blitzen gorge. In the low morning light, the west-facing gorge was dark and indistinct in detail. A mile or so south of the head of the canyon, we stopped and hiked a few hundred yards up the scree slope away from the gorge toward the edge of the mountain. As I said, there is no particular peakedness to the Steens Range. It has a highest point, a piece of rock that sticks up a bit above the surrounding terrain on the rim of the mountain, but that is a land surveyor's summit, not one that would be obvious to the human eye. But if the highest ground is a matter of subtle measurement, the edge of the mountain is an obvious fact.

I am not fond of high places. If a group I am with wants a photograph taken with their heels on the edge of a cliff, I volunteer to run the camera. Fear of heights is not necessarily a phobia; in my case it is just an excess of imaginative power combined with average human clumsiness. When obliged to go high, and for many summers and a couple of full years I worked in commercial construction, I lost (I never conquered) my fear after a week or so. The imagination ran dry, stifled by the daily ordinariness of being a hundred feet off the ground on a foot-wide beam.

As usual, I stopped several feet short of the knife-edge and left the straight-down view to Roy. To the south, the edge of the mountain curved out to where it could be seen from my position, and it was essentially vertical for the first 500 feet and steeply pitched for the next 4000 feet down to the Alvord basin. The edge of the block fault had, it appeared, once been vertical all the way to the basin below. The steep pitch was clearly all eroded rubble below the perpendicular solid rock. One useful human talent is the ability to make analogies, and I concluded that the face of the mountain in front of me was comparable to the mountain south of me and let it go at that. I was close enough to the edge to see the entire dry lake bed below us. For a moment there was a glint of sunlight on the windshield of a vehicle moving south along the road between the Steens and Alvord Dry Lake. We would be on that road tomorrow; there was no need to get closer to it.

Another mile down the loop road we came to a side road that went toward the technical summit of Steens Mountain and also to a turnaround that gave a view down Wildhorse Canyon. Several tourists were out walking, scattered along the trail to the summit and the path down to the Wildhorse Canyon overlook. There were five cars parked along this side road, and in three of them a single woman sat on the passenger side of the front seat, all three women staring straight ahead. They were pressed right up against the door, and I think one of them, from the position of her shoulders, was holding on to the door handle with both hands. This seemed odd, even to an acrophobe like me, because the cars were parked a considerable distance from the edge of the mountain or from the top of Wildhorse Canyon.

I began to understand when we left the summit and started down the last leg of the loop road to the Riddle Ranch. No one had passed us on the loop road where we had stopped to look down over the Alvord Desert, so the vehicles at the summit turnoff had come up the other way, counterclockwise around the loop. That made logistical sense; that end of the loop was the closest to Frenchglen. First we moved along the south side of Little Blitzen gorge in the direction from which the other cars had come, driving parallel to the Pruitt's camp across the gorge, and then we ran out of real estate. The only way off the mountain was down a knife-edge that separated the Little Blitzen gorge from Indian Creek canyon, and for the next several miles the Indian Creek gorge was on Roy's side. As I said, Roy is an excellent driver. The only problem that day was that we were going through old deer-hunting country and he had vivid recollections of every place where someone had killed a large mule deer. Memory, of course, requires expression and gesture, and every hairpin turn and yawning abyss seemed to be adjacent to some recollected trophy site on the uphill side of the road. So we motored slowly down the grade, with Roy occasionally checking the road ahead and, more often than seemed necessary, ignoring the unguarded shoulder of road that perched between us and perdition as he pointed to some long-dead buck's last bed. I understood why the women up by the summit were terrified: for most of their trip up the loop road, they would have been able to see nothing out of their passenger-side window but the airspace of Indian Creek canyon on their right.

The Riddle Ranch, when we visited it, was still managed as private property, although the Bureau of Land Management had just purchased it, leaving it in the owner's possession for what is accurately if morbidly called life tenancy. Shortly it will pass into BLM control, and you will be able to visit it without waiting for someone to come out and unlock the gate. It wasn't ever a big ranch, just about the right size to run a very nice dude operation, as Roy remarked more than once on our trip. Unfortunately, the BLM as always could outbid anyone who intended to make money and pay taxes. The Riddle was the last ranch the BLM bought before the temporary moratorium on land acquisition went into force. It does nicely round out their Steens Mountain property—everything inside the Loop Road is theirs now.

While we were waiting at the gate, a little bit of western history showed up to entertain us. Three wild horses, a pinto, a chestnut with a white blaze on its nose, and a roan, came trotting out of the junipers at the base of the mountain and crossed the ranch road a few hundred yards behind us, back toward the loop road. Roy took an immediate liking to the pinto; it had something to do with the rear end of the horse, a subtlety in the conformation that was not obvious to this untrained eye. The wild horses, like everything else, belong to the BLM, but if you acquire one discreetly no one makes much fuss about it. These three, we heard later, were ones that the BLM had missed when they'd taken a small herd out of the Little Blitzen the week before. The government has an active adopt-a-horse program in the West, although it frequently turns into a can-a-horse result.

Glen Davis, the sole surviving buckaroo of the Riddle Ranch, showed up at the gate in time to see the three ponies before they slipped on into another stand of junipers. He was less enthusiastic than Roy about catching one of the wild horses, in part because he already had two horses too many. One of them, he explained later, won't work until it's tried to buck him off; the other one's just as mean but too old to buck or work. I found out about the rank horses when we were walking around the Riddle corral and Glen offered me $10 if I'd ride his bay. I don't think he would have let me get on it, liability laws or the western equivalent—a natural human urge for revenge—being what they are, but he might have. Generally speaking, you should look any gift horse ride in the mouth from a safe distance if there's a $10 offer included. I fished around in my jeans and found two fives in the change and said I'd give him the ten bucks if he'd ride it first, which was when the truth came out.

Roy went into the house to say hello to Mrs. Clemens, the ranch owner, and surely he was going to rag her a little about selling out to the BLM. That was not a conversation I wanted to overhear. Catching a redband rainbow, even if the BLM did own the creek, seemed like a finer way to spend the afternoon. The Little Blitzen is exactly the right size—big enough for a real fish, small enough to wade across anywhere but in a deep pool. Just a few hundred yards upstream from the corral there is a sharp S bend in the creek with a deep hole on the upstream bend where the bank is undercut. Deep, in this case, means over your knees.

There are two ways to fish a place like that with a fly: one is right tight against the bank where the friction of the bank slows the current down to where a trout can rest, and the other is to run a fly down the slower water on the other side of the main flow. If you fish the undercut side, it's better to get on that side and just hang a fly down on the surface close to the bank and let it drift along while you stay well back and out of sight of the fish. Unfortunately, that means out of sight of your fly. If you can't see a fish come up and take the fly, you might as well put on a garden worm and be done with it. It is more fun to fish from downstream up into the slower water on your side of the main current because you get to see everything happen.

I squatted down on the gravel bar below the pool and frog-walked up until I could see exactly where the current on my side was the right speed for the biggest trout in the pool. Trout are like any animal, territorial and stuck in their own place in the pecking order. The big trout gets the best place to balance energy expended with food gathered. When water is as clear as the Little Blitzen it's sometimes deceptively deep. More than one tourist has discovered that just because you can see the rocks on the bottom, that doesn't mean it won't come up to your armpits when you step in. But it couldn't have been more than a foot deep where I wanted to float the fly. I had just reasoned all this out and decided how to fish the pool when Roy showed up on the far bank. He walked right up to the edge of the cutbank and pointed at the slower water on my side of the pool and said, "Trout like a place like that, right there in the slack." Walking up to the bank and pointing and talking is something that, in a hard-fished river, would bring considerable reaction from both trout and angler. One would flee; the other would complain.

I cast a little upstream of the place Roy was pointing at, and the fly came sliding down with the current to where the creek slackened and deepened. That is not much cover for a trout, and I was surprised even more than I was pleased when the floating fly disappeared in what looked like a large mouth. The trout was less pleased and more surprised when I set the hook. It came downstream a few feet toward me, creating slack in the leader and line, and then turned upstream, gathered speed, and jumped. I was still squatting when it came out of the water and for a moment it was as high as my head, two or three body lengths out of the water, above my eye level and above the far bank. It was the first time in my life I ever saw a jumping trout against the sky. In hand, before I slipped the hook out and put it back, it was a fourteen-inch fish, solid and deep and out of proportion to the size of the stream.

"Roy," I asked, "do they get much bigger up here?" He thought not often. "In that case," I said, "I think we'll call it a day." Given a choice between catching smaller fish and quitting while I'm the champ, I'll go look for arrowheads.

WHEN I AM HOME IN MASSACHUSETTS, I OCCASIONALLY LOOK FOR ARrow points or stone tools. Conservatively, a fair estimate of miles walked to artifacts found in the East would be on the order of a thousand to one. My loot, after twenty-five years in Massachusetts, consists of one crudely made arrowhead, probably abandoned as a bad job; a fine stone maul head, polished and grooved so it could be hafted securely; and two-thirds of a trough-shaped grinding stone from a Cape Cod beach. The last was as obvious as a white pigeon in a parking lot. It was the only piece of pink stone on a beach shingled with common gray granite rocks.

Henry David Thoreau acquired dozens of arrowheads in his lifetime, and not just because he averaged twenty miles a day for decades. In his time, our neighborhood (I live a mile from Walden Pond) was mostly farmland and pasture, much of it regularly plowed. Today what hasn't been paved or built upon is second-growth forest or hay field, and those are hard places to find worked stone. Henry had a great advantage over us; he was less than a century away from the Indians, and the additional 150 years of rain and leaf litter since he walked through Lincoln and Concord has been a great undertaker of manufactured debris. Ordinary modern human artifacts, beer bottles, bricks, barbed wire—disappear under the leaf mold within a few years.

Eight years ago, as part of a paleoanthropology course I was taking at Harvard, I made a few simple stone tools. (As a manufacturer, I am no further advanced than Peking Man most of the time, with occasional forays into Neandertal technology. I did not take honors in Neolithic arrowheads). Last summer, digging in my garden, I turned up an excellent scraper, a stone tool made out of a flake by serrating the edge with a series of scalloped retouchings.

Scrapers are one of the oldest of stone tools, and the longest-lived form—common everywhere in the world, left by humans who lived well over a million years ago and up until the moment of contact between stone technology and introduced metal tools. They are seldom found together with points; a scraper is a household tool, the arrowhead an expeditionary armament. Occasionally, though, just to prove that scrapers and more technically complicated arrow points overlap in time, one finds a snapped-in-half arrowhead with the fractured end retouched to make it over into a useful scraper. Some collectors look at these and imagine that the Indians made blunts to shoot and stun animals without tearing their skin. That is a pretty fallacy. I have one of these re-manufactured arrow points picked up in Oklahoma, and I admire it; it bespeaks a certain thriftiness and flexibility. I am pleased to know that recycling is an ancient human trait.

On closer inspection, after I washed it under the tap, the scraper from my garden looked familiar. The year I was taking the anthropology course, a friend had brought me some flint nodules from his family home in Oklahoma. They had a characteristic caramel-colored swirl in the dark brown stone, as did the tool in my hand. It was I who had made the scraper buried in my loam, I who had tossed it away. The undermining worms and the overlying mouldering leaves had taken just a dog's life to bury it.

In a desert, what little vegetation falls to ground is more likely to dry up and blow away in a dust storm than it is to stay in one place long enough to build new soil. If you have any eye for it at all, and particularly in a gray-brown desert like Harney County where most of the stone tools are made from shimmering black obsidian, the amount of Indian detritus is astonishing. After the Civil War, a young West Point graduate by the imposing name of Charles Erskine Scott Wood campaigned twice through Harney County during the Bannock disturbances in the late 1860s and 1870s. Wood was the first traveler, to my knowledge, to comment on the frequency of artifacts and flakes littering the landscape. He would become a popular writer in his own middle age, author of a curious perennial pre–World War II best-seller, *Heavenly Discourses,* which was exactly that, imaginary dialogues between

Socrates, Saint Augustine, Napoleon, and a host of similar ghosts.

C. E. S. Wood should be famous as a ghost writer. As an aide to general O. O. Howard (the famous "Christian general" of the western Indian wars), Wood trekked from Walla Walla, Washington, to Chinook, Montana, in pursuit of Chief Joseph, the Nez Perce leader. When Joseph surrendered in the Bear Paw mountains south of Chinook, a page was written into the history books by either C. E. S. Wood or Chief Joseph, depending on what you would prefer to believe. Two of General Howard's Nez Perce scouts (tribal disunity would come as no surprise to Howard or any veteran of the Civil War), Old George and Captain John, and a hired interpreter, Joseph Chapman, visited Chief Joseph's camp on the morning of October 5, 1877, and returned with some account of the great leader's emotions. By midafternoon, Charles Erskine Scott Wood, as aide-de-camp and official command historian, had rendered the various remarks into that famous speech:

> Tell General Howard I know his heart. . . . I am tired of fighting. Our chiefs are all dead. . . . It is cold and we have no blankets. The little children are freezing to death. My people, some of them, have run away to the hills, and have no blankets, no food. No one knows where they are—perhaps freezing to death. I want to have time to look for my children, and see how many of them I can find. May be I shall find them among the dead. Hear me, my chiefs! I am tired. My heart is sick and sad. From where the sun now stands I will fight no more forever.

Besides being an accomplished rewrite man, Wood was also a poet and years later worked his early memory of the Malheur country into a volume of verse, *The Poet in the Desert*. Anyone scouting Indian territory in a war situation is likely to be a close observer of native artifacts, even if the Bannocks had largely converted from stone to metal tools and weapons by the 1860s. The quantity of debris flakes (*débitage* is the technical term, from the

French) created while working flint or obsidian is substantial, approaching the ratio of mine tailings to ore. What Wood saw in the 1860s and 1870s is exactly what you will see tomorrow, walking across the rolling land by the Little Blitzen:

> *The ground with fragments is strewn,*
> *Just as they dropped them,*
> *The strokes of the makers undimmed*
> *Through the dumb and desperate years;*
> *But the hunters have gone forever.*

We picked up and then dropped hundreds of pieces of Glass Butte obsidian in a two-hour stroll just south of, and within hearing of, the rushing water of Little Blitzen. The temptation to walk toward the river was mild; as I get older, the sound of running water is often sufficient. The only finished artifact we found was also black and shiny—a Rayovac Workhorse plastic flashlight that someone had dropped under a juniper tree. It was no less obvious than the fragments, although it had not been there as long—the batteries were still charged.

The Blitzen River actually has a longer handle, now spelled Donner und Blitzen, although when it was named during a cavalry expedition against the Indians in 1864, the nominator remembered his German less accurately. After fording it a little downstream of the Riddle Ranch during a violent July thunderstorm, Col. George Currey called it the *Dunder und Blitzen*, thunder and lightning. It has always been a popular fishing spot. During the 1878-79 Bannock uprising that brought C. E. S. Wood back to the Steens, the main victims of the Bannocks were trout fishermen. A pair of anglers, whose names are not recorded in any source I have been able to find, were killed in June 1878. Then, on July 14 of that year, "the Paiutes killed Tom Dixon and a man named Harrison, who were fishing in the Blitzen River." Nonanglers will not understand why otherwise sensible people go trout fishing in the middle of an Indian conflict. On the other hand, they probably do not understand why we fly-fish in peacetime.

The only hostiles today are the rattlesnakes that hang around the Blitzen waiting for small mammals to come down for a drink. People who do not like snakes do not fish the Blitzen canyon below the Riddle Ranch. The problem with canyons and steep slopes, in case the reader is not familiar with rattlesnakes, is that we humans tend to surprise snakes when we are moving along steep terrain, and a surprised rattler is a problem. We slip down rock slides, climb back up with handholds, step over logs, and hop down from boulders. On level ground, you really have to work at it—be a bit of a fool—to get snakebit. Clambering up and down, the wisest can be struck. There is no sound more alarming than a snake's rattle by your boots, except one. It is much worse when you hear it at your own ear level. I have better luck with arrowheads than with rattlesnakes; except for carcasses (where I'm from in Montana, they are by far the most frequent roadkill), I haven't seen a rattler in the last dozen years. I've only heard but one or two and think one of them was likely a grasshopper tintinnabulating.

Toward midafternoon we headed on to Frenchglen. The bicycle tourers were gone; the new hotel guests were amicable; the old yellow-headed blackbird was still poaching crickets from the scratching mother hen and her chicks by the store; the beer in the store was cold—all was right with the world. In the morning, we would circle around Steens Mountain to the north end of the Alvord Desert and look for two things, aboriginal cutthroat trout and archaic Indian artifacts.

After dinner, a few local friends of Roy Pruitt stopped by the hotel to commiserate on several subjects having to do with the federal government in general and the national wildlife refuge in particular. There had been what amounted to an act of desecration that week. An old P Ranch juniper-wood corral next to the highway had been taken down by the refuge. The corral hadn't been used for half a century, but that wasn't the point.

"They just cut it up with chain saws, Roy," one of the visitors clucked. "Just cut it up and threw it in a pile."

It didn't make any sense to me, either. There is no antiquities law for buckaroo artifacts, but that doesn't mean you have to obliterate them. I suppose the corral amounted to something of an attractive nuisance. Somebody might want to trespass and look for horseshoe nails or sit on the fence and imagine the past. That someone might fall off the top rail and sue the refuge.

"I don't understand it," the visitor concluded. "It wasn't bothering anything."

We drove by it on the way to the Alvord in the morning, a heap of juniper posts and rails cut up in short lengths. The saw had cut through decades of desert bleaching to the bright heartwood of the logs, and the unweathered butt ends glowed in the low morning light. I expect they have burned it by now; another page, as my Montana friend Joey Caton would say, ripped out of the history book.

16

Bullbats and Beer

THE ROAD TO THE ALVORD DRY LAKE FROM FRENCHGLEN TAKES you up along the well-watered Malheur Refuge to Narrows, where once a blown-sand reef separated Malheur Lake from Harney Lake. Now a slowly moving irregular waterway connects the two vast reed-edged dead seas. We are always ignorant of the exact moment when two separate bodies of water are joined unless there has been human interference. In the early summer of 1881, a P Ranch buckaroo by the name of Martin Brenton was standing on the sand that formed the westernmost edge of Malheur Lake. It had been a wet year, and the lake was brimful. The human urge to join waters is not restricted to great deeds, to Panamas and Eries. Brenton kicked at the sand where the lake lapped at the shore and the water began to run west to Harney Lake. Except in the driest of years, they have been connected ever since.

From Narrows, a gravel road cuts due east below Malheur Lake and picks up pavement again at a junction with Oregon Highway 78 just south of New Princeton, a town that consists entirely of a closed gas station and an open barroom. For most of that drive, you will not be out of sight of agriculture; it is good hay country where the wells reach down to the Malheur aquifer and bring up water for the alfalfa fields. But heading south now, the highway tucks in behind the Steens range and climbs to a pass that separates the better-watered Malheur valley from the rainless land behind the mountains.

This is the smallest of divides and yet as important for life in the desert as the Continental Divide that separated Lewis and Clark's salmon-bearing rivers from the headwaters of the Missouri. The pass separates two dead seas: Harney/Malheur to the west, Alvord/Whitehorse to the east. In the deserts of the West, travelers are well advised to pay attention to such small details.

As you top over the pass, the mountains you see to the north, the Sheepsheads, have that peculiar barrenness that only comes with extreme winter cold and summer drought. There is no softness, not a hint of visible vegetation on the distant slopes, not even a lonely cottonwood in the dry washes.

A few miles southeast of the pass, a solitary gravel road bends off due south, heading into the drought shadow of the east scarp of the Steens. To take it means sixty miles of no services, no rest stops, no camp grounds, nowhere to spend money until you get to Fields Station well south of the Steens. It is not uninhabited. Four ranches—from north to south, Juniper Lake, Mann Lake, Alvord, and Wildhorse—are scattered between New Princeton and Fields. (There is an alleged town of Andrews on the map, a town in name only, not even a truck stop anymore.) The ranches prosper on snowmelt from the Steens and the few springs that run counter to the grain of the block fault and emerge to make up into small persistent streams.

What one is unprepared for, even after viewing it from the top of the Steens, is the vastness of the Alvord Dry Lake. As the road descends toward it, it begins to fill the twentieth-century viewing screen, the car windshield, from side to side. It is wide enough, over twenty miles, and long enough, nearly fifty, that it has its own horizon: like the sea viewed from a beach, it is visibly curved. A vehicle crossing it, like a ship at sea, will drop below the Alvord's horizon.

A series of smaller dry lakes precede it, first Tencent Lake and then Fifteen Cent Lake, which are, one supposes, a settler's estimate of their worth. Heading on south, we pulled over at Juniper Lake, where Roy was sufficiently acquainted at the ranch to trespass, and walked down to the lake bed over two successive ancient shores. The ground, although sagebrush covered, revealed old flat berms caused by waves. The country smelled like arrowheads.

Between the sagebrush, black and dark brown flakes of obsidian were scattered with almost the frequency of ordinary pebbles. The bed of the dry lake started abruptly at the edge of the second gravel bench. The lake bed was solid white with alkali, the surface cracked into the classic irregular three- to five-sided patterns of dried mud everywhere. A hundred feet out into the lake there was a cluster of heavy obsidian flakes sitting up on the surface of the white lake bed. One almost expected to see the footprints of the maker next to them, so fresh they looked, so recent. Who could count? Was it two hundred or two thousand years or deeper back into the archaic past when one hand held the obsidian core and and the other struck with a stone or antler hammer? In whatever time, why had they not sunk into the mud in a wet year? Roy was moving back and forth along the ancient beach, studying the ground between the sage, occasionally bending down to pick up a flake or perhaps an arrowhead. Roy is one of the few people I know who can pick up an arrowhead without a whoop of pleasure and surprise, so I had no idea what he was finding.

We had nothing much to do that day except find Mosquito Creek or Pike Creek (more likely named for the explorer than the fish; there are no pike west of the Rocky Mountains) and see if, by any chance, the presumably extinct Alvord cutthroat trout were in it. There were odd-looking cutthroat in the creeks; we had that piece of intelligence to work with. Also, a retired Oregon fisheries biologist, a friend of Roy's, had confided to him that Pike and Mosquito Creeks had "never been stocked." Being close to the creeks and in no hurry, I walked out toward the center of the Juniper Dry Lake, meandering back and forth, looking for something in the artifact line of work.

It was lying there, not exactly as if it had been dropped yesterday, but fully visible. It was very black and only dusted with an unconcealing film of alkali: a perfect arrowhead, small, thin, finely

236
worked, and ancient. The oldest arrow points found in the West are all of the same pattern but vary in dimension: they are the shape of willow leaves without the relatively modern Neolithic ears to use as convenient ways to lash them to the shaft. Instead of notching the points, the Old Ones carefully thinned the blade's rounded rear end and then slipped it into a slot in the shaft and bound it down with animal sinew. This style of point dates back to the last ice age in North America and mimics precisely even more ancient material from Siberia. Some have been found out West in the belly ribs of woolly mammoths and archaic buffalo, kills dated back to twelve thousand years before the present. The one in my hand was not so large as those, which would have been mounted on lances. This was a true arrow point, light, delicate, perfectly straight along its length and symmetrical in cross section. One assumes a bird was the target, given the site where it was lost, although such small points will easily pierce deerhide or sheepskin. Date it as you will, it had been at least two thousand years, as much as twelve thousand, since it was shot and left in the old water. And it was still sitting on the surface of the dry lake bed. It was a promising beginning. If the arrowhead was in hand, could the Alvord cutthroat trout be far behind?

THERE ARE TWO VAST BASINS EAST OF THE STEENS RANGE: ALVORD directly below the mountain and the Whitehorse, or Coyote, basin to the south and east. The Alvord is flat; the Whitehorse is as large, but more rolling and broken. Historically, and within living memory, each basin had a subspecies of cutthroat trout peculiar to it. They were offshoots of the Lahontan cutthroat *(O. clarki henshawi)*, and survived in tiny headwaters high in, of all places, the Trout Creek Mountains, a smaller east-west range south of the Steens. At this writing, the Alvord cutthroat is presumably extinct, having had the misfortune to encounter the gregarious and prolific stocked rainbow trout in all its waters except, of course, those waters from which cows had already evicted it. The Whitehorse trout may be alive in their aboriginal streams, although those headwaters were so badly overgrazed by lessees of the Bureau of Land Management (an oxymoron to rival "military intelligence") that survival is problematic at best.

What we knew, and it was all we could discover by using the blunt instrument of the telephone, was that two streams coming down out of the Steens range, Pike Creek and Mosquito Creek, had some kind of cutthroat in them, not rainbows (they are such small waters as to escape the notice of the peripatetic stocking truck). The closest stream heading south was Mosquito, and we stopped at the Mann Lake Ranch, where Roy was well acquainted, and asked directions. It was easy enough: head down to the next gate, turn right—toward the mountain—and then left on the service dirt road underneath the rural electrification lines and run south until we hit the creek. We had just closed that gate behind us (assuming all the while that the No Trespassing sign was a Mann Lake Ranch sign) when a very large and very angry young man roared up in a pickup truck, got out, hitched his jeans like John Wayne starting into a barroom brawl, and asked us what the hell we thought we were doing. As he asked, he slipped the loop off the top of the barbed-wire gate and threw the whole gate into a tangle. "You can drive right out of there," he offered, which was not going to be possible until someone moved the gate. Roy got out of the car and went up to reason with the pickup buckaroo while I opted for a long look at the distant horizon.

It turned out that Roy's friend at the Mann Lake Ranch was right about the directions; he just left out the little part about whose property the gate was on. It was an Alvord Ranch gate, and we were not exactly welcome. (To be fair to our informant, Mann

Lake and Alvord Ranches were once a single property and had been separated by that common cause, the divorce of our informant's parents.) We could have gone fishing, once we explained who told us to go through the gate and where we were going and how long we planned to be there and many other trivial details. About all we had going for us was that we were not government. And we would have gone to Mosquito Creek, except that when everything simmered down and the lad in the pickup had untangled the three-wire gate, Roy decided we didn't have enough gas to run the dirt trail to Mosquito Creek and then back to the road and down to Fields Station. This was due more to innate caution and conservatism (we had a quarter of a tank) than to bad planning. About the last thing we wanted to do was get so low on gas we'd have to pull into the Alvord Ranch and bum some.

Ordinarily, you can cut a creek from a road somewhere along its course and not have to go trailing off into the desert, but not these east-slope Steens creeks. They don't call it Alvord Dry Lake for nothing. The water comes down the hill, hits the sandy, gravelly rubble at the base of the mountain, and percolates down into the soil long before it reaches the old lake bed. Looking at the topographic map, it appeared that Pike Creek, down toward Fields, came all the way to the gravel highway, more because the road ran closer to the mountain than because the brook was any more powerful or the desert less absorbent. The other good news was that where Pike Creek came off the mountain, it went right through the middle of a square mile of Bureau of Land Management property. There shouldn't be a gate, and even if there was, there wouldn't be a hot buckaroo to go with it.

At about this moment, I voted for a nonstop trip to Fields Station, bypassing Pike Creek. We could run back up in the morning. It had something to do with beer as I recall, a substance which we had not bothered to bring up to Roy's camp and of which I am fond. Roy, who has seen the light in regard to alcohol, was just as eager for an ice cream. It would be suppertime before we got to Fields, anyhow, and there is only one place to eat and it closes early. We could come back in the morning. In the meantime, we would eat. We would drink. We would forget about the Alvord

Ranch's Mosquito Creek if we could find the trout in the national government's Pike Creek. Some people, and the kid in the pickup was one, get you to the point where you don't even want their simmered-down permission.

Fields Station is accurately named. It's a federal livestock inspection station, it's a gas station, and it's one of the most amazing feeding stations for bats and nighthawks I have ever encountered. This is partly due to a little water in the area, the same Trout Creek and a few tributaries, one of which trickles seasonally through Fields. Water means bugs in the desert, and outside the Fields Motel was a single large bright highway lamp making a pool of light in the black air. After beer and after hamburgers and after ice cream, we unfolded two lawn chairs and sat on the motel porch and watched the bats and the bullbats (which is what we call nighthawks out West; they are noticeably larger than North American bats).

Watching bats under artificial light turned out to be even better than seeing them on an ordinary evening in a purer nature. For one thing, your eye can pick up the prey in the incandescence while the bat is still circling out in the dark. Except for the occasional large moth that you can see when watching bats in natural twilight, humans have to assume what the bat is after. At night, under artificial light, it is easier to see what's happening. The mosquitos and bugs and moths make streaks of light. It is the same memory for vision—the same repeated firing of the retina that allows you to turn a television's scanned dots into a single picture— that makes the bugs look like tracer bullets or shooting stars. Then, as you watch the prey, from the edge of darkness the sudden bat appears. Bats are good at their trade, but not perfect. They appeared to average about 80 percent success. I assume this was more from their being confused by the numbers of flying insects than by any inaptitude. When they did miss, there were always two or three streaks of bug light crossing their flight path.

One or more nighthawks were working the same station. We never saw two at once, but we could not see a thing outside the streetlight's cone. There was something peculiar about the way the bullbat flew that puzzled me for an hour or so. It darted and turned as well or better than the smaller bats, but there was something unbirdlike about its flight. And then, with that insight which comes after much pondering and a little beer, it came to me: the nighthawk is the only bird I've ever seen that could flap its wings independently. It altered course just like Roy rowing his McKenzie River dory—pulling on just one oar while the other is turned down into the water to make a temporary keel. The bird would come into the light after a bug, drop a wing straight down, and take one or two quick beats with the other wing, spinning on its own alar axis in the desert air. I have seen birds make some quick turns, including over duck blinds, but I had never seen that trick before. It was a Zen koan: what is the flight of one wing flapping? (Well, it might have been a Coors question.)

In the morning we would go to Pike Creek on the edge of the Alvord Dry Lake and look for trout.

And so to bed.

17

Sitting in Paradise

Besides the (probably) extinct Alvord cutthroat trout (*O. c. henshawi* Alvord), the basin of that great dry lake is home to one other rare species of fish, the Borax Lake chub *(Gila alvordensis)*. It is the nature of chubs to live in lakes, and the only remaining constant standing water in the Alvord is formed by a borax-rich spring that rises from the lake bed some four and a half miles northeast of Fields.

The spring is actually visible from the road once you have seen it up close and know what to look for from a distance. About a half mile east of the improved gravel road there is a bump on the horizon with a perfectly flat top, parallel to the equally level dry lake bed. This is the shoreline of Borax Lake, an elevated berm formed by evaporating borax that increases minimally but annually, transpiring the spring flow into a solid chemical wall around the lake. It was the first spring in the West to be mined for borax, and Fields residents insist that it was here in Oregon, not down in California, that the first twenty-mule teams hauled evaporated borax to a railhead.

You can still see how it was done. The uplifted waters of the spring, imprisoned in a wall of their own making, were siphoned out into the desert and allowed to evaporate. Small canals, some with headgates still in place, lead away from the lake to evaporating beds. Near the lake there is still a ramp in place where the scraped-up borax could be brought up to wagon-bed height above the desert and the crystals pushed into the wagon. There was considerable hand labor involved, all of it done by Chinese laborers, refugees from the mines and the railroads. Until a few years ago, they say in Fields, you could see where these laborers' shacks had been. A similar deposit, also worked by evaporation and with an immigrant labor force, is near China Lake, California.

The edge of the lake supports a few peculiar sedges that can survive in the borated soil. The overflow from the lake makes up into a small reed and sedge marsh before the last of it percolates back into the desert. The water was clear enough and so shallow by the edge that we could have easily seen the infamous Borax Lake chub if one had chosen to swim by. The spring lake looked perfectly sterile, more like a chemical solution in a laboratory jar than a pond in the desert. No toad polliwogs, no diving beetles; none of the usual suspects that you expect in desert waterholes showed themselves. The water, when you reached down to touch it, felt exactly like what you would expect if you thought about it before you did it; it was like putting your hand in warm washing-machine water to which you had added a cup of borax.

The marsh, if not obviously populated with invertebrates and vertebrates, must have supported some kind of prey. A long-billed curlew *(Numenius americanus)* chattered at us and flew warily from fence post to fence post, as if we had gotten too close to its nest. This is a startling shore bird to encounter anywhere—the body is the size of a small hawk's, plus several inches of down-curving bill (the generic name is "new moon" in schoolboy Greek, from the sharp, although not quite semicircular, curve in the beak). In the middle of a desert lake bed, the curlew verged on the amazing. We admired the bird for a few minutes, and Roy Pruitt poked around in a desultory fashion for artifacts in what was evidently the old trash dump from the mining camp. Except for a small medicine bottle, he was not successful. The borated soil was as hard as a brick and discouraged excavation. I got my souvenir from the trip—by the time we had driven back to the gravel road and started north for Pike Creek, my fingers were chapped and dry from the borax-laden water. That was the second thing I had not thought about before washing my hands in the pond.

Pike Creek is just barely visible from the road. To be precise, there is a stubbly finger of green coming down from a narrow canyon, the remnants of willows not quite yet consumed by cattle. Absent large herbivores, the desert willows would have made a more obvious landmark. When Charles Erskine Scott Wood came into the Alvord country, striking down from Walla Walla, Washington, through the Nez Perce country to the desert, neither sheep nor cattle had come to the Steens range. What he saw—and the memory of it stayed with him until he began to commit poetry after leaving the army—was a healthy unbrowsed riparian community. It is only fair verse but excellent observation of the aboriginal streams that died into the Alvord:

> *The little rivers run away from the rugged Titans*
> *Who are jealously wrapped in cloaks of azure.*
> *They steal out into the bosom of the Desert,*
> *And the willows follow after, waving their hands,*
> *Calling to them, "Run not so fast away."*
> *They weave a green carpet in a barren place,*
> *And build a safe fortress for the birds.*

Besides the scrubby willows and the narrow gorge splitting the face of the mountain, we had a third landmark to find Pike Creek. The month before, a brushfire had started by the road and burned up the north side of the creek into the canyon. The ground north of the creek was covered with charred black sagebrush fragments, and that would interfere considerably with hunting for arrowheads.

The brush burn turned out to be a useful signal, given the lack of large numbers of healthy hand-waving willows near the road and because the lay of the land obscured the canyon mouth (it cuts out of the mountain at an angle to the north and is more obvious driving south toward Fields Station). We turned off at the fire-

blackened spot and found ourselves on the beginning of a graded
road that started up the north (burned) side of the creek toward
the narrow canyon mouth. A few hundred yards up the slope, at
the creek, the road became a turnaround and we stopped. The
ground was still scarred with Caterpillar tractor treads from the
previous month's fire-fighting crew. The unshaded creek was cold
to the touch, promising trout somewhere up higher.

ROY, WHOSE ENTHUSIASM FOR SMALL TROUT IN SMALL RIVERS IS ADE-
quate but not overwhelming, allowed as he would go looking for
stuff (meaning everything from ten-thousand-year-old arrowheads
to hundred-year-old glass bottles) to begin with, and I said I
would get serious about the fishing. I was still lugging my two
plastic laboratory bottles around, one with 100 milliliters of pure
formaldehyde in it, that small bottle inside a larger empty bottle.
This material was, should we find some, intended to embalm one
or two Pike Creek cutthroat trout. After two or three weeks of
pickling the fish in a 10 percent solution of formaldehyde, my instructions were to wash them thoroughly, repack them in distilled
water, and mail them to friend Behnke, author and professor of biology at Colorado State College in Fort Collins. Bob Behnke
knows more about western trout than anyone in the world, a fact
which has made him something of a thorn in the flesh of the Bureau of Land Management, the United States Forest Service, and
all state departments of fish and wildlife that insist on stocking
hybridized (and hybridizing) hatchery fish in otherwise pristine
environments. The washing procedure had two motivations—
formaldehyde is a noxious poison and can't be sent through the
mails, and Behnke, after thirty-odd years of preparing and studying pickled fish, had developed a nasty allergic reaction to the
preservative.

What looked like a foot trail up the creek turned out to be a
washed-out section of roadway, and where the track reached the
creek, some overhanging willow branches were thin enough that I
could see a serious graded road starting on the other side and par-
alleling the creek going up-canyon. I was admiring the roadway

ahead and starting to cross the creek when something flashed and caught my eye. There were trout or, to be precise, there had been trout in the shallow water where the road forded the creek. This seemed unusually generous of the stream—to put fish in six inches of water in the middle of a roadbed.

I say they were trout, that I knew they were trout the moment I saw them fleeing up the creek, but that was pure assumption at the time. Once across the creek, the road, which didn't have a tire track on it, looked even more impressive. Someone had put considerable effort into it and had carved it neatly into the south wall of the canyon, not quite wide enough to pass two cars everywhere but more than the usual jeep trail that you find in the West. I walked up half a mile, and with every step found myself farther from the water. The creek had carved a deep and narrow gorge, and the road stayed on the high ground, rising faster than the natural drainage below it.

What I was hoping to see ahead and could not find was a widening of the valley. I had an urge to find a meadow, a nice wet-ground *ciénaga* where one could fish easily in a meandering stream. Suddenly, without much reason to it, the road petered out as if someone had decided that this was far enough, no farther would they go. By then, it looked a steep 500 feet down to the stream. It was quiet up in the canyon, and when I stopped walking I could hear running water tumbling along far below. It was quite invisible; the creek was thoroughly overgrown and shaded by willows. The canyon, too steep to interest cows, had a thick green carpet in the bottom of its barren walls.

If there were trout at the very beginning of the walk, it made sense to go back and start up from the ford staying close by the creek. I strolled on down, the pickling bottle in the back pocket of my fly-fishing vest, bouncing gently against my spine, reminding me that this was not an entirely recreational event. It had the keener edge of amateur biology (speaking of the angler's job) and would soon have the acrid smell of formalin, that common denominator of academic icthyology.

I did not know what I was looking for, as I was unfamiliar at that point with the exact description of an Alvord cutthroat trout. But I had another kind of useful information, the sort that keeps you from mistaking, say, a harmless hognose snake for a rattlesnake. The trick in that case is to know exactly what a rattlesnake looks like. I knew what a typical Humboldt Basin cutthroat *(O. c. henshawi)* looked like. The classic parental strain of *henshawi* (there are several geographic sub-subspecies, including a pale unspotted one) is heavily spotted from eyeballs to tail fins, with somewhat more spots above the lateral line and some concentration of spots toward the tail. The spots are relatively large, numbering in the hundreds on each side, and are characteristic of the race.

For some reason, and you could probably get a minor-league doctorate out of speculating about it, the derivative sub-sub-species of the four major subspecies of cutthroat trout tend to start losing spots as they get farther from their ancestral stock. Parental *O. c. henshawi* has many large spots scattered all over it. When you take the next divergence, to the sub-subspecies like the Alvord cutthroat, spots seem to disappear from whole areas of the body. Both the Alvord sub-sub (derived from *O. c. henshawi*) and the Utah cutthroat (descended from *O. c. bouvieri*, the Yellowstone cutthroat) have done the same spot-dropping trick. But that was all I knew . . . if it were *not* a typical Humboldt *henshawi*, I would know it by its sparser use of spots. I would, at a minimum, know what it was *not*.

If someone wants to start wondering about the reason for fewer spots, there are some likely possibilities. In a very problematic setting like a small river in the middle of a desert, it might be energy saving. Spots require pigment, and manufacturing pigment uses up energy, and energy is made out of food, and food is scarce in these small waters. That conservation of energy, to use an example from animal husbandry, is the reason that almost all commercial poultry—chicken, duck, and goose alike—is pure white. Every colored feather eliminated is one less grain of corn you have to feed to the growing bird. Also, small desert streams attract fewer predators, especially predatory fish and mammals, than do larger and more productive waters. Fewer enemies may require fewer camouflaging spots, and that feeds back into the original energy equation.

Certainly the fish in Pike Creek were well protected from aerial predators. Unbrowsed, dense and overhanging and interwoven, the desert willows made a safe fortress for trout. I approached the stream a hundred yards above the ford with considerable caution. If there ever was a place that looked like rattlesnakes, this was it. Rattlesnakes are not aquatic, nor do they drink, but the water would concentrate small rodents who do drink. A narrow meadow, now grown into knee-high brown grass, bordered the stream on my bank. I shuffled through it deliberately and noisily. Snakes hate surprises.

There was a small break in the wall of willows, and I could see a narrow pool just downstream from the opening. At the lower end of the still water, the creek turned abruptly left and dropped over a boulder with an audible gurgle. Little athletic skill is involved in catching trout in water a foot wide and less deep. All that is required is some patience while you figure out how to float a fly down into the shade and then twitch it on the slack water above the rock.

The fish came up and swallowed the fly with the understandable enthusiasm of a trout that lives in unproductive water and sees only occasional meals sliding down toward it. Lying on the bank, I saw it was clearly *not* a typical Lahontan cutthroat. It was spotted, but not densely freckled. My notebook, slightly blurred by wet fingers, shows a count—on one side—of only ten spots on the body below the lateral line and only forty more spots above the line, and no spots forward of the pectoral fins.

This is entirely speculation on my part, but the few spots on the Pike Creek fish were not randomly scattered; there was a logic to the pattern, and one typical of the lightly spotted Rio Grande and Bonneville cutthroats as well. The spots increased in frequency toward the top side and the rear end of the trout. They were thickest around and on the dorsal fin and next to the tail fin, which was itself heavily spotted. The net effect was that the trout was best camouflaged when seen from above, as by a kingfisher or a heron, but much less camouflaged when seen from the side by an underwater predator—typically another fish. The denser spotting of the tail end was, it occurred to me, a camouflage of the part of the fish that is most often in motion. A trout hanging in the current will beat its tail constantly to hold position. Few as the spots were, they were cleverly arranged and economical. The various desert trout are usually the largest fish in their own small world and have only the sky to fear.

The fish, about seven inches long, fit neatly into the larger plastic bottle. One fish was good, but two fish would be better. The analysis of trout, besides newfangled and expensive genetic testing, involves some old-fashioned techniques. Taxonomists count things like the number of scales along the lateral line from the gills to the tail fin, the number of rays in a specific fin, or the numbers of small teeth that some trout grow behind their tongue on the floor of their throat. These numbers vary slightly between individuals in a population, and the more specimens, the better chance of getting the right average number.

One of the reasons I particularly love small trout in small water is that the whole activity of angling gets reduced back to what it really is—childlike. Many anglers and most professional guides have forgotten that fact, and to watch them at their sport you would think they were competing in some Olympic event. The bigger the river and the larger the fish the more they lose contact with reality.

Moving with appropriate adult concern for rattlers, I walked upstream, pausing every few yards to peer through the willows, looking for trout. At the head of the meadow, the stream came between two boulders and dropped into a pool. Through the branches I could see the trout. It had dropped back to the tail of the pool, a body of water about the size and shape of an old oval galvanized stock-watering tub. That fish was on its way to Fort Collins and didn't know it.

I knew that when I pushed through the willows the commotion would spook the fish, but that didn't matter. The trout wasn't going to leave the pool; it would just run up under a rock or hide under the bubbles where the water fell into the pool, and in a few minutes it would shift gears from fleeing to feeding and return to the end of the pool, where it could watch the whole surface for wayward ants or beetles. All I had to do was get in position, be ready to put the fly on the water, and wait like a heron until the trout had forgotten about me. There wasn't room to cast inside the willow tunnel; no wand waving would be allowed.

It was cool under the willows; only a few dapples of sunlight penetrated to the surface of the water, and the day's heat, approaching 90 on the barren hillside, could penetrate no better than the light. I reached down with my left hand and touched the water, and it was cold enough that my hand recoiled involuntarily, just as our hands will when we touch something hot. I settled down, crossed my legs like a Buddhist monk, and waited.

The world, one realizes after many years, has few places both large and perfected. Paradise was small; it was the work of an afternoon for Adam and Eve, "hand in hand with wand'ring steps and slow," to walk out of Eden and find their place of rest. What with the increase in population since then, things are considerably more cramped, even out West. It occurred to me that I was sitting in Paradise, although short one Eve to take off her shoes and cool her feet in Pike Creek. A very small pristine wilderness it was, I give you that, but an excellent one. I had shade in the desert and cold water. It mattered not at all that the stream was less than a foot wide where it came over the rocks at the top of the pool and no deeper where it ran below my feet. I have been on most of the big rivers of the West and never saw a better one, and never, ever, one that I could call my own. William Clark, you recall, noted in his journal that he was the "first white man" to walk the banks of the Bitterroot River. We think as proud a thought as we can in this less heroic age, and it occurred to me that I was likely the only fly fisherman to sit on this exact piece of ground and study this small and lovely washtub of a pool. I had come west. I was alone in the wilderness. I was the first.

I held the rod one-handed over the water and pinched the fly between the fingers of my left hand, holding it by the bend of the hook. When the fish came back, all I had to do was pull back on the fly, build a little tension against the rod, let go of the fly like an archer releasing an arrow (or a boy firing a slingshot), and it would land on the water upstream from my fish. And then the fish came back, and the fly went up the pool and floated down, and the fish ate it, and that was all there was to it. That is all there really ever is to it, no matter how fancy the fishing.

If anything, and I do not have a count in my notebook, this trout, a surprisingly large fish considering the minuteness of the water, had even fewer spots than the first one. Or appeared to have ... it was half again as big, both in length and depth, so there was twice as much surface area on which to scatter the fifty spots I had counted on the first fish. I had to bend it sharply to stuff it in the bottle. I filled the bottle nearly full of creek water and guesstimated the ratio—nine parts water to one part preservative—and topped off the larger bottle with pure formaldehyde. For a moment, the Alvord Desert reeked of high school biology class. When I screwed down the two bottle caps the scent of sagebrush returned.

As I walked back toward the car, the two fish and the 10 percent solution of pickling liquid in the bottle made a satisfying thump against my back with every step. I left the fishing vest and the rod by the car, waved to Roy— he was coursing back and forth across the unburned hillside south of the creek, looking for something interesting—and walked down to the gravel road. Pike Creek diminished with every yard I walked, sinking momently into the sand. By the time it reached the culvert under the state road it was trickling, not running. Below the road, it managed a few more yards and then collapsed completely, a long way short of the shining white surface of Alvord Dry Lake.

That pleased me. The water had come from up high where no one lived and it ran down a canyon that was too rocky and steep for cows, and then, before anyone could do anything useful with it, the stream stole away quite literally *into* the bosom of the desert. There was a beginning and an end to it, and only the trout knew the water. I admired the purity of the creek's life and the cleanliness of its death. It would never see a dam or an irrigation ditch or a sewerage pipe.

THE PREMONITION THAT I WAS THE FIRST FLY FISHERMAN ON PIKE Creek and that I had caught a rare and almost extinct trout turned out to have a higher proportion of reality than one usually gets from wishful thinking. Two weeks after leaving Oregon, I mailed two well-washed trout to Bob Behnke and with surprising speed got a reply. They were not the (probably extinct) Alvord subspecies. They were surely (their various body parts having been counted and compared) another local and endangered race of cutthroat trout. Everything from their guzzle to their zlatch, from their throat teeth to certain obscure cavities in their stomachs, matched the counts for Whitehorse cutthroats (*O. c. henshawi* Whitehorse), a very threatened species that is hanging on in those badly abused creeks in the Trout Mountains southeast of Fields Station. These creeks flow into and die into the Whitehorse Ranch country in the Coyote Basin, just south of the Alvord Desert.

I finally tracked down the source of these slightly displaced fish. Bill Hosford, a retired fisheries manager for the Oregon Department of Fish and Wildlife, was the cause of it all. I reached him at his home by telephone. Several years ago (he was a little vague on the dates), while monitoring the overgrazed streams up in the Whitehorse drainage, he had managed to arrange a helicopter evacuation flight from the Trout Mountains over to the Steens. He stocked several dozen Whitehorse cutthroats in the headwaters of Pike Creek and Mosquito Creek. He, as he put it, stashed these Whitehorse fish in the only two substantial creeks in the Steens that didn't already have trout.

I asked him if he'd ever been back to check on the success of his stocking, and he hadn't. "Fish from top to bottom," I told him. "You did a good job. There's a fish everyplace in Pike Creek that would hold one, right down to the Alvord.

"But," I continued, "didn't you tell Roy Pruitt that Pike and Mosquito had never been stocked?"

Yes, he had. He meant, of course, never stocked officially; that was why they were pure and secret places to hide a rare fish. It was a hint, not a fact, that he had related to Roy.

I was a little disappointed after hanging up the telephone. I had wanted the Alvord trout because it was always rarer and is very problematic at this late date. As with most ruefulness, it was an entirely selfish regret, and I have meditated my way out of it. I had been in Paradise for a day, and even Eden, as the story goes, had to be stocked.

L'Envoi

ONE OF THE THINGS YOU LEARN IN LIFE IS WHEN TO STOP. I HAVE been from Arizona to Montana, up the Missouri, down the Columbia, across the Colorado and the Rio Grande and into the Great Basin. When the last, best place turned out to be a brooklet on the edge of a dry, dead sea, I was not surprised. The world, as we are beginning to understand, is a collection of small things. Even our government now speaks of biodiversity and the need to protect whole zones of these small places. The great conservation movement that began with a few game refuges and a handful of scenic vistas out West has stopped, taken stock, and moved on to a higher level.

Most places we have been in this book are well known to regional biologists and land managers. Each one, along with thousands like it, is on the inventory, and that is the critical first step in the conservation of wildness. The struggle to preserve the West is hardly over, but now we have realized that national monuments, wildlife refuges, parks and wild and scenic rivers were necessary but incomplete steps. The old solution—preserve this, plunder that—is dying out. Everything, to use a metaphor from the game of poker, is on the table now: my fish, your birds, his cows, their hard-rock mine. I have lived long enough to see it then and see it now, and now is better. There are very few predator-control employees of the federal government anymore, and a great many new wildlife biologists, endangered-species officers, and systematic ecologists. I am not sanguine about the future, but I am comforted that at last we are arguing about the right things.

There is time now; I can stop for a while and be confident that somewhere the things I love will still swim and fly and bloom. Someone is watching out for them. There are a few special trout left to look for, and I know where they are and where, I do believe, they always will be. When there is time and gas money and I'm back in California, a state where I was partly raised, I will head over the Sierra toward Reno and find the Paiute trout *(O. c. seleniris)*, that spotless, truly immaculate trout of the moonlight rainbow. If things go well in New Mexico, there is the Gila cutthroat, and some spring when the saguaro cactus is in bloom down on the desert, I will go up into the piney hills and touch one.

And besides those desert-locked fish, I expect someday to meet up with the small but colorful California golden trout that swims high in the Kern River, up in what was once, and likely will be again, the mountain home of the California giant condor. The golden trout's scientific last name is *aguabonita*. One really should seek out a fish named after its home: "beautiful water." That comforting fluid is, after all, the best of all reasons to go back to wildness.

About the Author

M. R. Montgomery, known to the various government record keepers as Maurice R. Montgomery Jr., and to all his acquaintances as Monty, was born in eastern Montana in 1938, raised partly in California, and now lives near Boston for reasons that he cannot quite explain. Over the past twenty-five years he has written for the *Boston Globe* on every subject except politics, a clean record he hopes to maintain until retirement. Other than fishing and a little bit of gunning, he has no obsessive hobbies, although he has been known to plant the occasional tomato and a manageable number of antique rose varieties, these for the pleasure of his wife, Florence. He maintains small areas of both tallgrass and short-grass prairie in his yard that have attracted one moose, a coyote, and a few white-tailed deer. He has high if unrealistic hopes for a buffalo *(Bison bison)* someday.